A timely volume on the US–Australia alliance which provides fresh thinking on how the United States and Australia can navigate a more contested Indo-Pacific. This book will be of great value to scholars and practitioners alike.

Ben Schreer, *Professor of Strategic Studies,*
Macquarie University, Sydney, Australia

The timing of this volume on the US–Australia alliance relationship is impeccable. Written by some well-known scholars and practitioners, it offers an invaluable set of chapters that enhances our understanding of the new challenges and risks confronting the alliance and puts forth constructive ideas for Canberra and Washington to deal with them without compromising their vital interests and core values. It should be required reading not just for those interested in the fast-changing triangular Australia–America–China relationship but all those interested in the future of the Indo-Pacific regional order.

Mohan Malik, *Professor, National Defense College of the*
UAE and Visiting Fellow, NESA Center for Strategic Studies, USA

The Future of the United States–Australia Alliance

The United States–Australia alliance has been an important component of the US-led system of alliances that has underpinned regional security in the Indo-Pacific since 1945. However, recent geostrategic developments, in particular the rise of the People's Republic of China, have posed significant challenges to this US-led regional order. In turn, the growing strategic competition between these two great powers has generated challenges to the longstanding US–Australia alliance. Both the US and Australia are confronting a changing strategic environment, and, as a result, the alliance needs to respond to the challenges that they face. The US needs to understand the challenges and risks to this vital relationship, which is growing in importance, and take steps to manage it. On its part, Australia must clearly identify its core common interests with the US and start exploring what more it needs to do to attain its stated policy preferences.

This book consists of chapters exploring US and Australian perspectives of the Indo-Pacific, the evolution of Australia-US strategic and defence cooperation, and the future of the relationship. Written by a joint US–Australia team, the volume is aimed at academics, analysts, students, and the security and business communities.

Scott D. McDonald is a Non-resident Research Fellow at the Asia-Pacific Center for Security Studies and pursuing a PhD at The Fletcher School of Tufts University, USA. A retired US Marine Corps officer, his final active duty position was as a Military Professor at APCSS, where he taught Chinese philosophy and strategic thought, East Asia security dynamics, National Security Strategy, and strategic foresight.

Andrew T. H. Tan is Professor at the Department of Security Studies and Criminology, Macquarie University, Australia. He previously taught at the University of New South Wales, Australia, and Kings College London, UK, where he was based at the Joint Services Command and Staff College at Watchfield. Andrew has published 20 sole-authored, edited and co-edited books, and more than 60 refereed journal and chapter articles.

Europa Regional Perspectives

Providing in-depth analysis with a global reach, this series from Europa examines a wide range of contemporary political, economic, developmental and social issues in regional perspective. Intended to complement the Europa Regional Surveys of the World series, Europa Regional Perspectives will be a valuable resource for academics, students, researchers, policymakers, business people and anyone with an interest in current world affairs with an emphasis on regional issues.

While the Europa World Year Book and its associated Regional Surveys inform on and analyse contemporary economic, political and social developments, the Editors considered the need for more in-depth volumes written and/or edited by specialists in their field, in order to delve into particular regional situations. Volumes in the series are not constrained by any particular template, but may explore recent political, economic, international relations, social, defence, or other issues in order to increase knowledge. Regions are thus not specifically defined, and volumes may focus on small or large group of countries, regions or blocs.

Youth at the Margins
Perspectives on Arab Mediterranean Youth
Elena Sánchez-Montijano and José Sánchez García

Terrorism and Insurgency in Asia
A contemporary examination of terrorist and separatist movements
Edited by Benjamin Schreer and Andrew T. H. Tan

Russia in the Middle East and North Africa
Continuity and Change
Chiara Lovotti, Eleonora Tafuro Ambrosetti, Christopher A. Hartwell and Aleksandra Chmielewska

The Caribbean Blue Economy
Edited by Peter Clegg, Robin Mahon, Patrick McConney and Hazel A. Oxenford

The Future of the United States-Australia Alliance
Edited by Scott D. McDonald and Andrew T. H. Tan

For more information about this series, please visit: www.routledge.com/Europa-Regional-Perspectives/book-series/ERP

The Future of the United States–Australia Alliance

Evolving Security Strategy in the Indo-Pacific

Edited by
Scott D. McDonald and Andrew T. H. Tan

Routledge
Taylor & Francis Group

LONDON AND NEW YORK

First published 2021
by Routledge
2 Park Square, Milton Park, Abingdon, Oxon OX14 4RN

and by Routledge
605 Third Avenue, New York, NY 10017

First issued in paperback 2022

Routledge is an imprint of the Taylor & Francis Group, an informa business

Publisher's Note
The publisher has gone to great lengths to ensure the quality of this reprint but points out that some imperfections in the original copies may be apparent.

British Library Cataloguing in Publication Data
A catalogue record for this book is available from the British Library

Library of Congress Cataloging-in-Publication Data
A catalog record has been requested for this book

ISBN: 978-1-03-239987-4 (pbk)
ISBN: 978-0-367-32251-9 (hbk)
ISBN: 978-0-429-31752-1 (ebk)

DOI: 10.4324/9780429317521

Typeset in Times New Roman
by Taylor & Francis Books

Contents

Illustrations

Contributors

Alan Bloomfield is currently a Lecturer at Curtin University, and has also worked at UNSW and UWA in Australia, and at the UK campus of Queens University (Canada). His main research expertise is in foreign policy analysis (primarily Australia and India) and norm dynamics theory (especially regarding humanitarian intervention norms). He has written *India and the Responsibility to Protect* (Ashgate) and co-edited *Norm Antipreneurs* (Routledge). He has also published articles in leading international relations journals, including *Review of International Studies, Pacific Review, Contemporary Security Policy, India Review,* and the *Australian Journal of Politics and History,* and has written chapters for numerous edited volumes. In late-2020 Alan will leave academia to take up an Assistant Director's position in the Southeast Asia Division of Australia's Department of Foreign Affairs and Trade.

Shannon Brandt Ford is Lecturer in International Relations at Curtin University in Perth, Australia. He is also a Board Member for the Asia-Pacific International Society of Military Ethics and a Faculty Affiliate with the Program on Cybersecurity and Internet Governance at Indiana University. Previously, Shannon completed a Visiting Fellowship at the University of New South Wales, Canberra on the political, ethical, and legal dilemmas of emerging weapon technologies. He has also been a Research Fellow with the Centre for Applied Philosophy and Public Ethics. Before embarking on an academic career, Shannon worked in Strategic Policy Division at the Australian Department of Defence where he coordinated strategy planning work with the US Department of Defense. Before that, he was an analyst with the Defence Intelligence Organization specializing in North Asian security issues. His publications include: 'The Current State of Intelligence Studies' (with Rhys Crawley) in *Intelligence and the Function of Government* (2018); 'Weaponising Social Media' in *Ethics Under Fire* (2017); 'Military Ethics and Strategy: National Security, Moral Values and Cultural Perspective' (2015) in the *Routledge Handbook on Military Ethics*; and '*Jus Ad Vim* and the Just Use of Lethal Force Short-of-War' (2013) in the *Routledge Handbook of Ethics and War*.

Bates Gill has a 30-year global career as a scholar, policy advisor, and institution-builder, focusing on Asian and Chinese affairs. He is Professor of Asia-Pacific Security Studies at Macquarie University and Senior Associate Fellow with the Royal United Services Institute (RUSI) in London. Previous positions include: CEO, United States Studies Centre at the University of Sydney (2012–2015); Director, Stockholm International Peace Research Institute (2007–2012); Freeman Chair in China Studies, Center for Strategic and International Studies (2002–2007); and Senior Fellow in Foreign Policy Studies and inaugural Director of the Center for Northeast Asian Policy Studies, Brookings Institution (1998–2002). He is author, co-author, or co-editor of eight books including *China Matters: Getting it Right for Australia* (Latrobe University Press/Black Inc., 2017),*Governing the Bomb: Civilian Control and Democratic Accountability of Nuclear Weapons* (Oxford University Press, 2010), *Asia's New Multilateralism* (Columbia University Press, 2009), and *Rising Star: China's New Security Diplomacy* (Brookings, 2007). Among his international honours, Dr Gill holds the Royal Order of the Commander of the Polar Star, the highest award bestowed upon foreigners by the Swedish monarch. He received his PhD in Foreign Affairs from the Woodrow Wilson Department of Government and Foreign Affairs, University of Virginia.

Yves-Heng Lim is a Senior Lecturer at the Department of Security Studies and Criminology, Macquarie University. He is the author of *China's Naval Power: An Offensive Realist Approach*. His research has been published in the *Journal of Strategic Studies*, the *Journal of Contemporary China, Asian Security* as well as in several edited volumes.

Adam Lockyer is an Associate Professor in Strategic Studies at Macquarie University. He held the 2015 Fulbright Scholarship in US–Australian Alliance Studies at Georgetown University. Before joining the Department of Security Studies and Criminology, A/Prof. Lockyer was a Research Fellow in Defence Studies at the University of New South Wales. He has also held positions at the United States Studies Centre at the University of Sydney, at the Center for Strategic and International Studies, in Washington, DC, and was the Lowy Institute's 2008 Thawley Scholarship in International Security winner. He also spent four years serving in the Australian Army. A/Prof. Lockyer has published widely on issues relating to Australian defence strategy, US defence and foreign policy, post-conflict reconstruction, governance, and insurgency. His article titled 'The Logic of Interoperability: Australia's Acquisition of the F-35 Joint Strike Fighter' won the SAGE Award for the best international contribution to a Canadian academic journal in 2013. His article entitled 'Evaluating Civil Development in Counterinsurgency Operations' won the prestigious Boyer Prize for best original article published in the Australian Journal of International Affairs in 2012. His most recent book is titled: *Australian Defence*

Strategy: Evaluating Alternatives for a Contested Asia (Melbourne University Press, 2017).

Scott D. McDonald is a Non-resident Research Fellow at the Asia-Pacific Center for Security Studies and pursuing a PhD at The Fletcher School of Tufts University. A retired US Marine Corps officer, his final active duty position was as a Military Professor at APCSS, where he taught Chinese philosophy and strategic thought, East Asia security dynamics, National Security Strategy, and strategic foresight. He also led APCSS's first multilateral workshop in Taiwan. A China Foreign Area Officer (FAO), he has studied in Beijing, served as an attaché in Canberra, Australia, was the first Marine Corps Affairs Officer at the American Institute in Taiwan, established the Regional Engagement Branch at III Marine Expeditionary Force, and served as a Strategic Analyst in the Commandant's Strategic Initiatives Group. Among his publications are the co-edited *China's Global Influence: Perspectives and Recommendations* (APCSS, 2019) and co-written 'Phase Zero: How China Exploits It, Why the US Does Not' (*Naval War College Review*, 2012). Mr McDonald earned a BA in International Relations from The George Washington University, an MA in National Security Affairs from the Naval Postgraduate School, and completed the Massachusetts Institute of Technology's Seminar XXI Program for national security leaders.

Andrew O'Neil is Professor of Political Science at Griffith University and Research Dean in the Business School. He has published widely on international security issues, including alliances. Before entering academia, Andrew worked as a strategic analyst in the Australian government.

Fred Smith is Lecturer at the Department of Security Studies and Criminology, Macquarie University, Australia since 2013. He previously served in the United States Navy for 30 years, retiring as a Captain in 2012. During his career as a military intelligence officer, he had extensive experience in the Pacific and Middle East with tours in Europe, the Mediterranean, and with the North Atlantic Treaty Organization (NATO). He also served multiple tours in Australia (seconded to the Royal Australian Navy), Japan, and in London, UK. He has deployed to Bahrain on multiple occasions and conducted four at-sea deployments to the Pacific, Indian Ocean, Northern Arabian Sea, Arabian Gulf and Mediterranean Sea. He served multiple tours in the US, including ten years in Hawaii, postings on both coasts of the US and in the Pentagon, Washington, DC. His educational profile includes: Master of Arts (National Security & Strategic Studies), Naval War College, Newport, RI; Juris Doctor (Law Degree), Loyola School of Law, New Orleans, LA; Bachelor of Arts (Political Science), Auburn University, Auburn, AL. Fred has co-published (with Dalbir Ahlawat), 'Indo-Pacific Region: Evolving Strategic Contours', in D. Gopal and Dalbir Ahlawat (eds), *Indo-Pacific: Emerging Powers, Evolving Regions and Global Governance* (Aakar, 2016).

Paul J. Smith is Professor of National Security Affairs at the US Naval War College in Newport, Rhode Island. Prior to his current position, he was an associate professor and research fellow with the Asia-Pacific Center for Security Studies in Hawaii (1997–2006). He has published over 45 journal articles and chapters on subjects related to transnational security and the international politics of East Asia (with particular emphasis on the People's Republic of China, Japan, and Taiwan). His edited books include *Human Smuggling: Chinese Migrant Trafficking and the Challenge to America's Immigration Tradition* (Center for Strategic and International Studies, 1997) and *Terrorism and Violence in South-East Asia: Transnational Challenges to States and Regional Stability* (M. E. Sharpe/Routledge, 2004). He is author of *The Terrorism Ahead: Confronting Transnational Violence in the Twenty-first Century* (M. E. Sharpe/Routledge, 2007). He earned his Bachelor of Arts from Washington and Lee University, Master of Arts from the University of London (School of Oriental and African Studies-SOAS) and his JD and PhD degrees (political science) from the University of Hawai'i (Mānoa).

Andrew T. H. Tan is Professor at the Department of Security Studies and Criminology, Macquarie University, Australia. He previously taught at the University of New South Wales, Australia, and Kings College London, UK, where he was based at the Joint Services Command and Staff College at Watchfield. Andrew has published 20 sole-authored, edited and co-edited books, and over 60 refereed journal and chapter articles. Some of his latest books include: *The United States in Asia* (Edward Elgar, 2018), *US–China Relations* (Edward Elgar, 2016), *Security and Conflict in East Asia* (Routledge, 2015), *East and South-East Asia: International Relations and Security Perspectives* (Routledge, 2013), *Security Strategies in the Asia-Pacific* (Palgrave Macmillan, 2011) and *US Strategy Against Global Terrorism: How it Evolved, Why it Failed and Where it is Headed* (Palgrave Macmillan, 2009). His latest work (his 21st book) is an edited volume with some of the world's leading arms trade experts, entitled *The Arms Trade* (Edward Elgar, forthcoming). In 2013, Andrew was Chair of Global Security Asia, Asia's largest homeland security conference. He is also the co-commissioning editor of Edward Elgar's New Horizons in East Asian Politics series.

Dr Alexander L. Vuving is a Professor at the Asia-Pacific Center for Security Studies. His main areas of research include great power competition, Chinese strategy, Vietnamese politics and foreign relations, the South China Sea dispute, and the history of human power. He has published in major scholarly journals and policy magazines in addition to presenting at leading universities and think tanks around the world. Numerous newspapers and news agencies, including the *New York Times*, the *Financial Times*, the Associated Press, Bloomberg, and other media outlets, have featured and quoted his views. Prior to APCSS, Dr Vuving was an Assistant Professor at Tulane University and a Post-doc Fellow and Associate of Harvard University's Belfer Center for Science and International Affairs. He is an Editorial Board member of the journals *Asian Politics and Policy* and *Global Discourse*. His most recent publications include two book chapters entitled 'China's Strategic Messaging: What It Is, How It Works, and How to Respond to It' and 'Great Power Competition: Lessons from the Past, Implications for the Future', as well as an article titled 'Will China Set Up an ADIZ in the South China Sea?'

Acknowledgements

The editors would like to thank the contributors to this volume who have taken the time to participate in this project. Drawn from US and Australian institutions, the contributors are united in their strong belief in the merits of the US–Australia alliance relationship, one that has served not just the interests of both countries, but has also been a vital lynchpin to stability in the Indo-Pacific.

The editors would also like to thank the referees who commented on and supported the original book proposal, as well as the referee who read the final manuscript, resulting in an improved volume.

Last, but not least, the editors are grateful to Cathy Hartley for commissioning this work, and to the team at Routledge which enabled this volume to be published.

Scott D. McDonald (LtCol (ret), US Marine Corps;
Non-resident Research Fellow, Asia-Pacific Center for Security Studies,
Honolulu, HI, USA)
Andrew T. H. Tan (Professor of Security Studies,
Macquarie University, Australia)
September 2020

1   The United States–Australia alliance

Scott D. McDonald and Andrew T. H. Tan

The United States–Australia alliance is an important component in the security architecture of the Asia-Pacific and Indo-Pacific regions. This close-knit relationship has been an important component of the US-led hubs and spokes system of alliances cobbled together in the early 1950s.[1] The resulting security architecture has underpinned regional security and stability, enabling Asia to develop and prosper following the aftermath of the Second World War. However, geo-strategic developments since the end of the Cold War, particularly the economic and military rise of the People's Republic of China (PRC), accompanied by its growing confidence and assertiveness, have posed significant challenges to this US-led regional order. This challenge from China has been exacerbated by the coronavirus disease 2019 (COVID-19) global pandemic of 2019–2020, which led to worsened relations between the United States and China. In turn, the growing strategic competition and intensifying tensions between these two great powers have generated challenges to the long-standing US–Australia alliance.

Given the combination of a changing strategic environment and increasing calls in Australia to re-evaluate its relationship with the US and the PRC, there is a need to clearly identify the common interests and challenges in the US–Australia strategic and military relationship. This relationship has been important both to Australian security planning and as a vital component in the US-led regional order, which is now coming under challenge (White 2010; White 2017).

Benefits of the US–Australia alliance

The United States has been the central plank in Australia's defence and foreign policies since the signing of the Australia, New Zealand and United States Security Treaty (or ANZUS Treaty) in 1951. As Bisley observed, Australia sought the security pact with the United States because of perceived threats to Australian interests after 1945, emanating from the threat of communism and fears over a re-armed Japan (Bisley 2013: 405). Additionally, Britain could no longer provide the required security guarantees, and Australian decision-makers recognized that only the United States could uphold the post-1945 global and regional orders. Although the ANZUS Treaty began to unravel when the US suspended its treaty obligations towards New Zealand following the latter's declaration of its territory as a nuclear-free zone, the US and Australia both reaffirmed that they would continue to honour their treaty obligations to one another (Office of the Historian n.d.).

Since then, the alliance has provided several major benefits to Australia: the prospect that the United States would come to Australia's aid in the event of an external threat or attack; privileged access to US military hardware and training; access to US intelligence networks; and direct access to Washington, capital of the world's largest economy and pre-eminent military power for much of the post-1945 era (Bisley 2013: 405–406). Australia also belongs to the Five Eyes intelligence network, which 'in terms of breadth, depth and coherence … easily surpasses all other intelligence networks'. All told, in terms of the number and strength of linkages, the 'strength of the commitment arguably exceeds NATO as an alliance' (O'Neil 2017: 540).

On the part of the United States, the Asia-Pacific has been acknowledged as the most important region for its future. In a seminal foreign policy speech to Australia's parliament in November 2011, President Obama announced the 'Pivot to Asia' (later rebranded as 'rebalancing'). The speech was significant in that it strongly reaffirmed the United States' determination to stand its ground in Asia and maintain its dominant position. Obama declared that the US presence in the Asia-Pacific was its top priority and that reductions in US defence spending as a result of its budget and debt crises would not be at the expense of the region (Australian 2011). After his speech, the US sought to strengthen its presence in Asia through the rotation of US Marines through the Northern Territory and US Air Force assets through Australian bases (Stars and Stripes 2013).

Australia is clearly important to the United States as a key ally in the region most important for its future. Significantly, by delivering his Pivot speech before the Australian Parliament, Obama chose to highlight the importance that the United States has placed on the long-standing alliance relationship with Australia. Australia has been a reliable ally in most major conflicts that the United States has been involved in, such as the Second World War, the Korean War, the Vietnam War and, more recently, the US wars in Afghanistan and Iraq. As Obama noted in his Canberra speech, 'from the trenches of the First World War to the mountains of Afghanistan, Aussies and Americans have stood together, we have fought together, we have given lives together in every single major conflict of the past hundred years … every single one' (Australian 2011). Indeed, the Trilateral Security Dialogue involving the United States and its two closest allies in Asia, Japan and Australia, are committed 'to working together to maintain and promote a free, open, prosperous and inclusive Indo-Pacific region' (Department of Foreign Affairs and Trade 2019).

A clear example of Australia and the US working together has been the defence relationship, the symbiotic nature of which has led to an increasing array of information sharing, personnel exchanges, combined exercises and shared engagement with partner nations across the Indo-Pacific (Church n.d.). At present, there are almost 600 Australian Defence personnel embedded in the US military, working side-by-side with their US counterparts (Australian Embassy, Washington). This integration extends to leading US forces in the Indo-Pacific, through an Australian officer serving as one of the Deputy Commanding Generals of US Army Pacific (Guardian 2012).

A common challenge: China's rise

The problem is that since the end of the Cold War, there have been significant developments in the international system, leading to changes in the regional strategic environment. China's dramatic economic rise has underpinned its growing challenge to the current US- and Western-dominated international order. China has also become an important economic player in every major continent in the world, due to its voracious appetite for energy and raw materials, as well as its proactive search for new markets.

At the same time, the 2008 global financial crisis revealed political, fiscal and economic issues in the United States, raising allies' concerns regarding its capacity to meet its global military and security commitments. In addition, America's controversial wars in Afghanistan and Iraq after the 11 September 2001 terrorist attacks have to some extent damaged American soft power. Yet, the United States remains an unrivalled global military power and has managed its dominance in such a way that it has not sparked a balancing coalition against it by other great powers (Telegraph 2013). China also does not have the attributes necessary to replace the US as the new global hegemon (Tan 2014). Nonetheless, China has posed a serious challenge to US regional dominance in Asia, through military actions, assertive diplomacy and the use of economic instruments. Most visibly, PRC aggressiveness has manifested in establishment of control over the disputed South China Sea through construction of artificial islands and military bases (Yahuda 2013). Moreover, China's behaviour in the South China Sea poses a threat to international sea lanes, which the US and Australia share an interest in protecting.

The challenge to Australia is complicated by the fact that China's dramatic economic rise has resulted in it becoming Australia's largest trading partner. Indeed, the economic relationship has been buoyant, with China's continued purchase of Australia's resources driving a 23 per cent increase in bilateral trade, reaching A$180 billion in 2017 (Sydney Morning Herald 2018). China is Australia's largest trading partner and a key market for Australia's mining resources, agricultural produce and education services. Some argue this gives China increasing leverage over Australia. Yet, at the same time, the US remains Australia's principal security partner. Indeed, despite calls from some quarters for a more equidistant relationship between China and the US, Australia has chosen to deepen its security relationship with the United States (see, for example, White 2010). This ongoing conversation within Australia calls attention to the importance of alliance management.

To engage with the new challenges, Australia and the US have made recent progress in bilateral security cooperation, for instance, through the Defence Trade Cooperation Treaty in 2013, which provides substantial benefits such as reducing red tape, minimizing procurement delays and improved data sharing. Significantly, only the United Kingdom has a similar arrangement with the US, which underlines the strategic importance of Australia to the US. For Australia, such a unique status provides special levels of access and engagement, particularly regarding advanced defence technologies (Church n.d.).

Australia has thus seemingly taken America's side in the Sino-US strategic rivalry. This appears to stem from a cold calculation of its own interests. According to its latest *Foreign Policy White Paper*, 'the Australian Government judges that the United States' long-term interests will anchor its economic and security engagement in the Indo-Pacific', and that 'its major Pacific alliances with Japan, the Republic of Korea and Australia will remain strong' (Department of Foreign Affairs and Trade 2017: 26). In short, the US–Australia alliance is perceived to be pivotal for both countries in the Indo and Asia-Pacific strategic context. Moreover, because this is part of the wider regional alliance system led by the United States, the strength of this alliance has serious implications for other US alliance partners in Asia, as well as for other states in the region.

Challenges within the US–Australia alliance

Yet, the alliance is fundamentally unequal, with the United States shouldering a much heavier financial and operational burden due to its size. As the US revaluates the budgetary balance between defence and domestic spending – a discussion exacerbated by neo-isolationist tendencies – Australia will likely be asked to do even more as a US partner (Church n.d.). This however, raises conundrums for both the United States and Australia.

On Australia's part, will it continue to free-ride on its bigger ally, or will it increase defence spending and procure capabilities that could make a better contribution to regional defence arrangements? As Richard Armitage observed in 2013: if there was any future neuralgia in the Indo-Pacific, then the US would start looking at Australia and ask, 'What's up with that – you're spending 1.56 per cent of GDP? You expect America to be there for you on defence, but you have to be there for yourself as well' (cited in Leah 2016: 532). Thus, the question for Australia is: what can it do to sustain this relationship and play an even greater role in the maintenance of the regional order that has existed since 1945 and which has served it so well? At the time of writing, the geostrategic impact of the COVID-19 global pandemic that swept the globe in early 2020 was unclear. However, China–Australia relations worsened in 2020 due to Australia's championing of an international enquiry into the origins of the global pandemic, leading to unusually strong language from China directed at Australia as well as threats of economic retaliation (ABC 2020a). This manifested itself in the banning of beef imports, an 80 percent tariff on barley and official discouragement of tourism and students from travelling to Australia. As Townshend asserted, this was accompanied by a disinformation campaign, with China accusing Australia, for instance, of cooperating with the United States in its alleged propaganda war against China (Townshend 2020). In response, Prime Minister Scott Morrison declared that he would not 'trade our values in response to coercion from wherever it comes'. This was followed by moves to reinvigorate the Five Eyes intelligence network comprising the US, the UK, New Zealand, Canada and Australia and to coordinate efforts in building trusted supply chains for vital materials (ABC 2020b).

On the part of the United States, Australia is a vital partner for its continued engagement in Asia. In the context of an increasingly complex and dynamic security environment, mixed with growing appetite for partnership among regional states and contrasted with mounting budget challenges and increasing domestic support for isolationism, the US finds itself in need of a reliable partner, who shares its values and has the capability to share the tasks of regional leadership. The region has benefitted from the US-led ruled-based regional order, which has sustained stability and underwritten prosperity since 1945. However, to sustain that order in a time of rising requirements and little chance of budgetary increases the US needs regional allies, such as Australia, to play an increasingly important role in sustaining regional security. The US and its allies will need to increase the extent of their cooperation and integration in order to improve the regional security architecture and ensure this pivotal region continues to grow prosperous and free. The question then is: what are the risks that might lead to a de-emphasis on the bilateral relationship and how can these risks be managed? Just as significant is the question of the implications of the future of the Australia–US alliance for other alliance partners and the entire regional security architecture.

To provide insight into these challenges, this book seeks to identify the common interests and similar security perspectives that sustain the relationship, the key factors underpinning its evolution and potential futures, both for this alliance and the implications for regional order. Moreover, as the US explores a more interest-based and assertive strategy in Asia, albeit complicated by growing neo-isolationist sentiments, it is important that it understands Australia's unique interests and contributions to enable better strategy, efficient division of responsibility and realistic alliance expectations. Meanwhile, as with the past several US administrations, Australia may find itself navigating through US inconsistency in regional engagement, driven by domestic uncertainty and balancing global commitments. All these possibilities will have implications for alliance defence and strategic policies, including strategy, spending and procurement on both sides of the Pacific.

This research is timely, as there are no competing works on this topic and the alliance relationship is a vital component to both regional order and the

US position in Asia. This work is also the first volume on the alliance to appear following the COVID-19 pandemic in 2020. Both countries have to confront a changing strategic environment, and the alliance needs to respond to the challenges that they face. The United States cannot continue to take Australia for granted. It must understand the challenges and risks to this vital relationship, which is growing in importance, and take steps to manage it. On its part, Australia now needs to clearly identify its core common interests with the United States, and start exploring what more it really needs to do to match its stated policy preferences.

Structure of this work

Chapter 2, by Alexander Vuving of the Asia-Pacific Center for Security Studies, evaluates the strategic environment of the US–Australia alliance in the Indo-Pacific era. According to Vuving, the most powerful factors shaping the strategic environment are related to climate, demographic, technological and economic changes, great power relations, big catastrophes, and human dynamics. The ongoing COVID-19 pandemic will have the largest impact on the strategic environment in the short to medium term. Although the directions of many changes brought about by the global plague are still unfathomable as the pandemic continues to unfold, four trends accelerated by the pandemic – the growth in importance of the cyber domain, the bifurcation of the world economy, the intensification of great power competition, and the transformation of international architecture – are constituting the shape of things to come. In the medium to long term, the hegemonic contest between China and the United States will have the largest impact on the strategic environment. This chapter argues that, contrary to the belief of many, there is no Thucydides Trap – the structural cause of war – in this hegemonic contest because it is structured as a game of chicken, not a prisoner's dilemma. It is important for any player in this environment to recognize the strategic structure of the US–PRC hegemonic contest and apply the best strategy for it as suggested by this structure. China has masterfully played the game of chicken with its grey zone tactics, its pursuit of 'war by other means', i.e., its weaponization of the non-military, even of risks. The US–PRC hegemonic contest will not resemble the Cold War much beyond this strategic structure. It will be very different from the Cold War in important aspects, including the ideological and economic realms. Most strikingly, the main front lines of the contest will be in the maritime and cyber domains and, consequently, will be far more fluid and unstable than that of the Cold War.

Chapter 3 examines the United States' security perspectives in the Asia-Pacific and the value of its alliance with Australia, and is written by Paul J. Smith of the United States Naval War College. According to Smith, the United States considers Australia as its closest and most dependable ally in the Indo-Pacific region. For the United States, the alliance provides significant benefits, including intelligence sharing, military support, a market for US defence articles, among others. Thus, when Australian Prime Minister Scott Morrison visited President Donald Trump in September 2019, the two leaders emphasized the strategic convergence and historical depth of the two countries' relationship. However, it is also clear that the two countries have divergent views about the People's Republic of China. Canberra's drive to maintain its 'comprehensive strategic partnership' with Beijing contradicts Washington's more competitive posture vis-à-vis Beijing. Consequently, Australia may be faced with uncomfortable choices if Beijing-Washington ties continue to deteriorate.

Chapter 4 assesses the security threats and challenges to Australia, and is authored by Andrew T. H. Tan. As a middle power, Australia's security and the future challenges that it faces are linked to developments in both its regional and global environments. The fundamental changes in the international system present serious challenges for Australia, a country that has had a long-established pattern of reliance on a great power ally and on a Western-dominated international system. The key drivers that will shape Australia's security environment to 2035 include: the roles of the US and China, and their relationship; challenges to the stability of the rules-based global order; the enduring threat of terrorism; state fragility (especially within Australia's immediate neighbourhood); the pace of military modernization and development of more capable regional military forces; and the emergence of new complex, non-geographic threats, such as cyber threats and pandemics, such as COVID-19. The current Australian policy of continuing security reliance on the United States while taking steps to build a multilateral coalition of like-minded states to help bolster the faltering regional order and maintain the status quo in the face of China's attempts to reshape the regional order to better serve its interests looks to be, on balance, a calibrated and correct one. Whether this will serve Australia in the future as the strategic balance continues to shift, particularly in the wake of the global pandemic in 2020 and worsening relations between China and Australia as well as between China and the United States at the time of writing remains to be seen.

Chapter 5 examines the common interests that bind the United States and Australia, and is written by Bates Gill, one of America's leading experts on China. As Gill observes, the Australia–United States relationship is grounded in a lengthy history of shared experiences, interests and values. In recent years, the alliance relationship has deepened in many ways and become more important to Canberra and Washington. However, the strategic interests between Australia and the United States have never fully overlapped and at times diverged considerably. Moreover, new pressures have mounted in recent years to challenge some of the long-held fundamentals for Australia–United States relations. These emergent pressures include the rise of China and persistent uncertainties surrounding US global and regional leadership. This chapter examines this conundrum for Australian and US interests by identifying and analysing Australian and US geopolitical and security interests at the global level, at the Indo-Pacific regional level and at the level of bilateral ties. The article concludes that Australia and the United States share many interests, but this could change. Canberra and Washington should not be complacent, and have much work to do – through greater transparency, more frank consultation, a broadened definition of the alliance and clearer understanding of one another's strategic objectives – to sustain this exceptional partnership into the 21st century.

Chapter 6, by Shannon Brandt Ford, discusses the evolution of the US–Australia strategic relationship. This relationship has evolved from more or less an adversarial position in the 19th century to an Australia largely dependent on the US during the Cold War to the interdependent partnership we see today. Strategic interdependence means the US–Australia relationship is not merely a one-sided affair; and that Australia has something of substance to offer to the strategic relationship. The strong relationship is founded on a shared language, similar social values and compatible political-legal systems. Moreover, the relationship has been institutionalized through intelligence cooperation, defence science collaboration and extensive personal relationships. But what the US really seems to value is Australia's reliability as an ally. Ford argues that Australia best demonstrates its reliability as an ally when it follows US strategic decision-making for the right reasons. This sense of reliability is more akin to trustworthiness than it is to loyalty. History demonstrates that Australia has not always agreed with the US, but agreeing does not matter so much when Australia has established a track record of consistently applying sound reasoning to its strategic decisions and has made substantive contributions to jointly sought after strategic outcomes.

Chapter 7, written by Alan Bloomfield, examines defence co-operation between Australia and the United States. It surveys the state of Australia–US defence co-operation in four main ways. First, it considers the broad strategic relationship and finds that while the two states' interests do not align perfectly, mainly because Australia relies much more heavily than the US on trade with China. However, the allies' identities are very similar, and they are core members of the Anglosphere security community, which provides a very firm basis for defence co-operation in more discrete policy realms. The chapter then examines bilateral defence co-operation in training and combat operations, in intelligence-sharing and operation of the Joint Facilitates in Australia and in defence procurement. It concludes that not only is it likely that Australia and the United States will increase defence policy co-operation as China rises and threatens the status quo they both seek to protect, but that there is also little chance Australia would move to end the alliance in the foreseeable future because doing so would require a radical change in Australian strategic culture.

Chapter 8, entitled 'China–US–Australia: Redefining the Strategic Triangle', is jointly authored by Adam Lockyer, Scott D. McDonald and Yves Heng-Lim. Australia's security is acclimated to its relationship with the United States (US), while its economy is increasingly oriented on the People's Republic of China (PRC). Despite this apparently awkward position between the two powers, Australia has considerable say in both of these relationships. Drawing on the concept of strategic triangles offered by Lowell Dittmer, this chapter explores the value of viewing the Australia–US–PRC relationship under this paradigm. Using Dittmer's typology, the Australia–US relationship will remain a 'stable marriage'. This relationship is grounded in shared values and is believed by both sides to remain beneficial. The Australia–PRC leg of the relationship has greatly benefitted the Australian economy, but led to fears that the PRC's economic pull could undermine Australia's relationship with the US. However, this fear appears overstated, as a PRC-led Indo-Pacific order remains unattractive to Canberra. Instead, it is the US–PRC leg of the relationship itself that could have the largest impact on Australia's economy and security. Concerns over the increasingly competitive nature of the relationship, as well as concern it would be forced to pick a side are more likely to cause a re-evaluation of its cost and benefits than Australia's bilateral relationship with either partner. Consequently, it is in Australia's interests to attempt to move the triangular relationship in the direction of Dittmer's '*ménage à trois*'. The chapter concludes by drawing out recommendations for all three parties on how they might restructure the triangular relationship and develop a more stable and prosperous Indo-Pacific.

Chapter 9, entitled 'The US–Australian Alliance and its Implications for Australian Defence Strategy and Procurement', is jointly authored by Fred Smith (Captain, US Navy retired), Yves-Heng Lim and Adam Lockyer. As the authors note, Australia's alliance with the United States has long been the cornerstone upon which its defence strategy and many of its procurement decisions rest. Indeed, there are few stages within Australia's defence planning process where the US alliance is not a prominent – if not the primary – factor in the decision-making process. However, the US–Australia alliance is entering a new era and the expectations of each partner are shifting quickly. This chapter sketches some likely possible futures for Australia, in terms of both the US alliance and procurement. It examines the historical antecedents of the relationship before outlining how changes in the military balance in Asia are affecting the US–Australia alliance. The chapter also outlines some possible future options for Australia in regards to the alliance and procurement.

Chapter 10, by Andrew O'Neil, examines the future of Australia–US strategic and defence cooperation from an Australian perspective. As the regional security environment in the Indo-Pacific becomes increasingly unstable, Australian policy makers face serious challenges in the coming years, particularly the management of the US alliance. O'Neil examines the key drivers of the Australia–US alliance and discusses three potential options for Australian policy makers to recalibrate the country's strategic policy – armed neutrality, bandwagoning with China, and deeper commitment to the US alliance – all of which would have major implications for the alliance. While the logic of path dependency points to deeper commitment being most likely, the US alliance will incur greater costs for Australia irrespective of who is in the White House from January 2021.

Chapter 11, by Scott D. McDonald, assesses the future of the Australia–US strategic and defence cooperation from the US perspective. Although the US–Australia alliance remains strong, the end of the Cold War and changes in the region necessitate a reorientation and reinvigoration of the partnership. The world that confronts Australia and the US today is not one of imminent military threat. While security issues remain, they tend to be of a less existential nature. Moreover, the application of military power is insufficient to meet present security challenges, or nurture a desired regional order. Therefore, this chapter presents a new vision for the Australia–US alliance. This updated alliance will be based around four foundational principles. First, it must be a whole-of-government effort, nested in the grand-strategic level of statecraft. Second, the alliance must operate from a positive, pro-value orientation, rather than focused on countering any specific adversary. The principles behind the Free and Open Indo-Pacific concept are widely accepted in the region and well-suited as a vision to promote regionally. In order to accomplish this, the third principle is integration. This must occur at the policy level, ensuring allied ideas are raised early and often in the policy-development process, as well as at the functional level, ensuring the allies are acting in concert across the elements of national power – diplomatic, informational, military and economic. Finally, the alliance will implement its vision by serving as a catalyst for developing a network of partners across the region, leveraging the 'partnerships for a purpose' concept to bring like-minded states together around a variety of interests. The chapter then notes several risks to the alliance, but argues that mitigation for these, though not fool proof, lie in tighter integration and more robust exchange proposed by the chapter's concept for the alliance.

Note

1 ANZUS, 1951; US–Japan, 1951; US–Philippines, 1951; US–Korea, 1953; SEATO, 1954 (though the organization dissolved, the Manila Pact remains the basis of the US security relationship with Thailand); US–Republic of China (Taiwan), 1955–1979.

References

ABC (2020a), 'China's "Wolf Warrior Diplomacy" With Australia Over COVID-19', www.youtube.com/watch?v=9NC9fL72PYI accessed 30 April 2020.

ABC (2020b), 'China Seems Intent on Using its Economic Heft to Intimidate Australia – But the Government is Eyeing Off a New Plan', 13 June, available at www. abc.net.au/news/2020-06-13/coronavirus-china-australia-foreign-students-threats-fed eral-gov/12350738 accessed 16 June 2020.

Air Force, Australia (n.d.), 'F35 Joint Strike Fighter', available at www.airforce.gov.au/ technology/aircraft/strike/f-35a-joint-strike-fighter accessed 5 January 2020.

Australian (2011), 'US President Barack Obama's Speech to Parliament', *The Australian*, 17 November.

Australian Embassy, Washington (n.d.). 'Australia–US Defence Relationship', available at https://usa.embassy.gov.au/defence-cooperation accessed 1 April 2020.

Bisley, Nick (2013), 'An Ally for all the Years to Come: Why Australia is not a Conflicted US Ally', *Australian Journal of International Affairs*, 67 (4).

Church, Nathan (n.d.), 'The Australia–United States Defence Alliance', Parliament of Australia, available at www.aph.gov.au/About_Parliament/Parliamentary_Departm ents/Parliamentary_Library/pubs/BriefingBook44p/AustUSDefence accessed 5 January 2020.

Department of Foreign Affairs and Trade (2017), *Foreign Policy White Paper*, available at www.fpwhitepaper.gov.au/ accessed 5 January 2020.

Department of Foreign Affairs and Trade (2019), 'Trilateral Security Dialogue Joint Ministerial Statement', media release, 9 August, www.foreignminister.gov.au/minis ter/marise-payne/media-release/trilateral-strategic-dialogue-joint-ministerial-stateme nt accessed 4 September 2020.

Guardian (2012), 'Australian General to Help Lead US Military Push into Pacific', *The Guardian*, 20 August, www.theguardian.com/world/2012/aug/21/australia n-general-us-army-pacific, accessed 10 January 2020.

Leah, Christine M. (2016), 'Deterrence Beyond Down-under: Australia and US Security Guarantees since 1955', *Journal of Strategic Studies*, 39 (4).

Office of the Historian (n.d.), 'The Australia, New Zealand and United States Security Treaty (ANZUS Treaty), 1951', available at https://history.state.gov/milestones/ 1945-1952/anzus accessed 5 January 2020.

O'Neil, Andrew (2017), 'Australia and the "Five Eyes" Intelligence Network: The Perils of an Asymmetric Alliance', *Australian Journal of International Affairs*, 71 (5).

Stars and Stripes (2013), 'US Increasing Number of Marines on Rotation to Aus-tralia', 14 June, available at www.stripes.com/news/pacific/us-increasing-number-of-marines-on-rotation-to-australia-1.225843 accessed 5 January 2020.

Sydney Morning Herald (2018), 'China Trade with Australia Soars, Along with War of Words', 12 January, available at www.smh.com.au/world/china-trade-with-austra lia-soars-along-with-war-of-words-20180112-h0hfkq.html accessed 5 January 2020.

Tan, Andrew T. H. (2014), 'Why China is Not a Global Power', *The RUSI Journal*, 159 (5).

Telegraph (2013), 'China May Not Overtake America This Century After All', *The Telegraph*, 8 May, available at www.telegraph.co.uk/finance/comment/10044456/ China-may-not-overtake-America-this-century-after-all.html accessed 5 January 2020.

Townshend, Ashley (2020), 'China's Pandemic-Fuelled Standoff with Australia', United States Studies Centre, 20 May, available at www.ussc.edu.au/analysis/china s-pandemic-fuelled-standoff-with-australia accessed 16 June 2020.

White, Hugh (2010), 'Power Shift: Australia's Future Between Washington and Beijing', *Quarterly Essay*, 39.

White, Hugh (2017), 'Without America: Australia in the New Asia', *Quarterly Essay*, 68.

Yahuda, Michael (2013), 'China's New Assertiveness in the South China Sea', *Journal of Contemporary China*, 22 (81).

Part I

US and Australian perspectives of the Indo-Pacific

2 The strategic environment of the US–Australia alliance in the Indo-Pacific era

Alexander L. Vuving

As the US–Australia alliance connects a global power with a regional power, its ambit is global with a regional focus. This region was called the 'Asia-Pacific' in the decades extending from the last stage of the Cold War (the 1980s) to the last stage of the post-Cold War period (the 2010s). Australia was a strong proponent of the idea of the Asia-Pacific, a posture that manifested not least in Australia's driving role in the creation of the Asia-Pacific Economic Cooperation (APEC). During the 2010s, the idea of the Indo-Pacific emerged to replace that of the Asia-Pacific, and Australia is again a promoter of the new idea (Medcalf 2020). In both constructs, Australia retains its geographic position as one of the pivots of the region: a hinge country between Asia and the Pacific, and between the Indian and Pacific Oceans. Like the Asia-Pacific before it, the Indo-Pacific is both a region and an idea, a fact and a vision. If the Asia-Pacific anticipated a trough in great power competition and strived for an economically integrated and prosperous region, the Indo-Pacific is a response to the rise of great power competition with the vision of a region free of domination by any great power and open to all.[1] Only partly fulfilled, the vision of the Asia-Pacific has already been overcome by the contestation of the Indo-Pacific, One Belt One Road, and possibly other visions to come. This incompleteness resulted from the changing strategic environment. The fate of the Indo-Pacific, One Belt One Road, and other visions will also hinge on the evolution of the strategic environment in the decades to come.

This chapter will examine the strategic environment of the US–Australia alliance in the Indo-Pacific era. It starts with a general framework that teases out the chief currents shaping the strategic environment. One of these currents is the ongoing coronavirus disease 2019 (COVID-19) pandemic with its tremendous destructive – and creative – forces. The second section will identify the trends triggered or accelerated by this pandemic that will have a large impact on the post-COVID-19 world. Key questions about peace and war and about strategy will be given an analytic foundation in the third section. This section will discuss the strategic structure of great power competition while the fourth section will address the implications of this structure for the strategies of the players and the outcomes of their game. It argues that, contrary to the belief of many, the Thucydides trap, i.e., the structural cause of war, does not exist in all cases of hegemonic contest. If war is inevitable in some cases, peace is equally attainable in some others, depending on the strategic structure of the competition. Based on the previous sections, the fourth section will further characterize the strategic environment by comparing it with the last peak period of great power competition – the Cold War. As with the Cold War, there is no Thucydides trap in the hegemonic contest between the United States and the People's Republic of China (PRC). But the next 'Cold War' will be very different from the last in important aspects, including the ideological and economic realm. Most strikingly, the main front lines of the contest will be in the maritime and cyber domains and, consequently, will be far more fluid and unstable than those of the Cold War.

The multi-current river that is the strategic environment

The strategic environment is the totality of factors that affect the strategic trajectories of the actors concerned. These factors change at different paces, ranging from very rapid changes measurable in days and months to very slow changes that become visible only in several decades. One characteristic of the strategic environment is that it never stops changing. Its change results from a myriad of changes that occur at very different paces and the interaction of these multi-speed changes. These two characteristics make the strategic environment a multi-current river: it is interwoven and driven by multiple interacting currents residing at various depths and moving with different speeds. The currents that make up this river are numerous, but the most powerful ones can be grouped under six headings: climate change, demographic change, technological and economic change, great power relations, catastrophes of a large magnitude, and human dynamics in each society.

Climate change deeply shapes the strategic environment. Not all changes in the climate shape the strategic environment, and the ones that do often move very slowly; their effect on the big picture can only be felt in the very long term, in many decades. Many effects of climate change on the strategic environment have their harbinger in the melting of the ice cap in the Arctic and Antarctica. Between 1989 and 2019, the Arctic ice cap lost 2.69 million square kilometre, or 38.4 per cent of its area, and is now declining with a rate of 12.85 per cent per decade. The land ice sheets in Antarctica also lost mass an average of 147 giga-tonnes per year between 2002 and 2020 (NASA n.d. a; NASA n.d. b). These trends are likely to continue in the next decades.

The melting of the Arctic icecap has opened a new transoceanic trading route – the Northeast Passage – that is the shortest sea route connecting Western Europe and Eastern Asia. The opening of the Northeast Passage has intensified power competition in the Arctic, drawing not just resident great powers Russia and the United States, but also China, a non-resident great power, into a 'great game' in the region.

The melting of ice at Antarctica makes it easier to exploit the natural resources under its soil as well as the location of its land. China has been the most active to grasp this opportunity. Its action is certainly driven by its hunger for natural resources, but it may also reflect the instinct of a master *go* player searching for strategic places and of someone who wants to impress the world with a special feat. Replicating the South China Sea plot, China can multiply, enlarge, and turn its scientific bases in Antarctica into hybrid bases in a few decades. As the shortest routes from China to Antarctica run through Australia's waters, China's interests in Antarctica has added more strategic importance to Australia on the chessboard – or more precisely, the *go* board – of great power competition. China's strategic interests in the Arctic and Antarctica also helps to redefine the US–Australia alliance as an alliance 'from the Arctic to the Antarctic'.

A major consequence of the melting of ice at the Arctic and Antarctica is the rise of sea level. Although the sea does not rise equally in all places and some coral reefs such as Tuvalu, the proverbial sinking nation, actually grew larger despite sea level rise, the narrative that small islands in the middle of the ocean are sinking remains powerful particularly among the nations of the South Pacific, which are mostly small islands with vast exclusive economic zones (EEZs) (Nield 2018). Playing on this narrative, China can offer to help with its superior land reclamation capabilities, demonstrated spectacularly in the South China Sea, in return for certain rights on some strategically located islands and privileges in the vast EEZs of the Pacific islands. Australia and the United States must not be surprised by such bargains and ready for solutions.

Demographic change is a vast category for migrations and changes in different demographic structures of the population related to age, education, ideological orientation, etc. These changes affect the vitality and coherence of nations, the balance of power among them, and the shape of the strategic environment in the long term. Japan, South Korea, and China are the most rapidly ageing nations in the Indo-Pacific, while Pakistan, India, and Indonesia continue to have a youth bulge for one or more decades (United Nations, Department of Economic and Social Affairs, Population Division 2019). Ageing societies are faced with problems of a shrinking workforce, while violent extremism challenges countries with a sizable unemployed young population, and people tend to migrate from youthful countries to ageing ones. Being immigrant nations, Australia and the United States stand to win if they let in hard-working and talented people and leave out those whose attitude or aptitude may cause problems for the society. In the long term, population growths in India, Pakistan, Indonesia, Australia, and the United States and population losses in Japan and China will shift the balance of power in the Indo-Pacific in favour of the former at the expense of the latter, provided that the former maintain their national coherence.

Technological and economic changes move in waves, and the most powerful wave that will shape the strategic environment in the decades to come is the Fourth Industrial Revolution. Starting in the 1990s, this fourth wave of the Industrial Revolution is characterized by the high speed of change and the intensity of innovation in the fields of information and communication technology. New technologies like big data, artificial intelligence, blockchain, the Internet of Things, and autonomous vehicles/weapons are revolutionizing our lives and the world and bringing in revolutionary changes in society, economy, military, and governance. With their help, humanity will reach new heights in our capabilities to produce resources, connect people, organize people, and coerce each other.

Each wave of the Industrial Revolution makes a new domain available to human activities: the Second Industrial Revolution added the air domain to the land and maritime domains; the Third Industrial Revolution opened up the space domain; the Fourth Industrial Revolution created the cyber domain. Like the other non-land domains, the cyber domain is more of a global commons than a national territory. A virtual domain, the cyber domain cannot be militarized in the traditional sense because it cannot host the traditional military means, but it has already been weaponized and can carry non-traditional military means that may be developed in the future.

Great powers are the most powerful actors in the system and their relations, whether cooperative or competitive, have the strongest direct impact on the overall balance of power that shapes the strategic environment. Unlike most other actors, which are 'system-takers', great powers are 'system-makers'. Prior to the nuclear age, an upswing phase in production and technological innovation was often accompanied by a hegemonic war (Goldstein 1988). The Fourth Industrial Revolution is bringing a production upturn in a cycle that returns only in several decades, and since the 2010s, great power competition has also been on the rise. The hegemonic contest of our time is between the United States and the PRC. Russia and Islamic fundamentalists are also major global challengers of the United States but they are not system-makers like America and China.

The strategic competition between China and the United States is most intense in the Indo-Pacific, where both countries have a part or whole of their territory. The system-makers of this region include China, America, Japan, and, increasingly, India. The United States, Japan, and India are united in their determination to thwart China's bid for predominance. Most other states in the region are behaving like swing states – hedging between the two superpowers or taking a side temporarily. China is building an alliance system with Chinese characteristics through a complex web of *guanxi* – the reciprocity of favours and the primacy of relationships – and 'debt traps' created by its One Belt One Road programme. The United States is recruiting allies by strengthening ties with its Cold War allies and nurturing strategic partnerships with emerging regional powers.

A catastrophe of a large magnitude can upset the strategic environment. We are experiencing such a catastrophe – the COVID-19 pandemic. But such catastrophes can come in many forms. About 75,000 years ago the Toba volcanic eruption caused a years-long winter in large parts of the world and may have had an immense impact on the evolution of humanity. The Third

Industrial Revolution had added radioactive contamination to the list, and the Fourth Industrial Revolution, still unknown catastrophes in the Internet of Things and disasters caused by artificial intelligence and autonomous weapons. These 'black swan' events change the world enormously in directions we cannot predict while affecting the world and humanity unevenly.

Human dynamics in each society contribute many deep currents that make up the strategic environment. History has plenty of examples when a charismatic leader like Napoleon, a social movement like socialism, an appealing ideology like nationalism, a far reaching reform like that of Genghis Khan, or 'new kids on the block' like the Islamic fundamentalists transformed the strategic environment. These dynamics often are unknown unknowns to the contemporaries and change the world in unpredictable ways.

The post-COVID-19 world

Like other catastrophes of a large magnitude, the COVID-19 pandemic will leave a gigantic scare on humanity. It will cause tremendous changes in the ways people live and the institutions they create, and it will force people to rethink their ideas and habits and adjust to the new normal. The post-COVID-19 world will be different from the pre-COVID-19 one in many aspects, most of which have yet to become visible. But six months after the first outbreak in Wuhan, some changes triggered or accelerated by the pandemic that will have a significant impact on the strategic environment are already discernible.

First, the cyber domain, already indispensable for human life and a critical domain of human activities, has gained more importance and will be more so in the future. The cyber domain has become a lifeline during the pandemic, carrying much of human communications and social activities – tens of millions of people depend on it when working from home or in lockdown. The Fourth Industrial Revolution, with its reliance on the Internet of Things and mobile networks, renders the cyber domain essential for economics, politics, and security. In some respects, it has become more important than the air and space domains because it carries information that everyone relies on.

Human communications and social activities are present in the form of data in the cyber domain. These data can be collected, controlled, and manipulated by those that provide the software, user devices, physical networks, and virtual platforms for the communications and activities to take place. As it stands today, a small number of 'big tech' companies dominates the markets for these goods and services. Their access to data and devices and their control of networks and platforms make them critical actors in the geopolitical system. These 'new kids on the block' have the power to *change* the system, though the power to *make* the system still lies in the hands of great powers.

Second, the COVID-19 pandemic has laid bare the vulnerability and, in some cases, fatal dependency of many countries on China, urging some to diversify the supply chains and reduce their dependence on China. The United States, which boasts the world's largest economy, and Japan, which has the world's third largest, are leading effort to diversify their supply chains, even decouple their economy, from the world's second largest economy – China. As a part of its economic stimulus package to cushion the negative impact of the pandemic, Japan has earmarked \$2.2 billion to help its firms to shift production out of China (Bloomberg 2020). In late April 2020, alluding to a video conference initiated by the United States and including six other Indo-Pacific countries – Australia, India, Japan, South Korea, New Zealand, and Vietnam – which make up a new grouping called the 'Quad Plus' by observers, US Secretary of State Mike Pompeo said that Washington was working with these 'friends' to explore 'how we restructure these supply chains to prevent something like this from ever happening again' (Pompeo 2020a). In early May 2020, Reuters reported that 'the US Commerce Department, State and other agencies are looking for ways to push companies to move both sourcing and manufacturing out of China'. According to a senior US official cited by the Reuters report, 'the United States is pushing to create an alliance of "trusted partners" dubbed the "Economic Prosperity Network"' (Pamuk and Shalal 2020). These efforts are unlikely to achieve their objectives in the short term, and decoupling will not happen overnight, but with the intensification of power competition between China and its global, regional, and subregional rivals, the bifurcation of the world economy will be a long-term trend in the next decades.

Third, the COVID-19 pandemic presents a golden opportunity for hard and soft power competition between strategic rivals both at the global and the regional level. China and the United States have engaged in a blame game regarding who is responsible for causing and worsening the pandemic. The global preoccupation with the health crisis appeared to give China an opportunity to step up aggression on the conflict zones along its land and sea frontiers. In the South China Sea, China continued to be more assertive, a trend that started around 2007 and ratcheted up every two years or so since. Examples of PRC aggression during the first six months of the COVID-19 pandemic include the survey of a vast swath of waters within Malaysia's EEZ, the sinking of Vietnamese fishing boats, and large-scale military drills simulating island seizure (Asia Maritime Transparency Initiative 2020; Al Jazeera 2020; Japan Times 2020). The United States responded with rare actions that clearly sent a strong signal of US commitment to the region. US warships were seen in the scenes of 'cat and mouse' games between Chinese, Vietnamese, and Malaysian vessels. In July 2020, for the first time since 2014, two US aircraft carriers were present at the same time in the South China Sea; moreover, they conducted exercises when China also carried out military drills in the region (Trevithick 2020). In July, the United States for the first time explicitly rejected a large part of China's maritime and territorial claims in the south and east South China Sea (Pompeo 2020b). Also during the pandemic, although no shot was fired, a deadliest clash between China and India since their border war of 1962 broke out in the Ladakh section of their Line of Actual Control. Tellingly, Washington extended 'deepest condolences' to New Delhi and accused Beijing of escalating border tensions with India (PTI 2020; Basu 2020).

Fourth, the pandemic has strengthened the role of the nation-state and weakened that of the existing international organizations. The strongest and most effective responses to the pandemic came from the state, while most multilateral institutions receded into the sideline. As nation-states badly need the cooperation of others, it is unlikely that multilateral institutions will fade away in the post-COVID-19 world. Rather, the pandemic will accelerate major changes in the international architecture, shaking up the foundations of many existing international organizations, throwing some into irrelevance, while facilitating the creation of new groupings and giving a new face to international architecture.

This transformation of the international architecture had already started well before the coronavirus ravaged humanity. International organizations work well if the great powers that sponsor them cooperate. But if their competition intensifies, international organizations will either become the arena of their competition or be weaponized by one against the other. As a result, these organizations will be paralyzed by the power rivalry, sometimes abandoned by a great power that has previously sponsored it. Great powers unsatisfied with existing multilateral institutions will create new ones under their leadership. This trend had started in the 2010s and will be even stronger in the 2020s.

The transformation of the international architecture will be most salient in the Indo-Pacific region, the core region of China's rise and the Australia–US alliance. The regional architecture of the Asia-Pacific era, dominated by APEC, the Asean Regional Forum (ARF), the East Asia Summit (EAS), and the Asean Defence Ministers' Meeting Plus (ADMM+), will be replaced by new architecture that better reflects the efforts of regional great powers and middle powers to realize their new visions and to cope with the changing strategic environment. The Association of the Southeast Asian Nations (ASEAN) will continue to work at the level of the lowest common denominator, which will be even lower in the future, as all members of the group need it in their coping with the vicissitude of great power relations. But given the growing diversity of their higher interests, ASEAN will be less united and Southeast Asia cannot avoid becoming a battlefield of the struggle for spheres of influence between the two opposing great power camps.

These trends – the growth in importance of the cyber domain, the bifurcation of the world economy, the intensification of great power competition, and the transformation of international architecture – have already begun before the outbreak of the new coronavirus, but the pandemic is giving them strong impetus to accelerate. They are now integral parts of the contour of the post-COVID-19 world, although the directions of many changes brought about by the global plague are still unfathomable as the pandemic continues to unfold.

The strategic structure of great power competition

If the COVID-19 pandemic will have the largest impact on the strategic environment in the short to medium term, the US–PRC hegemonic contest will have the largest impact in the medium to long term. Although the future is open and everything is possible, not all possibilities are created equal. Some possibilities are more likely than others because the field of possibilities is shaped by structures. In particular, the strategic structure of a hegemonic contest ensures that some outcomes of the competition are more stable than others and some strategies of the contenders are more effective than others. Understanding the strategic structure of great power competition will help us answer key questions related to war and peace and strategy.

The inevitability of war is a structural feature of most cases of hegemonic contest in the past (Vuving 2020). Most great powers in the 5,200-year-long history of great power competition saw their own predominance as the best option and their own subordination as the worst. For them, nothing, including war, was worse than subordination, because the subordinated was guaranteed to lose everything she valued most in life: honour, material wealth, independence, freedom. War with one or more peer challengers was their next worst option. Their second best option was a peaceful division of power that was acceptable to the great powers involved. We can symbolize this preference order as: P > D > W > S. When two great powers having this preference order engage in a strategic competition, they are locked in a situation that game theorists call 'prisoner's dilemma'.

This situation has a distinctive structure that renders the best strategy for each player invariably to 'defect' – to pursue its self-interest regardless of whether the opponent will cooperate or not. Hence the outcome of this game is inevitably the third best option for both players, which is confrontation. This outcome is evolutionarily stable and called a 'Nash equilibrium' after John Nash, who has shown mathematically how the structure of a strategic game dictates the best strategies for the players and thus determines the stable outcomes of their game. (Nash was awarded a Nobel Prize in economics 40 years later for this work.) In the language of game theory, the prisoner's dilemma has only one Nash equilibrium, and that is war when the players are great powers and their game is great power competition. The Greek historian Thucydides in his book, *The History of the Peloponnesian War*, left a famous comment on the inevitability of war between the hegemonic contenders of his time and place. He wrote, 'it was the rise of Athens and the fear that this inspired in Sparta that made war inevitable'. This was a 5th century BC statement of the Nash equilibrium of the prisoner's dilemma.

Recently, Graham Allison invoked this quote and coined the term 'Thucydides's trap' to describe the inclination to war of great power competition. He raised the spectre of war between the United States and China and asked, 'Can America and China escape Thucydides's trap?' (Allison 2017). But the talk about the Thucydides trap is misplaced at best because it is based on a fundamentally flawed assumption. It assumes that the Thucydides trap exists whenever great powers engage in intense competition. This assumption ignores the fact that not all cases of great power competition share a similar structure as illustrated by Thucydides's quote about the inevitability of war between Athens and Sparta.

Indeed, some factors such as technology and geography can transform the prisoner's dilemma into a game of chicken (Vuving 2020). The two games are very different in terms of their outcomes and the best strategies for the players. How does technology transform the prisoner's dilemma into a game of chicken? Nuclear weapons, due to its 'overkill' effect, render war between nuclear-armed states worse than subordination. An all-out nuclear war between great powers can destroy all human life on Earth, first and foremost the lives of the great powers involved. How does geography transform the prisoner's dilemma into a game of chicken? Distance of the domain of contest from the home territory of a great power can make this contender perceive the value of predominance in that domain smaller than the cost of war in the home area. If leaders of great powers have this perception – that war is worse than subordination – then their preference order is P > D > S > W. When two great powers having this preference order engage in a strategic competition, they are locked in a situation that theorists call a 'game of chicken'.

The most striking difference between the prisoner's dilemma and the game of chicken is the reverse of their outcomes. If both players in the prisoner's dilemma are bound to clash, they are bound to avoid their clash in the game of chicken. Unlike the prisoner's dilemma, the game of chicken has three Nash equilibria (Colman 2017). Accordingly, the stable outcome of great power competition structured as a game of chicken can be either a division of power that both contenders more or less honour or the predominance of one of the contenders.

Two of the major cases of great power competition in the past 500 years, the Cold War between the nuclear-armed United States and Soviet Union (USSR) and the hegemonic contest between Portugal and Spain over colonial supremacy in the 'new world' of the late 15th and early 16th century, perfectly fit this model. Their results are well predicted by the Nash equilibria of the chicken game. The Cold War took the form of an extremely tense but relatively stable division of Europe, its central theatre of contest, throughout the length of the conflict and eventually resulted in US hegemony when the Soviet Union imploded. The hegemonic contest between Spain and Portugal resulted in the 1494 Treaty of Tordesillas, which gave each contender the exclusive right to trade directly with and conquer a half of the globe. This agreement held well into the 16th century even when it turned out that Spain had gotten the better end of the deal.

Two other cases in the 16 cases examined by Allison to advance the Thucydides's trap thesis also resulted in no war: the competition between the United Kingdom and the United States over naval supremacy in the Western Hemisphere in the late 19th and early 20th century and the competition

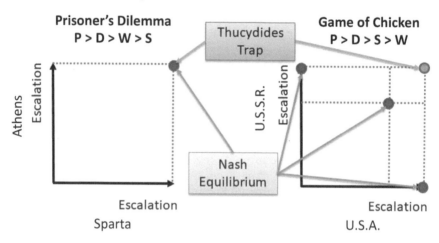

Figure 2.1 Strategy and outcome of great power competition.

between the UK and France on one side and Germany on the other over leadership in post-Cold War Europe. The US vs UK rivalry was an asymmetric game where for the UK, war was worse than subordination to the US in the Western Hemisphere (the UK preference order was P > D > S > W), while for the US, subordination to the UK was worse than war (the US preference order was P > D > W > S). In accordance with the Nash equilibrium of this game, the UK conceded to US naval supremacy in the Western Hemisphere rather than resort to war with the US. The UK/France vs Germany competition was structured as a game called 'concord' by game theorists. Their leaders and elites, especially those of Germany and France, have deeply learned the bloody lessons of the First World War, the Second World War, and the many wars that ravaged Europe in the preceding centuries. This deep historical learning combined with the fear of a nuclear war has changed their preference order to D > P > S > W, rendering their great power competition a 'concord', not a prisoner's dilemma or a game of chicken.

Yet, these 'peace' cases are treated as anomalies in the Thucydides's trap thesis, while the 'war' cases are regarded as normal (Allison 2017).[2] In light of the strategic game structure, however, war was avoided in these cases because they did not share the structure of the rivalry between Athens and Sparta in the 5th century BC or that between Britain and Germany in the early 20th century, as Allison claims. In other words, there was no Thucydides's trap in the four cases that did not result in a war in the Thucydides's trap case file. The risks of war still exist in the games of chicken, especially when both players escalate, but they lie in human errors, machinery defects, or other non-structural factors, not in Thucydides's trap.

Are we entering a new Cold War?

One powerful way to imagine the coming hegemonic contest is to compare it with the last – the Cold War. This question is not just an intellectual exercise, but it has a practical purpose. If the current great power competition is a new Cold War, then we can mine the Cold War for good strategies and good lessons. But if it is not, then we would rather find wisdom elsewhere. So, are we entering a new Cold War? The truth is mixed. The hegemonic contest between China and the United States is similar to the Cold War in some aspects, but it differs from the Cold War in many others.

The key similarity between the US–PRC competition and the US–USSR rivalry is that both are structured as games of chicken. This is because for both the United States and the PCR, like the United States and the Soviet Union during the Cold War, an all-out nuclear war is worse than their acceptance of the other's supremacy. Both the PRC and the United States are nuclear-armed to the extent that their weapons arsenals are enough to destroy both of them many times over. Each possesses the capability to strike back after being first hit by the other. And, most importantly, their political elites are well aware of this 'overkill' effect of nuclear weapons (Kristensen and Koda 2019; Pearce and Denkenberger 2018; Fravel and Medeiros 2010; Xu 2016: 24). Moreover, all the major powers involved in this strategic competition – the United States, China and Russia at the global level, and China, Russia, the United States, India, and Japan at the regional level in the Indo-Pacific – are all nuclear-armed, or, in the case of Japan, is under the nuclear umbrella of the United States. According to the logic of the chicken game, the Third World War is unlikely to occur, although high tensions and dangerous crises will abound and localized, conventional conflicts are possible.

With regard to strategy, if one side escalates and the other side deescalates, the more aggressive side will gain and the gains tend to be frozen into the status quo. But if both sides escalate, they will eventually reach some sort of agreement, expressly or tacitly. Knit together, these agreements will form a division of power between the main contenders, creating their spheres of influence in the major domains of contest.

Interactions in the East China Sea, the South China Sea, and along the Sino-Indian land border in the past decades followed neatly these patterns. China seized the Scarborough Shoal in 2012 after the Philippines, brokered by the United States, agreed to withdraw its Navy vessel from the scene (Heydarian 2015). During 2013–2017, China built several artificial islands in the disputed Spratly and Paracel Islands without any kinetic opposition by others. These are now parts of the 'new normal' in the South China Sea (Beech 2018). By contrast, China's unilateral deployment of a giant oil rig, the HYSY-981, in waters claimed by Vietnam near the Paracels was met with vehement resistance from the latter, which held the line throughout the standoff by not only sending its law enforcement vessels to challenge Chinese ships on the ground, but also bringing the matter to international forums and international journalists to the scene. In the end, China had to withdraw its oil rig and tension was defused while China-Vietnam relations plummeted to the lowest point since 1988 (Vuving 2014a). In 2017 as well as 2020, China's attempt to change the status quo of the Sino-Indian border in the Doklam Plateau and Ladakh, respectively, was halted after India upped the ante (Myers, Barry and Fisher 2017; Hernandez 2017; Hutcheon, Doman and Palmer 2020).

Different perceptions about the propensity of the US–China strategic competition lead to different implications for strategy. If war is a structural tendency, as Allison in the United States and Hugh White in Australia believe, then in order to avert the worse, America, the ruling power, must be ready to share power with China, the rising power (Allison 2017; White 2013). This will turn a symmetric prisoner's dilemma into an asymmetric game in which China can still be aggressive but the United States will play chicken. The new structure eliminates the structural cause of war, but it also creates a structural tendency for Chinese hegemony and US acceptance of Chinese dominance. If the US–PRC rivalry is a symmetric game of chicken, US de-escalation in front to Chinese escalation and, at the macro level, US offer to share power with China in response to China's rising power or assertiveness remain a sensible strategy for one of the game's three Nash equilibria – but the worst of the three for America. A better strategy that can prevent both war and Chinese dominance is holding the line when China is testing your resolve and matching its escalation with your own while maintaining a channel for talks.

The PRC's actions since its birth in 1949 indicate that China is a master player of the game of chicken. Beijing plays the 'aggressive but not very aggressive' actor, which cautious commentators call 'assertive'. As a true inheritor of Sun-tzu, who is famous for dictums such as 'all warfare is based on deception' and 'the supreme art of war is to subdue the enemy without fighting', China pursues psychological campaigns to disarm the mind of its opponents, making them think de-escalation is the best way to respond (Vuving 2019). When its opponent deescalates, China continues to escalate but just a few steps further than its opponent in order to reap strategic gains, then it stops short of open conflict. Its primary use of grey zone tactics is proof that China has full intent to keep the conflict below the threshold of an open military clash (Vuving 2017).

Grey zone approaches play on the gap between the fluid nature of reality and the rigid character of rules, norms, and conventions. Salami slicing, a tactic that flourished during the Cold War, was a chief source of success for China in the South China Sea and the Sino-Indian border. Another grey zone tactic – surrounding a target like a cabbage wrapping itself with layers of non-military forces on the front and paramilitary forces in the middle, supported by military forces over the horizon – has helped China to seize Scarborough Shoal and enlarge its dominance in the South China Sea. Leveraging the third dimension of the grey zone – creating a fait accompli by stealth or surprise – also has a high success rate in the South China Sea. Based on the principles of deniability, camouflage, stealth, indirection, gradualism, and fait accompli, these tactics and others that will be invented or reinvented will gain strategic importance in the coming decades.

As kinetic war becomes too risky in the nuclear age, war by other means, such as economic warfare, information warfare, psychological warfare, 'law-fare' (the use of law as a weapon of conflict), and the weaponization of the non-military will be critical to future power competition (Blackwill and Harris 2016; Qiao and Wang 1999; Vuving 2019). An effective tactic in the game of chicken is 'riskfare' and China has been adept at this tactic in the East and South China Seas (Odom 2019). Riskfare is the deliberate use of risks that plays on the opponent's fear of escalation. As the fear of escalation tends to spread more freely and more quickly in open societies and smaller countries, China has a strong edge in weaponizing risks to achieve its objectives without the use of kinetic force.

The learning curves of other countries, especially the United States, Japan, India, and Australia, will be longer than China's to various extents, but they are also learning – everybody is learning. Due partly to this long learning process, but also to the nature of great power competition, the struggle over leadership in Asia and the world that broke to the surface in the 2010s will likely last for several decades. At the end of this decades-long competition, the final victor is likely the anti-China coalition led by the United States, India, and Japan. This coalition has more chance to win in the end because in its combination it is better positioned and better resourced than China.

Had China confined its hegemonic ambitions to Asia only and accepted US global primacy, the United States would have conceded supremacy in Asia to China, similar to the UK concession to US hegemony in the Western Hemisphere a century earlier. But China has already and aggressively challenged US power around the globe, not least with its extensive Belt and Road Initiative and its combative 5G domination campaign. That has brought home to the United States the China threat, raising the costs of US subordination to China globally, and rendering war the only force that can stop escalation.

The coming hegemonic contest between China and the United States will not resemble the Cold War much beyond its strategic structure. There will be an ideological conflict, with Washington and Beijing each promoting a different sets of values and principles of governance. As a Leninist regime, the PRC has never ceased to regard the 'capitalist-imperialist' America as its ideological enemy. The Trump administration has started a counteroffensive on the ideological front (O'Brien 2020). But the PRC's official ideology of 'socialism with Chinese characteristics' is unlikely to be an effective rallying cry in the international arena, while Beijing lacks an attractive ideology that champions universal, as opposed to nationalistic, values. To expand its soft power, China can rely not so much on the appeal of some universal values or the commitment to a shared ideology but primarily on the ethnic allegiance of the Chinese diaspora, *guanxi* with foreign partners, the attraction of the

Chinese model, and the solidarity of those who share feelings of anti-Americanism.

Like the Soviet state, the PRC state also occupies the 'commanding heights of the economy'. But unlike the Soviet bloc, which was an autarky, China today trades extensively with the outside world and penetrates the world economy like no other states. By 2010, China overtook the United States as the larger trading partner of most countries in the world, including major US allies like South Korea, Australia, and Japan (Leng and Rajah 2019). Efforts to decouple from the Chinese market, if successful, will not result in two independent economic blocs as in the Cold War, but in two interconnected economic blocs that have little to no precedent in history.

The biggest difference between the current great power competition and the Cold War is related to the central domain of contest. During the Cold War, it was Europe because of the industrial capacity of the region and its proximity to the industrial core areas of the Soviet Union. For similar reasons, the great power competition of today is taking place most intensely in East and South Asia and in a new domain that did not exist in the Cold War – the cyber sphere. Most consequently for the stability of the contest, a key difference between the two peak periods of great power competition concerns the places of their main frontlines. The main frontlines of the Cold War were in the land domain and cut across Central Europe. It was relatively stable throughout the conflict because generally defence has the advantage over offense on land. Today, the main frontlines of hegemonic contest are in the maritime domain of the Western Pacific, cutting across the East and South China Seas and running through the Taiwan Strait, and in the cyber domain, cutting across individual countries. The East Asian seas are home to the lifeline of Asia, while the Internet is increasingly a critical lifeline of the world. Major efforts by the hegemonic contenders in these areas are to maintain and enlarge their own sphere of influence while trying to roll back and destroy that of the opponent.

The struggle for spheres of influence has no start and no end. In the East Asian seas, American advantage, gained after the Second World War, has gradually been eroded, in the manner of the salami slicing and the fait accompli, by China's stealthy occupation of the eastern part of the Paracel Islands in 1956, China's seizure of the western group of the islands from South Vietnam in 1974, China's occupation of six reefs in the Spratly Islands in 1988, China's stealthy occupation of Mischief Reef in 1995, China's 'cabbage' seizure of Scarborough Shoal in 2012, and China's building of large artificial islands in the Paracel and Spratly Islands during 2013–2017 (Vuving 2014b). The disputed land border between China and India in the Himalayas also takes centre stage in the contemporary great power competition. But because generally defence has the advantage on land while offense has the advantage in the sea, we will see, as we have seen in the last decade, more dramatic changes in the East Asian seas than on the Sino-Indian land border.

In the cyber domain, the Great Fire Wall of China has not only protected the regime from unfavourable ideas, but it has also helped to turn China into a great incubator for the country's leading tech companies to become world giants. When they go global, as they have since the early 2010s, they help expand the Chinese sphere of influence far beyond the border of China. In September 2018, former Google CEO Eric Schmidt predicted that 'the most likely scenario now is not a splintering, but rather a bifurcation into a Chinese-led internet and a non-Chinese internet led by America' (Kolodny 2018). Today, the division of the cyber domain into a Chinese sphere of influence and a US sphere of influence is well underway, with Huawei, the world's largest producer of 5G equipment, leading the effort to enlarge the Chinese sphere of influence. Like the British East India Company, Huawei is a private company that expands the power of its sovereign by conquering vast and critical areas, this time in the physical backbone of the cyber domain.

Non-existent before the 1990s, the cyber domain is virtual but not non-physical because it has a physical layer. Spheres of influence in this physical layer often reflects and reinforces those in the land domain. Once established, they are also far harder to change than spheres of influence in the maritime domain and the virtual space of the cyber domain. In all these domains, the logic of the game of chicken will apply: if you deescalate, your opponent will get a strong incentive to escalate and the more aggressive player will gain; but if both escalate, both will reach an agreement at the very end. Grey zone operations and hybrid warfare will be the critical instruments in this game of chicken.

Conclusion

One of the strategic objectives of Australia's *2020 Defence Strategic Update* is to shape the country's strategic environment (Australian Government, Department of Defence 2020). Successive US National Security Strategies, at least from the Clinton to the Trump administration, also specify shaping the international environment to protect American interests and advance American values as an overarching foreign policy goal (White House 1998; White House 2017). How can one shape one's geopolitical environment effectively? Effective shaping of the environment is not the same as causing changes or making differences. Much of the time, it is like swimming efficiently in a river.

The river that is the strategic environment has numerous currents residing at different depths and moving at different speeds. These currents, some of which result from the effort to shape the strategic environment by various actors, create vortices large and small in the river. The hegemonic contest between China and the United States is forming the largest vortex in the strategic environment of the decades to come. Given its strategic position as a hinge country between the Indian and Pacific Oceans, Australia will be drawn into this vortex, with or without the US–Australia alliance. It is important for any player in this environment to recognize the strategic structure of the

US–PRC hegemonic contest and apply the best strategy for it as suggested by this structure.

Disclaimer

The views expressed in this chapter are the author's own and do not reflect the official policy or position of the US government, the US Department of Defense, or DKI APCSS.

Notes

1 Japan was the first to announce the vision of a free and open Indo-Pacific, an idea that was soon embraced and further developed by the United States. Australia and India, where the idea of the Indo-Pacific had circulated before it gained currency in the United States, followed suit and, in a 'shared vision' issued in June 2020, endorsed a 'free, open, inclusive and rules-based Indo-Pacific region'. As a response to the US initiative and driven by Indonesia, another hinge country between the Indian and the Pacific Ocean, ASEAN adopted in 2019 an 'outlook on the Indo-Pacific' that emphasizes ASEAN centrality, openness, and inclusivity, among others.
2 In his fullest statement of the Thucydides trap thesis, Allison explained these anomalies by recourse to a plethora of ad hoc factors ranging from the Pope's authority, to economic, political, and security institutions, to the role of statesmen, timing, cultural commonalities, to nuclear weapons and economic interdependence (Allison 2017: 187–286). From the perspective of Occam's razor, Allison's explanations are clearly inferior to an explanation based on the strategic structure of hegemonic contest.

References

Al Jazeera (2020), 'Philippines Backs Vietnam after China Sinks Fishing Boat', 8 April, www.aljazeera.com/news/2020/04/philippines-backs-vietnam-china-sinks-fishing-boat-200409022328432.html accessed 23 July 2020.

Allison, Graham (2017), *Destined for War: Can America and China Escape Thucydides's Trap?*Boston, MA: Houghton Mifflin Harcourt.

Asia Maritime Transparency Initiative (2020), 'Update: Chinese Survey Ship Escalates Three-Way Standoff', 18 May, https://amti.csis.org/chinese-survey-ship-escalates-three-way-standoff accessed 23 July 2020.

Australian Government, Department of Defence (2020), '2020 Defence Strategic Update and 2020 Force Structure Plan', www.defence.gov.au/strategicupdate-2020 accessed 23 July 2020.

Basu, Nayanima (2020), 'Pompeo Cites Ladakh Tensions, Accuses China of Playing 'Rogue Actor' Around the Word', *The Print*, 20 June, https://theprint.in/diplomacy/pompeo-cites-ladakh-tensions-accuses-china-of-playing-rogue-actor-around-world/445643 accessed 23 July 2020.

Beech, Hannah (2018), 'China's Sea Control Is a Done Deal, 'Short of War with the US' ', *The New York Times*, 20 September, www.nytimes.com/2018/09/20/world/asia/south-china-sea-navy.html accessed 23 July 2020.

Blackwill, Robert D. and Jennifer M. Harris (2016), *War by Other Means: Geoeconomics and Statecraft*, Cambridge, MA: Harvard University Press.

Bloomberg (2020), 'Japan to Fund Firms to Shift Production Out of China', *The Economic Times*, 8 April, https://auto.economictimes.indiatimes.com/news/industry/japan-to-fund-firms-to-shift-production-out-of-china/75053048 accessed 23 July 2020.

Colman, Andrew M. (2017), *Game Theory and Its Applications: In the Social and Biological Sciences*, New York: Routledge.

Fravel, M. Taylor and Evan S. Medeiros (2010), 'China's Search for Assured Retaliation', *International Security*, 35 (2).

Goldstein, Joshua S. (1988), *Long Cycles: Prosperity and War in the Modern Age*, New Haven, CT: Yale University Press.

Hernandez, Javier C. (2017), 'China and India Agree to Ease Tensions in Border Dispute', *The New York Times*, 28 August, www.nytimes.com/2017/08/28/world/asia/china-india-standoff-withdrawal.html accessed 23 July 2020.

Heydarian, Richard Javad (2015), *Asia's New Battlefield: The USA, China, and the Struggle for the Western Pacific*, London: Zed Books.

Hutcheon, Stephen, Mark Doman and Alex Palmer (2020), 'High Stakes in a Himalayan Hotspot', ABC News, 9 July, www.abc.net.au/news/2020-07-10/high-stakes-in-china-india-himalayan-border-hotspot/12417248?nw=0 accessed 23 July 2020.

Japan Times (2020), 'China to Conduct Major Military Drill Simulating Seizure of Taiwan-Held Island', 14 May, www.japantimes.co.jp/news/2020/05/14/asia-pacific/china-military-drill-taiwan accessed 23 July 2020.

Kolodny, Lora (2018), 'Former Google CEO Predicts the Internet Will Split in Two – And One Part Will Be Led by China', *CNBC*, 20 September, www.cnbc.com/2018/09/20/eric-schmidt-ex-google-ceo-predicts-internet-split-china.html accessed 23 July 2020.

Kristensen, Hans M. and Matt Koda (2019), 'Chinese Nuclear Forces, 2019', *Bulletin of the Atomic Scientists*, 75 (4).

Leng, Alyssa and Roland Rajah (2019), 'Chart of the Week: Global Trade Through a US–China Lens', *The Interpreter*, Lowy Institute, 18 December, www.lowyinstitute.org/the-interpreter/chart-week-global-trade-through-us-china-lens accessed 23 July 2020.

Medcalf, Rory (2020), *Contest for the Indo-Pacific: Why China Won't Map the Future*, Carlton, VIC: La Trobe University Press.

Myers, Steven Lee, Ellen Barry, and Max Fisher (2017), 'How India and China Have Come to the Brink Over a Remote Mountain Pass', *The New York Times*, 26 July, www.nytimes.com/2017/07/26/world/asia/dolam-plateau-china-india-bhutan.html accessed 23 July 2020.

NASA (n.d. a), 'Arctic Sea Ice Minimum', https://climate.nasa.gov/vital-signs/arctic-sea-ice accessed 21 July 2020.

NASA (n.d. b), 'Ice Sheets', https://climate.nasa.gov/vital-signs/ice-sheets accessed 21 July 2020.

Nield, David (2018), 'This Pacific Island Was Expected to Disappear, But It's Actually Growing Larger', *Science Alert*, 15 February, www.sciencealert.com/pacific-island-nation-expected-to-sink-is-getting-bigger accessed 23 July 2020.

O'Brien, Robert C. (2020), 'The Chinese Communist Party's Ideology and Global Ambitions', remarks delivered by National Security Advisor Robert C. O'Brien, 24 June, Phoenix, Arizona, www.whitehouse.gov/briefings-statements/chinese-communist-partys-ideology-global-ambitions accessed 23 July 2020.

Odom, Jonathan G. (2019), 'China's "Riskfare"', *Proceedings of the United States Naval Institute*, 145 (3).

Pamuk, Humeyra and Andrea Shalal (2020), 'Trump Administration Pushing to Rip Global Supply Chains from China: Officials', *Reuters*, 3 May, www.reuters.com/a rticle/us-health-coronavirus-usa-china/trump-administration-pushing-to-rip-global-s upply-chains-from-china-officials-idUSKBN22G0BZ accessed 23 July 2020.

Pearce, Joshua M. and David C. Denkenberger (2018), 'A National Pragmatic Safety Limit for Nuclear Weapon Quantities', *Safety*, 4 (2).

Pompeo, Michael R. (2020a), 'Secretary Michael R. Pompeo at a Press Availability', remarks to the press, Washington DC, 29 April, www.state.gov/secretary-micha el-r-pompeo-at-a-press-availability-4 accessed 23 July 2020.

Pompeo, Michael R. (2020b), 'US Position on Maritime Claims in the South China Sea', press statement of the Secretary of State, 13 July, www.state.gov/u-s-positio n-on-maritime-claims-in-the-south-china-sea accessed 23 July 2020.

PTI (2020), 'Pompeo Extends Deepest Condolences to Indians for Loss of Soldiers' Lives in Clashes with Chinese', *Times of India*, 19 June, https://timesofindia.indiatim es.com/india/pompeo-extends-deepest-condolences-to-indians-for-loss-of-soldiers-liv es-in-clashes-with-chinese/articleshow/76456099.cms accessed 23 July 2020.

Qiao Liang and Wang Xiangsui (1999), *Unrestricted Warfare*, Beijing: PLA Literature and Arts Publishing House, translated by FBIS, www.c4i.org/unrestricted.pdf accessed 23 July 2020.

Sun Tzu (1963), *Art of War*, trans. Samuel B. Griffith, New York: Oxford University Press.

Thucydides (5th century BC), *The History of the Peloponnesian War*, translated by Richard Crawley, www.gutenberg.org/files/7142/7142-h/7142-h.htm accessed 23 July 2020.

Trevithick, Joseph (2020), 'Here Are Photos of Two US. Navy Carriers in the South China Sea for the First Time in Six Years', *The War Zone*, 6 July, www.thedrive. com/the-war-zone/34598/here-are-photos-of-two-u-s-navy-carriers-in-the-south-chin a-sea-for-first-time-in-six-years accessed 23 July 2020.

United Nations, Department of Economic and Social Affairs, Population Division (2019), *World Population Prospects 2019, Vol. II: Demographic Profiles*, New York: United Nations, https://population.un.org/wpp/Publications accessed 23 July 2020.

Vuving, Alexander L. (2014a), 'Did China Blink in the South China Sea?', *The National Interest*, 27 July, https://nationalinterest.org/feature/did-china-blink-the-south-china-sea-10956 accessed 23 July 2020.

Vuving, Alexander L. (2014b), 'China's Grand Strategy Challenge: Creating Its Own Islands in the South China Sea', *The National Interest*, 8 December, http s://nationalinterest.org/feature/chinas-grand-strategy-challenge-creating-its-own-islan ds-the-11807 accessed 23 July 2020.

Vuving, Alexander L. (2017), 'How America Can Take Control in the South China Sea', *Foreign Policy*, 13 February, https://foreignpolicy.com/2017/02/13/how-the-u-s-can-take-control-in-the-south-china-sea accessed 23 July 2020.

Vuving, Alexander L. (2019), 'China's Strategic Messaging: What It Is, How It Works, and How to Respond to it', in Scott D.McᶜDonald and Michael C. Burgoyne (eds), *China's Global Influence: Perspectives and Recommendations*, Honolulu, HI: Daniel K. Inouye Asia-Pacific Center for Security Studies, https://apcss.org/wp-content/up loads/2019/09/10-Chinas_strategic_messaging-vuving.pdf accessed 23 July 2020.

Vuving, Alexander L. (2020), 'Great Power Competition: Lessons from the Past, Implications for the Future', in Alexander L. Vuving (ed.), *Hindsight, Insight,*

Foresight: Thinking about Security in the Indo-Pacific, Honolulu, HI: Daniel K. Inouye Asia-Pacific Center for Security Studies.

White, Hugh (2013), *The China Choice: Why We Should Share Power*, Oxford: Oxford University Press.

White House (1998), 'A National Security Strategy for a New Century', October, www.hsdl.org/?view&did=2959 accessed 23 July 2020.

White House (2017), 'National Security Strategy of the United States of America', December, www.whitehouse.gov/wp-content/uploads/2017/12/NSS-Final-12-18-2017-0 905.pdf accessed 23 July 2020.

Xu Weidi (2016), 'China's Security Environment and the Role of Nuclear Weapons', in Li Bin and Tong Zhao (eds), *Understanding Chinese Nuclear Thinking*, Washington, DC: Carnegie Endowment for International Peace.

3 The United States' security perspectives in the Asia-Pacific and the value of the alliance with Australia

Paul J. Smith

Introduction

On 20 September 2019, Australian Prime Minister Scott Morrison conducted a state visit to the White House in Washington, DC, where he was hosted by President Donald Trump and members of his administration. In remarks delivered at the official arrival ceremony, President Trump stated that 'the unbreakable bond between America and Australia is rooted in eternal ties of history, culture and tradition'. Morrison echoed Trump's kindness by asserting: 'Australians and Americans understand each other like few other people'. In a reference to the historical depth of the two countries ties, Morrison stated: '[f]rom the cornfields of Hamel, to the jungles of Southeast Asia and the Pacific, to the dust of Tarin Kowt, and now, even in the Straits of Hormuz, Australians and Americans continue to stand together' (White House 2019a).

The visit by Morrison, his spouse and other Australian officials to the White House came at a particularly sensitive and tumultuous period for the Trump Administration. Just ten days earlier, Trump's National Security Adviser, John Bolton, had resigned after being requested to do so by the President. About a month before that, Dan Coats, the Director of National Intelligence, left his position. Moreover, the US House of Representatives, led by the opposition Democratic Party, was contemplating impeachment proceedings against the President (which would be officially launched just four days later on 24 September).

Video images of the visit, released by the White House, show a festive atmosphere and good rapport between Trump and Morrison as the two men participated in ceremonies and delivered speeches (YouTube 2019). The visit's official status gave the White House and its staff a chance to display the iconic building's historic grandeur and military pageantry. A state dinner – only the second ever conducted by the Trump Administration since its inception – featured performances by various military ensembles representing the Army, Marines, Navy and Air Force. In remarks during the dinner, Trump stated: '[w]e give thanks to all the sons and daughters of Australia who have toiled and sacrificed for a strong, vibrant and sovereign nation'. In response,

Morrison proposed a toast in which he said: '[t]o 100 years of mateship, and to 100 more, to the people of the United States, to the President and his magnificent First Lady and may God bless America' (Morrison 2019c).

Morrison's visit to the White House was not merely important for its ceremonial value, it held profound geopolitical significance. Two years earlier, the Trump Administration released its National Security Strategy, which characterized US relations with Australia in the following way: 'Australia has fought alongside us in every significant conflict since World War I, and continues to reinforce economic and security arrangements that support our shared interests and safeguard democratic values across the region' (NSS 2017). Given Australia's location, the topic of the People's Republic of China (PRC) was raised frequently during the visit. Trump was keen to emphasize the tariffs that he had applied against Chinese imports and the difficult state of the Chinese economy. By contrast, Morrison emphasized the trade linkages that Australia enjoyed with China. At one point he stated that 'Australia has benefited greatly from the economic growth of China' (Morrison 2019b).

Apart from the China topic, it was clear that one of the objectives of the visit was to re-emphasize and coordinate US and Australia joint approaches to Asia and the Pacific and Indian Oceans. A fact sheet produced by the White House stated that the visit reaffirmed and strengthened 'the long-standing partnership between the United States and Australia'. The fact sheet also extolled Australia's valuable role in the overall US strategy toward the Indo-Pacific region: '[o]ur two countries have agreed to develop a new mechanism to strengthen and align coordination of our Indo-Pacific strategies to promote peace and stability in the region' (White House Fact Sheet 2019).

Overall, Morrison's visit to the White House emphasized the fact that America's alliance with Australia is probably its tightest and most dependable in the world. It provides Washington with significant benefits, including intelligence sharing, military support, a market for US defence articles, among others. However, as was apparent in the dialogue between Trump and Morrison, the growing rift in the US–China relationship is creating tensions in the dynamic. Canberra's drive to maintain its 'comprehensive strategic partnership' with Beijing contradicts Washington's more competitive posture vis-à-vis Beijing. Consequently, Australia may be faced with uncomfortable choices if Beijing-Washington ties continue to deteriorate.

This chapter will proceed with an examination of US security perspectives on the Indo-Pacific region and US strategy, then turn to an assessment of the value of the US–Australia alliance. Finally, the chapter will examine differences in how Australia and the United States view the People's Republic of China and assess whether differences in those views pose longer term or structural challenges to the larger bilateral relationship.

US security perspectives of the Asia-Pacific

On 10 November 2017, while attending the APEC CEO Summit in Vietnam, President Donald Trump unveiled his administration's vision and strategy toward the Indo-Pacific region. Having meticulously avoided the strategic labels of his predecessor, notably 'rebalance' and 'pivot', Trump elicited much interest and anticipation from the audience. 'What an honor it is to be here in Vietnam – in the very heart of the Indo-Pacific – to address the people and business leaders of this region', Trump began (Trump 2017b). As he continued, Trump explained that his travels through the region had provided an opportunity for him to share America's vision for a 'free and open Indo-Pacific', which would be 'a place where sovereign and independent nations, with diverse cultures and many different dreams, can all prosper side-by-side and thrive in freedom and in peace'. He went on to say that he was offering the region a 'renewed partnership' with the United States 'to strengthen the bonds of friendship and commerce between all of the nations of the Indo-Pacific, and together, to promote our prosperity and security' (Trump 2017b).

The Trump Administration's Free and Open Indo-Pacific strategy or FOIP was a new approach to the region that featured, among other things, a key innovation in terms of labelling and associated narratives. Instead of the more conventional and traditional term 'Asia-Pacific', the US would henceforth refer to the region as the Indo-Pacific. Moreover, it would re-name its oldest and largest unified command from US Pacific Command (USPACOM) to US Indo-Pacific Command (USINDOPACOM). The re-naming exercise was designed to highlight both the Pacific Ocean and the Indian Ocean and the latter's growing importance, not to mention America's heightened emphasis on building a strategic relationship with India. On this latter point, the Trump Administration's National Security Strategy states that the United States will 'expand [its] defense and security cooperation with India, a Major Defense Partner of the United States, and support India's growing relationships through the region' (NSS 2017). However, in many respects the FOIP strategy pursues goals that are consistent with objectives the US has always had in the region since the end of the Second World War and earlier. A State Department elaboration of the FOIP strategy acknowledges this when it states that the FOIP vision 'is based on values that have underpinned peace and prosperity in the Indo-Pacific for generations' (Pompeo 2019b).

The FOIP strategy is based on three pillars, which provide a useful framework to understand US strategy in the region as it has been practiced across multiple administrations. The first of these pillars is economics. A key theme underlying US strategy in the Indo-Pacific is the emphasis on (and preference for) open trade and markets. Asia's economic vibrancy is viewed as a key rationale for extensive US presence and engagement in the region. The USINDOPACOM website states that 'the [Indo-Pacific] region is a vital driver of the global economy and includes the world's busiest international sea lanes and nine of the ten largest ports' (USINDOPACOM 2020). The

United States had once advocated for the creation of the Trans-Pacific Partnership (TPP), but eventually political support for that initiative declined in the US and the proposed economic grouping was subsequently rejected by the Trump Administration. Nevertheless, freedom of commerce (including shipping) is a key tenet of US foreign policy. This partially explains why the US is so concerned about Chinese expansion in the South China Sea, which is a world shipping transit zone (O'Rourke 2020: 4–5).

The second pillar is effective and representative governance and in this regard there is little mystery that the US has consistently supported and advocated for democracies and democratic values. During the Cold War, the preference for democracy was a key rationale for the strategy of containment, particularly as it related to Communist expansion from the Soviet Union and, subsequently, the People's Republic of China. This explains America's persistent relationship with Taiwan, notwithstanding the increasingly fraught shift in the balance of power across the Taiwan Strait that has occurred in recent years. As Kurt Campbell, former Assistant Secretary of State for East Asian and Pacific Affairs, said in 2011: '[t]he foundation of our political ties with Taiwan is our common values and shared belief in democracy, and Americans have been deeply impressed by Taiwan's open, exuberant democratic policy and society' (Campbell 2011). The preference for democracy also explains American attempts to upgrade its relationship with India and integrate it into its larger security architecture. In 2016, the US designated India as 'Major Defense Partner', a designation that positioned India to be on par with America's other allies. An official US Department of Defense press release characterized the 'Major Defense Partner' designation as a 'status unique to India' which 'institutionalizes the progress made to facilitate defense trade and technology sharing with India' (Department of Defense (United States) 2016).

America's preference for democracy is often paired with an idealized conception of the international system that is governed by rules and norms where institutions play a major role. In furtherance of this objective, according to Assistant Secretary of State David Stilwell, the 'Trump Administration is committed to maintaining ASEAN centrality at the core of our engagement with broader regional institutions such as the East Asia Summit, the ASEAN Regional Forum and the Asia Pacific Economic Cooperation forum' (Stillwell 2019). The State Department's official description of the FOIP strategy states that the 'United States actively participates in and supports ASEAN-centered institutions', including East Asia Summit (EAS), US-ASEAN Summit, ASEAN Regional Forum (ARF), ASEAN Defense Minister's Meeting Plus (ADMM Plus) and the Expanded ASEAN Maritime Forum (EAMF) (Department of State 2019a). Such institutions are seen as critical in the promotion of 'sound, just and responsive governance', which the Trump Administration hopes to encourage with its Indo-Pacific Transparency Initiative (Trump 2018).

The third pillar of America's Indo-Pacific strategy is security, which from an American perspective is provided by a web of alliances that the US has cultivated since the early 1950s. Such alliances facilitate forward deployment and America's extended deterrence guarantees to a number of countries. In a 1954 memorandum, Secretary of State John Foster Dulles described the rationale and purpose of the US security structure in the Asia-Pacific region: '[w]e have negotiated since 1951 a series of mutual security treaties covering Japan, South Korea, the Philippines, Southeast Asia, Australia and New Zealand ... These various measures in aggregate substantially cover the free world position, in the Western Pacific and East Asia.' The purpose of this treaty system was to keep 'these areas out of Communist control [which] is essential to the maintenance of the Pacific Ocean as a friendly body of water with our defenses far from and not close to the continental United States' (National Security Council 1954).

One could easily argue that there is a fourth, perhaps unwritten pillar in the FOIP and earlier US strategies directed at the region. That pillar would be an outsized American emphasis on, and deep concern about, the People's Republic of China. A 1953 National Security Council memorandum, for example, described as the 'central problem' for the US as the takeover of China by 'an aggressive and dynamic Communist regime closely aligned with and supported by the Soviet Union' (National Security Council 1953a). For US officials, the Korean War, in which American and Chinese troops clashed directly, helped to solidify the view that China was not merely a satellite of the Soviet Union, but in the words of the Director of Central Intelligence, Allen Dulles, a 'voluntary and genuine ally' of the USSR (National Security Council 1953b). Former Secretary of State Dean Rusk described how the Korean War transformed American views of China: '[t]he Korean War hardened American attitudes toward Peking; it certainly hardened mine' (Rusk 1990: 284). In addition, at a 1966 ANZUS meeting, Rusk explained that China was among the core reasons that the US maintained its vast defence commitments in the Asia-Pacific: '[w]e have solemn treaty commitments in the Far East with a number of key countries (Korea, GRC, Japan, Viet-Nam, etc.). It might be said that these came about in part as a result of Communist Chinese efforts to seize the continent of Asia, but it was also an effort to bring stability to the Pacific' (Department of State 1966). In a 1967 news conference, Rusk reportedly revealed that the 'basic motivation' for American involvement in Vietnam was the 'containment of Chinese aggression' (Melby 1968: 421).

One way of thinking about US–China relations is to use a historical framework, which allows the US–China relationship to be viewed through the lens of four distinct and discrete phases (Liu and Ren 2014). The first phase, lasting from 1949 to 1971, could be characterized as the Cold War hostility era. This phase would last for nearly 22 years and feature a multi-decade attempt by the United States to deny international space and legitimacy to the government of the People's Republic of China, namely by keeping Beijing out of the United Nations among other measures. This era also featured multiple military crises, most notably within the Taiwan Strait. The first

Taiwan crisis, lasting from 1954–1955, would lead to Taiwan's formal entry into the US alliance system after Taipei and Washington signed a Mutual Defense Treaty, which would last until 1980 (Chang 1988; Yale University 1954). This was followed by a second Taiwan crisis in 1958. However, the US and China continued to have dialogue through various 'back channels' – such as Geneva or Warsaw – during this phase. Moreover, the US was aware of a growing fissure in the relationship between Beijing and Moscow, which later it sought to exploit (Cline 1963; Fredman 2014).

The end of the 1960s created the environment for the second key phase in US–China relations, lasting from 1972 to 1990. This phase officially began when Chinese Premier Mao Zedong and US President Richard Nixon agreed to have a meeting in Beijing in 1972 (MacFarquhar 1972). President Richard Nixon's abrupt policy shift changed the direction of US–China relations, although his attitudes toward China had been evolving for years. In 1967, for example, Nixon published an essay in *Foreign Affairs* that foreshadowed policy changes to come; specifically he wrote: '[t]aking the long view, we simply cannot afford to leave China forever outside the family of nations, there to nurture its fantasies, cherish its hates and threaten its neighbors ... The world cannot be safe until China changes. Thus our aim, to the extent that we can influence events, should be to induce change' (Nixon 1967). Similarly, attitudes were changing in China, especially as military tensions grew along the Sino-Soviet border in the late 1960s. In 1969, the study group commissioned by Mao Zedong concluded that in order for China to prepare for a possible clash with the Soviet Union, the 'card of the United States' should be played (Xia 2006).

When President Jimmy Carter assumed office in 1977, he largely continued the momentum of rapprochement begun six years earlier by the Nixon Administration and subsequently continued by the Ford Administration. Secretary of Defense Harold Brown, in a memorandum to Carter, stated that 'we [the United States] have gained important security benefits from our new relationship with Peking. We have substantially reduced the danger of a conflict in northeast Asia and eliminated the friction that our China policy caused with major allies such as Japan' (Brown 1977). Moreover, Brown emphasized the effect that the new realignment had had on the Soviet Union, America's primary antagonist at the time. 'At least by comparison with what would otherwise have been the case, the Soviets have so far been forced to divide their military strength ... the most important factor for the next decade is that the US–PRC relationship will be a major influence on US-Soviet relations', Brown wrote (Brown 1977). It was during this second phase that the two countries issued their three communiques, which would define their relationship for subsequent decades. The first of these was the Shanghai Communique, issued during Nixon's historic trip; the second was the Joint Communique on the Establishment of Diplomatic Relations, which led to the establishment of formal diplomatic relations in 1979. The third, known as the US–China Joint Communique, was issued on 17 August 1982.

However, with the end of the Cold War, notwithstanding hopeful celebrations and anticipation of a 'peace dividend', the strategic ballast that guided Beijing and Washington – common antipathy toward the Soviet Union – no longer existed. Thus, the third phase, bifurcation and frigid estrangement, slowly materialized. With the US having reduced its interactions with the People's Liberation Army (PLA) due to the latter's violent role in the 1989 Tiananmen Square protests, military-to-military engagement declined (Liu and Ren 2014: 262). On the economic side, however, bilateral ties actually deepened as the two countries' economies became more interdependent. American officials believed that open trade with China (including a willingness to tolerate trade deficits) would ultimately pay off by resulting in a deep transformation of China's economic and political system. In testimony before Congress, Deputy Assistant Secretary of State Kent Wiedemann articulated the rationale behind this notion:

> Last year the President [Clinton] decided to renew China's most favored nation trade status because he concluded that strengthening broad engagement between the US and China offers the best way, over the long term, to promote the full range of US interests with China, including our human rights, strategic, economic and commercial concerns.
>
> (Wiedemann 1995)

On the other hand, however, the deterioration of security and military ties during this era was accelerated by a series of incidents and crises. One of these was the 1993 seizure by the US Navy of the Chinese-flagged ship *Yinhe*, which was believed to be carrying chemical weapons to Iran. Two years later, a crisis would erupt in the Taiwan Strait in which Chinese forces attempted to coerce Taiwan with missile tests and other exercises. The US deployed two carrier strike groups in or around Taiwan to demonstrate support for the fledgling democracy. From that point on, PRC military strategists pursued ever more vigorous A2AD (anti-access, area-denial) measures, essentially attempting to achieve sea control from the land by relying on a growing arsenal of ballistic missiles. In 1999, the US bombed the Chinese embassy in Belgrade, Yugoslavia. The US announced that the bombing was an accident, but many Chinese never accepted that explanation. Moreover, the 1990s witnessed a number of claims, counterclaims and leaks regarding Chinese missile export activities and alleged espionage pursuits within the United States. On 3 January 1999, Congress released the Report of the Select Committee on US National Security and Military/Commercial Concerns with the People's Republic of China (also known as the 'Cox Report'). The report alleged, among other things, that 'the People's Republic of China (PRC) has stolen classified design information on the United States' most advanced thermonuclear weapons' (Select Committee 1999).

The end of the decade marked the transition from phase 3 to phase 4 of the US–China relationship. In January 2000, Condoleezza Rice, who would later serve as President George W. Bush's national security advisor and secretary of state characterized China as a 'strategic competitor'. She wrote: '[w]hat we do know is that China is a great power with unresolved vital interests, particularly concerning Taiwan and the South China Sea … This means that China is not a "status quo" power but one that would like to alter Asia's balance of power in its own favor' (Rice 2000). Bush himself had also characterized China as a competitor and, upon assuming office, bilateral relations appeared to be reflecting that mood, culminating in the EP-3 plane incident near Hainan in April 2001. Following that incident, US–China relations appeared to be headed in a downward trajectory until two key events appeared to generate a 'strategic pause' in the overall deterioration of diplomatic ties.

The first strategic pause was the impact of the 9/11 attacks in the United States. The attacks had one major effect: they diverted Washington's gaze from China to the Middle East and South Asia. China even rode the counterterrorism wave by asserting its status as a terrorism victim, an argument that the US initially accepted. The second strategic pause occurred with the 2008 election of Barack Obama, who saw himself, due to his childhood experiences in Southeast Asia, as particularly well-positioned to advance US relations with Asian powers, including China. Obama's initial approach to China was hopeful and optimistic, to include a town hall meeting in Shanghai with Chinese college students. However, eventually Obama's optimism was tested by Chinese resolve to advance its interests in the South China Sea and other areas. Secretary of State Hillary Clinton offered what was widely seen as a rebuke to China when she emphasized, in a 2010 speech in Vietnam, that the United States, 'like every nation', had important national interests in the South China Sea (Clinton 2010). Obama's transformation from 'China optimist' to 'China realist' culminated in his 2011 decision to rebalance US forces toward the Asia-Pacific (Landler 2012: 1). In January 2012, the Pentagon released a document that formalized the shift in US strategy: '… while the US military will continue to contribute to security globally, *we will of necessity rebalance toward the Asia-Pacific region*', it stated (Department of Defense (United States) 2012). Although Obama Administration officials sought to downplay the military dimensions of the rebalance, its military flavour was nonetheless apparent in Beijing.

The election of an unconventional politician, Donald Trump, to the US presidency unleashed a number of uncertainties regarding the future of US–China relations. Would the phase 4 trend of competition and confrontation continue? Or would the businessman adopt a more pragmatic and transactional approach to foreign policy, as many Chinese scholars and pundits had initially anticipated (Global Times 2016)? Although it appeared that Trump and Chinese President Xi Jinping had established good relations following mutual visits to Mar-a-Lago and Beijing, the differences in trade policy began to emerge. In what was considered a major announcement of US China policy, Vice President Mike Pence stated, among other things, that 'Beijing is employing a whole-of-government approach, using political, economic and military tools, as well as propaganda, to advance its influence and benefit its interests in the United States' and China is 'applying this power in more proactive ways than ever before, to exert influence and interfere in the domestic policy and politics of our country' (Pence 2018). Perhaps even more significant from a long-term perspective was the announcement, in March 2018, by the US Department of Justice of its China Initiative, which was designed to advance the Attorney General's 'strategic priority of countering Chinese national security threats … [including] trade secret theft, hacking and economic espionage' (Department of Justice 2019).

Thus, the US has maintained a security architecture in the Asia-Pacific (now Indo-Pacific) for more than seven decades originally intended to contain Communism from the Soviet Union and, subsequently, the People's Republic of China. Following the end of the Cold War, it appeared that this security system had persisted despite not having a compelling rationale. Now that US–China relations have become more fraught and contentious, the temptation may be to see the relationship as having come full circle. But comparing today's situation to the 1950s and 1960s era of US–China relations has limited utility. Today's China represents about 15% of the global economy; it has trade and investment linkages throughout the world. It is a major political actor on the world stage, which has a vast and survivable nuclear arsenal. In short, today's China cannot be contained. This leaves the United States with the next best (but far from perfect) option of balancing with allies. 'Balancing is alignment against the threatening power to deter it from attacking or to defeat it if it does' (Walt 1988: 278). However, balancing works best with allies that have a common perception of threat (Walt 1997: 158). In today's Indo-Pacific, however, it is unclear whether such common perception exists, even among America's closest allies and partners.

The value of America's alliance with Australia

When President Barack Obama delivered his historic 'rebalance' speech in Canberra in 2011, he emphasized the value of the US–Australia alliance, which he described as 'our unbreakable alliance' (Obama 2011). The bonds between the two countries run deep, Obama asserted, and 'in each other's story we see so much of ourselves'. Moreover, the two countries shared a common creed: 'no matter who you are, no matter what you look like, everyone deserves a fair chance', he stated (Obama 2011). Obama's choice of Australia to unveil his administration's re-orientation toward the Asia-Pacific region was appropriate. Australia has been America's most steadfast ally in the region for decades, underpinned by the two countries' 'ideological solidarity' in addition to balancing motives (Walt 1985: 18). In fact, the United States has been able to count on Australia's support in all of its major wars in the 20th century. On 4 July 2018, the US and Australia celebrated '100 Years of Mateship', a date that marked the 100 year anniversary of the first instance (in France during the First World War) in which the two countries fought side by side (US Embassy (Australia) 2018).

In the aftermath of the Second World War, US–Australia relations became closer than they had ever been before. In 1948, three years after the surrender of Japan, the US State Department produced a policy statement regarding US objectives toward Australia. Among other things, it described three fundamental objectives vis-à-vis Australia: (1) maintaining and strengthening 'the close ties of friendship which exist between the United States and Australia', (2) to encourage Australia 'to collaborate closely with us on matters of mutual concern, especially in the Pacific', and (3) encourage Australia to engage in economic development and to increase its level of foreign trade (Department of State 1948). Three years after the publication of that document, Australia, New Zealand and the United States signed the ANZUS Treaty, which stipulates, among other things, that the signatories 'will consult together whenever in the opinion of any of them the territorial integrity, political independence or security of any of the Parties is threatened in the Pacific' (ANZUS Treaty 1951). ANZUS continues to provide the legal underpinning of the Australia–US alliance relationship, which continues to the present day. On 8 September 1954, Australia, along with six other countries, signed the treaty that created the Southeast Asia Treaty Organization (SEATO) (Mackerras 2014: 226). The US always viewed Australia as one of the most important members of this group. A US National Security Council report in 1961 (NSC 6109) characterized Australia as follows: 'Australia has generally proved a bulwark of strength in the SEATO alliance and can be depended upon to support its words with action should the need arise to defend the area' (Lay 1961).

In 1957, the National Security Council published a report that assessed the value of Australia vis-à-vis US operations in Southeast Asia: 'Australia's geographic location, near Southeast Asia; its political orientation and general stability are such that Australia would provide us with secure logistic and defence production bases overseas for operations in Southeast Asia' (National Security Council n.d.). The report went on to characterize Australia in much the same way that American observers consider valid today: '[g]iven Australia's record in times of crisis, there is little question as to its reliability and effectiveness as an ally'. More importantly, the report highlighted the possibility that Australia could play the role of a backup option to the US military presence in Japan in the event that the 'converging forces of nationalism, neutralism and atomic fear' caused anti-US sentiment in Japan to rise, thus forcing the withdrawal of US forces (National Security Council n.d.).

Throughout the Cold War, the United States consistently characterized the US–Australia alliance as 'one of the cornerstones of peace and stability in the Pacific. It is on par with our Mutual Security Treaty with Japan in its global implications' (Eagleburger 1976). Moreover, cooperation between the United States and Australia was viewed as 'vital to the maintenance of a favorable balance of power in the Pacific and thus in the world' (Eagleburger 1976).

Australia demonstrated its commitment by fighting alongside the US in the Korean War and subsequently in the Vietnam War. In a 1967 speech, President Lyndon Johnson characterized Australia's role in Vietnam as follows: '[y]our forces stand in Vietnam alongside our own, to preserve for one small nation the right to determine its future without external force or interference' (Johnson 1966).

In the latter half of the Cold War, the US continued to emphasize Australia's importance in the context of Washington's larger strategic objectives vis-à-vis the Soviet Union and the containment of Communism. Some US diplomatic language characterized Australia's role in the context of a type of division of labour. While the US focused on global issues, Australia was expected to manage regional challenges. 'Australia is committed to assisting the US in its global role by what Australia does in the region', noticed one Department of State briefing paper. This meant that Australia would handle 'problem areas' in the regional neighbourhood, such as Timor, Papua New Guinea (and with New Zealand's cooperation) the South Pacific (Eagleburger 1976). Moreover, given its unique geographic position and internal geography, Australia was viewed as critical for advancing US strategic goals. 'We welcome close security cooperation with Australia', noted the State Department briefing paper:

> [Australia's] continent-sized land mass is strategically located off Asia at the junction of the Indian and Pacific Oceans, and provides unique locations for joint defence-related installations important to the common defence, to the maintenance of the global balance and to the negotiation of strategic arms limitations.
>
> (Eagleburger 1976)

In the contemporary context, the relationship is no less tight and focused, in contrast with some of Washington's other defence relationships in the region in which strategic convergence exists but not necessarily complete trust at the operational and tactical levels. Australia is in stark contrast with that scenario. For example, one key benefit that Australia brings to the alliance is its critical intelligence gathering role as part of the overall '5-eyes' structure. The arrangements predate ANZUS; signals intelligence cooperation and exchange were formalized by the UK–US–Australian Agreement (UKUSA) of 1947–1948 (Brown and Rayner 2001). The US and Australia operate certain joint facilities in Australia, including Pine Gap. Australia views its intelligence role as its 'most meaningful contribution to the [ANZUS] alliance', which is reciprocated by Washington's provision of 'sophisticated technology necessary for Australian self-reliance in credible defence contingencies' (Brown and Rayner 2001).

However, perhaps the most substantive aspect of the US–Australia alliance exists in the military realm. The primary element of the ANZUS alliance that determines military relations is the Australia–United States Ministerial

(AUSMIN) process. AUSMIN meetings occur almost annually and alternate between the United States and Australia. The joint declarations, produced as a product of each meeting, highlight common visions and concerns about contemporary security issues. The 2017 Joint Statement, for instance, articulated US and Australian common views about the South China Sea (without specifically mentioning China). The statement urged, among other things, that 'all parties ... refrain from further militarization of disputed features, including in the South China Sea (SCS)' (AUSMIN 2017). The statement also emphasized the importance of freedom of navigation and 'adhering to the rules-based order'. It also described the 2016 Arbitral Tribunal decision, which was unfavourable to China, to be a 'useful basis for further efforts to peacefully resolve disputes in the SCS [South China Sea]' (AUSMIN 2017). The 2019 Joint [AUSMIN] Statement also made reference to the South China Sea, again without specifically mentioning China. It stated: '[t]he principals expressed serious concerns at continued militarization of disputed features in the South China Sea'. It further stated that the principals 'strongly objected to coercive unilateral actions by any claimant state that could alter the status quo and increase tensions' (AUSMIN 2019). In addition to high-level consultations, the US and Australian militaries benefit from the fact that the Australian Government assigns a full-time General Officer to USINDOPACOM and a separate full-time General Officer to US Army Pacific (Harris 2018: 39).

One tangible indicator of close Australia–United States relations is the fact that Australia is a major purchaser of US arms, defence articles and associated services. For the United States, 'arms transfers are foreign policy' (Kaidanow 2019). Such transfers not only affect regional balances of power, they also send a 'signal of support' and suggest a sustained relationship with the recipient state 'that may last for generations and provide benefits for an extended period of time' (Kaidanow 2019). In the United States, arms transfers, such as those related to Australia, occur generally under a framework known as the Foreign Military Sales (FMS) and Direct Commercial Sales (DCS) programs. The US–Australia defence relationship is further underpinned by the US–Australia Defense Trade Cooperation Treaty (2007) that was designed to 'facilitate defense industrial collaboration by permitting the license-free export of defense goods and services between the Australian and US governments' (CSIS 2012). The treaty essentially fast-tracks – by omitting the requirement of a license or other authorization – the export of defence articles that fall within the treaty (US–Australia Defense Trade Cooperation Treaty 2007). One Australian report noted that the Australian Government had spent more than $10 billion on American defence articles during the periods from 2012–13 and 2016–17, including purchases of the GBU-53/B Small Diameter bomb and upgrades to the ADF MH-60R Multi-Mission helicopters (Greene 2017).

Arms transfers can indicate larger strategic trends in alliance relationships. One key trend evident in US–Australia military relations is the drive to expand interoperability and to widen operational networks. In January 2020, for instance, the US Department of Defense provided notice to Congress regarding a proposed sale of 'defense articles and services', related to the AEGIS Combat System (ACS) to Australia in the amount of $1.5 billion. The Department of Defense letter stated that 'the proposed sale will enhance Australia's surface combat capability by modernizing their existing three AEGIS capable Hobart Class Destroyers with the latest technology and capability, and delivering the first three (of nine) AEGIS capable Hunter Class Future Frigates' (Federal Register 2020). This would provide Australia and the United States with 3 key advantages: (1) it would greatly enhance Australia's overall self-defence capability; (2) it would improve interoperability between Australian forces and US Navy AEGIS combatants operating in the area and (3) it would significantly improve Australia's network-centric warfare capability because of the incorporation of Cooperative Engagement Capability (CEC) into its surface fleet (Federal Register 2020). Cooperative Engagement Capability refers to a 'real time sensor netting system' that allows ships or other units in similar or distant areas to integrate their surveillance information and awareness (US Navy 2020). Such a system, among other things, allows multiple surface ships (along with US Marine Corps land units) 'to form an air defense network by sharing radar target measurements in real time' (US Navy 2020).

On the naval aviation side, there are similar trends toward greater interoperability between Australian and US forces as well as greater networking capabilities. In September 2019, the Department of Defense notified Congress of an Australian request 'for additional sustainment and upgrades' to its F/A-18 E/F fleet (Federal Register 2019). The upgrades involved modifications that added three key systems: (1) infrared Search and Track (IRST) Block II. This technology 'detects targets over long distances and operates in environments where radar isn't an option' (Lockheed Martin 2020); (2) distributed Targeting processor-Networked (DTP-N); and (3) Multifunctional Information Distribution System Joint Tactical Radio Systems (MIDS/JTRS), which is described as a 'four-channel radio [that] runs Link 16 waveform and up to three additional communications protocols … [that increase] situational awareness for enhanced survivability and mission effectiveness' (Collins Aerospace 2020). These improvements suggest a trend where the navies of both countries will have even greater interoperability and situational awareness.

In addition to arms transfers, perhaps the most visible change in US–Australia relations has been the rotational stationing of significant numbers of US troops inside Australia itself. In November 2011, the US and Australia announced the United States Force Posture Initiatives, which were designed to gain 'new opportunities for combined training and improved interoperability' between the two forces. Specifically, the initiatives were (1) the Marine Rotational Force-Darwin (MRF-D) and (2) the Enhanced Air Cooperation (EAC) (Department of Defence (Australia) n.d.). Regarding the first initiative, in July 2019, the Australian Government announced that the Marine Rotational Force-Darwin had reached its full strength (2,500 Marines) following the additional arrival of US Marines that month. According to Minister of Defence Linda Reynolds: 'the Marine Rotational Force-Darwin improves interoperability between Australian and US defence forces, and enhances our ability to work together with regional partners in the interests of stability and security in the Indo-Pacific' (Department of Defence (Australia) 2019b). Regarding the second initiative, the Enhanced Air Cooperation (EAC), the US deployed F-22s to the Royal Australian Air Force to be integrated with the latter's E/A-18G, F/A-18F and/or E-7A. The deployments were intended to 'build upon the initial activities that occurred in 2017 by increasing the complexity of mutual tactics, techniques and procedures' (Harris 2018: 39).

Overall, the United States considers recent upgrades in defence relations with Australia to be particularly valuable. In 2012, a DOD-commissioned report assessed Australia's strategic value to the United States in the following terms: 'Australia's geography, political stability and existing defense capabilities and infrastructure offer strategic depth and other significant military advantages to the United States in light of the growing range of Chinese weapons systems, US efforts to achieve a more distributed force posture and the increasing strategic importance of Southeast Asia and the Indian Ocean' (CSIS 2012). A more recent (2020) US Department of Defense assessment of Australia is that it 'is one of our most important allies in the Western Pacific. The strategic location of this political and economic power contributes significantly to ensuring peace and economic stability in the region' (Federal Register 2020).

Geopolitical cognitive dissonance? The China factor

During Prime Minister Scott Morrison's visit to the White House in September 2019 (referenced in the introduction), a press conference occurred that involved both President Donald Trump and the prime minister. Trump began the official remarks by praising the US–Australia alliance. 'We've been great allies for a long time. There's no better partnership', he stated. Reporters subsequently asked questions about Iran, Ukraine, the whistleblower and former Vice President Joe Biden, which appeared to unnerve the president. Then a reporter asked about China: '[w]ill you be asking Australia to do more when it comes to China?' Trump replied that 'we're talking about China all the time' (White House 2019b). At Trump's request, Morrison intervened. 'We have a comprehensive strategic partnership with China. We work well with China', Morrison stated (White House 2019b).

The exchange between the reporter, Trump and Morrison highlighted a geopolitical reality that underpins the US–Australian relationship as China emerges as a major third player. For Australia, as reflected in Morrison's remarks, China is seen more as an opportunity, while for the US, as reflected in Trump's remarks, China is viewed through a competitive lens. On the US side, a litany of strategy documents characterize China in language that suggests sinister and adversarial motives on the part of Beijing. First, the National Security Strategy of 2017 categorizes China (alongside with Russia) as a revisionist power that challenges 'American power, influence and interests, attempting to erode American security and prosperity' (NSS 2017). Not only is China seeking to erode American influence and power, according to the NSS, it is also seeking to 'displace the United States in the Indo-Pacific region, expand the reaches of its state-driven economic model and reorder the region in its favor' (NSS 2017). A subsidiary strategic document, the National Defense Strategy paints a similarly ominous picture regarding Chinese intentions: 'China is leveraging military modernization, influence operations and predatory economics to coerce neighboring countries to reorder the Indo-Pacific region to their advantage' (NDS 2018). The Pentagon's Indo-Pacific Strategy also characterizes China as a revisionist power, arguing that 'the People's Republic of China (PRC), under the leadership of the Chinese Communist Party (CCP), undermines the international system from within by exploiting its benefits while simultaneously eroding the values and principles of the rules-based order' (Indo-Pacific Strategy Report 2019: 7).

In addition to cautious descriptions of China featured in various US strategy documents, American officials and business leaders have proposed a new narrative of 'decoupling', which is posited as a long-term process of separating American and Chinese technology standards, encouraging US disinvestment from China (as well as Chinese disinvestment from the United States) and reducing other forms of social and economic interdependence. As if on que, China announced its own decoupling strategy in December 2019 when it promulgated rules designed 'to decouple its technology sector from the US' by nudging Chinese contractors to use indigenous technology instead of the foreign variety (Kubota and Lim 2019). The decoupling narrative also underpins America's international campaign to limit Chinese companies, such as Huawei, from dominating the global 5G infrastructure market (although China already dominates 40 per cent of this market) (Barr 2020). The decoupling concept was also mentioned in the context of China's struggle with the coronavirus disease 2019 (COVID-19) and the resulting pandemic in 2020. While expressing his sympathy toward the victims of the epidemic, Secretary of Commerce Wilbur Ross nevertheless stated that the COVID-19 epidemic would 'accelerate the return of jobs to North America' (Ward 2020).

In dramatic contrast with the emerging American narrative on China is Australia's much more sanguine assessment of its relationship with China. The website of Australia's Department of Foreign Affairs and Trade (DFAT) states that 'the Australia–China bilateral relationship is based on strong economic and trade complementarities, a comprehensive program of high-level visits and wide-ranging cooperation'. It further describes a range of 'consultation mechanisms' that underpin the relationship and 'advance cooperation and manage differences', such as the Annual Leaders' Meeting that involves China's Premier and Australia's Prime Minister (DFAT 2020). One area that is particularly promising in the two countries' relationship is two-way trade. In 2017, Prime Minister Malcolm Turnbull told an audience in China that 'we [Australia] have a $150 billion two-way trade relationship, making China our largest trading partner by a wide margin, and almost 2 million people travel between our countries each year' (Turnbull 2017).

Trade relations were greatly bolstered when the two countries signed the historic China–Australia Free Trade Agreement (ChAFTA), which went into force 20 December 2015. According to the Australian Government, the ChAFTA 'has built on Australia's large and successful commercial relationship with China, by securing markets and providing Australians with even better access to China across a range of our key business interests, including goods, services and investment' (DFAT 2019).

In addition to mutually beneficial trade relations, Australia also enjoys relatively good relations with China in the defence and security realm. According to DFAT: '[o]ur international security engagement with China aims to improve mutual understanding, foster open communication and encourage cooperation'. In 1997, Australia and China began holding an annual 'Defence Strategic Dialogue', which is designed to provide a forum in which both sides can discuss 'a range of regional security matters in frank and open terms' (Department of Defence (Australia) 2019a). The 2019 dialogue, which was held on 14 November 2019, was designed to examine 'the many benefits of [Australian–Chinese] defence cooperation' and to explore ways in which engagement could continue in the future.

However, not everything is perfect in the Australia–China relationship and DFAT acknowledges this reality: '[a]t the same time, both sides acknowledge that Australia and China have different histories, societies and political systems, as well as differences of view on some important issues' (DFAT 2020). Some of those issues involve differences in how each views the issue of human rights, or activities in the South China Sea. In recent years, some Australians have become concerned about allegations of Chinese interference in Australia's political system. In February 2020, the director-general of the Australian Security Intelligence Organization, Mike Burgess, announced that 'the level of threat we face from foreign espionage and interference activities is currently unprecedented' (Packham 2020). Although Burgess did not list specific countries, it is widely believed that China would be on the list if such naming had occurred. Given these and other concerns, some in Australia argue that a debate should occur to determine the proper status and role of the Australia–China relationship (White 2012; Dittmer and He 2014: 215–222; Medcalf 2016: 6–13). Relations between Beijing and Canberra also took a hit in 2020 when the Australian Government called for an inquiry into the facts surrounding COVID-19's origins and spread; Beijing reacted furiously by threatening to boycott Australian products.

Notwithstanding these misgivings and counter-currents, however, it is probably reasonable to assert, based on recent official statements and strategic documents, that Australia–China relations are on a much more positive foot-ing, compared to the US–China relationship. Thus, the question becomes: does such dissonance create challenges or opportunities for the US Australia relationship? First, on the challenges side, Australia may feel pressure from either the United States or China to 'tilt' more their way instead of toward the other. When the Gillard government announced in 2011 the agreement to host US Marines in Darwin for six-month rotational periods, China protested that such move 'would have a negative impact on Australian relations with China' (McDougall 2014: 339). Nevertheless, Australia proceeded anyway as part of its hedging and soft balancing strategy. Alternatively, many Aus-tralians are concerned about the extent to which the ANZUS alliance would require Australian intervention in the event of a US–China conflict. When asked 'does Washington still believe unequivocally that the ANZUS alliance obliges Canberra to America's side in the event of a conflict', Secretary Mike Pompeo answered, 'Yeah, the ANZUS Treaty is unambiguous'. When the same question was posed to Australian Foreign Minister Marise Payne, she deflected the question by emphasizing the extensive discussions she had had with Pompeo regarding the 'depth and breadth of the US relationship' (Pompeo 2019a).

It cannot be denied that in certain Australian political circles, excitement about Australia's alliance with the United States is sometimes muted and, moreover, the risks that such relations may pose to Australia are often high-lighted. In a 2016 television interview, former Prime Minister Paul Keating urged that Australia pursue an independent foreign policy that was oriented toward its Asian neighbors. 'What we have to do is to make our way in Asia ourselves, with an independent foreign policy … Our future is basically in the region around us. It's in Southeast Asia' (Keating 2016). Keating questioned the idea that Australia should be drawn into the China–US antagonism dynamic. Geographically, Australia and China are far from each other; he emphasized that China was more than 11 flying hours away from Australia's capital, and thus there are no 'geostrategic problems with China in this respect'. However, he said, 'we're being hounded on by American admirals who run ships through the South China Sea and create all these sorts of issues'. He characterized the Australia–US alliance as merely granting 'tag-along rights' for the Australians (Keating 2016).

Such attitudinal differences between Washington and Canberra may be felt especially in the evolution of the Quadrilateral Security Dialogue, or Quad. The Quad, originally started in 2007, was intended to be an informal security dialogue involving four countries: the United States, Australia, India and Japan. However, China protested when military exercises were conducted under the aegis of the Quad and the group atrophied. A recent initiative to revive the Quad, what some call 'Quad 2.0', has gained more traction (Le Thu 2019). However, due to concerns about China's reactions, the Quad members have not reached a consensus on whether the group will evolve into anything more substantive than an informal consultative mechanism. At their

November 2019 meeting in Thailand, Quad members focused on largely non-military topics including 'counter-terrorism, cyber, development finance, maritime security, humanitarian assistance and disaster response' (Department of State 2019b).

One area where US–Australia divergence on China could manifest is in the realm of arms transfers. If the US perceives Australia to be too 'friendly' toward China – especially elements of the Chinese military – it may feel compelled to restrict certain transfers of defence articles, particularly those of the high-end variety. However, Australia might have counter-leverage by being in a position to diversify its arms mix by including Chinese systems, especially in cases where the US might refuse to sell key items or technologies. Similarly, pressure could emerge in intelligence sharing. The US may be more reluctant to work with Australia if it knows it is sharing information with China. Australia might also face pressure from China in the economic realm if Canberra hews too closely to Washington's preferences. Beijing may attempt to use its economic leverage against Canberra to achieve certain policy goals (Medcalf 2017).

However, such dissonance might have positive implications as well. A positive Australia–China relationship might have a stabilizing effect on US–China relations, particularly in acute situations. In light of the growing absence of US–China defence cooperation, Australia might be in a position to propose a trilateral exercise oriented toward a commonly-accepted objective (such as a humanitarian mission), which in turn could build trust. Derek McDougall has argued that it is possible for Australia to develop its relationship with China and maintain its relationship with the Americans, but it must do this 'by encouraging both China and the US to resolve differences peacefully, and to cooperate in the pursuit of relevant political, strategic and economic goals at both global and regional levels' (McDougall 2014: 320).

Conclusion

At a news conference following the 2019 meeting of AUSMIN, Minister of Defence Linda Reynolds reiterated Australia's position with regard to both the United States and the People's Republic of China. She said, among other things, that Australia believes the 'presence of the United States and its military forces in this region has been a force for stability for decades, and that Australia has consistently welcomed that force and that presence' (Thai News Service 2019). At the same time, however, she emphasized the importance that Australia accorded to its relationship with China. 'We see China as a vitally important partner for Australia. We are strongly committed to our comprehensive strategic partnership [with China], which continues to grow', she stated. Then she made what appeared to be a plea to both countries:

> It's in no one's interests for the Indo-Pacific to become more competitive or to become adversarial in character. So we work closely with our key

partners – with our strongest alliance partner, the United States, and our key partner, China – to pursue those issues of stability and security and prosperity.

(Thai News Service 2019)

From this statement, one can deduce three key conclusions. First, the United States-Australia relationship continues to be strong and Washington views Canberra as a critical component of its larger Free and Open Indo-Pacific (FOIP) strategy. Or to characterize matters more directly, Washington regularly lists many allies, partners and friends in the Indo-Pacific region. But there are three that matter the most due to their capabilities and geopolitical heft: Japan, Australia and India. Former Secretary of State Rex Tillerson once used the image of a 3-position 'pinpoint' to describe how these countries help facilitate the larger FOIP strategy. Under this construct, Japan serves as the northern pinpoint, India the western pinpoint and Australia the southern pinpoint (Tillerson 2017). It does not require much imagination to reasonably infer that the referent within this model, or its *raison d'être*, is China, although it is not clear that all of the various pinpoint partners share Washington's enthusiasm for a structure that ostensibly acts as a balancing mechanism against China.

Second, the growing discord and animosity between the United States and China, evidenced by the recent trade war and adversarial statements in official documents and speeches on both sides, are generating some tension and anxiety within Australia. Australia's 2017 Foreign Policy White Paper states that the United States and China 'have a mutual interest in managing strategic tensions but this by itself is not a guarantee of stability' (Australian Government 2017). It further states that 'Australia will encourage the United States and China to ensure economic tension between them does not fuel strategic rivalry or damage the multilateral trading system' (Australian Government 2017).

Third, while Australia cannot control actions that Beijing and Washington take against each other – including acrimonious rhetoric or policy measures – it still potentially plays a powerful mediating role by virtue of the fact that it maintains close ties with both. The 2016 Australian Department of Defence White Paper clearly describes Australia's intention of maintaining its links with China: '[t]he [Australian] Government will seek to deepen and broaden our important defence relationship with China while recognizing that our strategic interests may differ in relation to some regional and global security issues' (Department of Defence (Australia) 2016). But the White Paper also acknowledges that the US–China relationship factor, which it cannot directly control, will shape Australia's future choices. 'The relationship between the United States and China continues to evolve and will be fundamental to our future strategic circumstances' (Department of Defence (Australia) 2016). Thus, the future health and vibrancy of the US–Australian alliance will likely depend extensively on the forthcoming trajectory of US–China relations and the question of whether

Washington and Beijing can transcend the competitive dynamics of their fourth phase and, instead, establish a mutually-beneficial modus vivendi.

Disclaimer

The views and positions in this chapter are solely those of the author and do not represent or reflect those of his employer.

References

ANZUS Treaty (1951), 'ANZUS Treaty – Full Text', https://australianpolitics.com/1951/09/01/anzus-treaty-text.html accessed 26 February 2020.

AUSMIN (2017), 'Joint Statement (Australia–United States Ministerial Consultations)', 5 Junehttps://dfat.gov.au/geo/united-states-of-america/ausmin/Pages/joint-statement-ausmin-2017.aspx accessed 26 February 2020.

AUSMIN (2019), 'Joint Statement: Australia–US Ministerial Consultations (AUSMIN)', 4 August, www.defense.gov/Newsroom/Releases/Release/Article/1925222/joint-statement-australia-us-ministerial-consultations-ausmin-2019/ accessed 9 February 2020.

Australian Government (2017), *2017 Foreign Policy White Paper*, www.fpwhitepaper.gov.au accessed 28 February 2020.

Barr, William P. (2020), 'Attorney General William P. Barr Delivers the Keynote Address at the Department of Justice's China Initiative Conference', 6 February, www.justice.gov/opa/speech/attorney-general-william-p-barr-delivers-keynote-address-department-justices-china accessed 12 February 2020.

Bloomberg (2020), 'Australia Blasts China for Creating "Disinformation" in Pandemic', June 16, www.bloomberg.com/news/articles/2020-06-16/australia-blasts-china-for-creating-disinformation-in-pandemic.

Brown, Gary and Laura Rayner (2001), 'Upside, Downside – ANZUS: After Fifty Years', Current Issues Brief, 3, www.aph.gov.au/About_Parliament/Parliamentary_Departments/Parliamentary_Library/Publications_Archive/CIB/cib0102/02CIB03# negative 17 February 2020.

Brown, Harold (1997), 'Memorandum from Secretary of Defense Brown to President Carter, Subject: The People's Republic of China and US National Security Policy', 9 February, (contained as an attachment in Document 9, Memorandum from the President's Assistant for National Security Affairs (Brzezinski) to President Carter, 14 February 1977), in Foreign Relations of the United States, 1977–1980, Volume XIII, China. https://history.state.gov/historicaldocuments/frus1977-80v13/d9 accessed 28 January 2020.

Campbell, Kurt (2011), 'Why Taiwan Matters, Part II', Testimony of Kurt Campbell Assistant Secretary of State for East Asian and Pacific Affairs, US Department of State, Congressional Documents and Publications (Lexis-Nexis), 4 October.

Chang, G. (1988), 'To the Nuclear Brink: Eisenhower, Dulles, and the Quemoy-Matsu Crisis', *International Security*, 12 (4), 96–123. doi:10.2307/2538996, accessed 3 July 2020.

Cline, Ray S. (1963), 'Memorandum by the Deputy Director for Intelligence (Cline), Subject: Sino-Soviet Relations', January 14, 1963, in Foreign Relations of the United States, 1961–1963, Volume XXII, Northeast Asia, https://history.state.gov/historicaldocuments/frus1961-63v22/d163 accessed 26 February 2020.

Clinton, Hillary Rodham (2010), 'Remarks at Press Availability, National Convention Center, Hanoi, Vietnam', 23 July, https://2009-2017.state.gov/secretary/20092013clinton/rm/2010/07/145095.htm accessed 26 February 2020.

Collins Aerospace (2020), 'Multifunctional Information Distribution System, Joint Tactical Radio System (MIDS-J)', Collins Aerospace, www.rockwellcollins.com/Products-and-Services/Defense/Communications/Tactical-Data-Links/Multifunctional-Information-Distribution-System/MIDS—Joint-Tactical-Radio-System.aspx accessed 16 February 2020.

CSIS (2012), *US Force Posture Strategy in the Asia-Pacific Region: An Independent Assessment*, Washington, DC: Center for Strategic and International Studies, 27 June, p. 32, https://csis-prod.s3.amazonaws.com/s3fs-public/legacy_files/files/publication/120814_FINAL_PACOM_optimized.pdf accessed 31 January 2019.

Department of Defence (Australia) (2016), *2016 Defence White Paper*, www.defence.gov.au/WhitePaper/Docs/2016-Defence-White-Paper.pdf accessed 23 January 2020.

Department of Defence (Australia) (2019a), '22nd Australia–China Defence Strategic Dialogue', 13 November, https://news.defence.gov.au/media/media-releases/22nd-australia-china-defence-strategic-dialogue accessed 28 February 2020.

Department of Defence (Australia) (2019b), 'Record US Marine Contingent Stationed in Darwin', 25 July, www.minister.defence.gov.au/minister/lreynolds/media-releases/record-us-marine-contingent-stationed-darwin accessed 9 February 2020.

Department of Defence (Australia) (n.d.), 'United States Force Posture Initiatives in Australia', www.defence.gov.au/Initiatives/USFPI/ accessed 23 January 2020.

Department of Defense (United States) (2012), 'Sustaining US Global Leadership: Priorities for 21st Century Defense', Washington, DC, Department of Defense, January, p. 2, https://archive.defense.gov/news/Defense_Strategic_Guidance.pdf accessed 25 February 2020.

Department of Defense (United States) (2016), 'Joint India-United States Statement on the Visit of Secretary of Defense Carter to India', 8 December, www.defense.gov/Newsroom/Releases/Release/Article/1024228/joint-india-united-states-statement-on-the-visit-of-secretary-of-defense-carter/ accessed 13 February 2020.

Department of Justice (2019), 'Attorney General China Initiative Fact Sheet', www.justice.gov/opa/press-release/file/1179321/download accessed 26 February 2020.

Department of State (1948), 'Policy Statement of the Department of State: Australia, [Washington] 18 August', in *Foreign Relations of the United States, 1948, The Far East and Australia, Volume VI*, https://history.state.gov/historicaldocuments/frus1948v06/d1 accessed 22 November 2019.

Department of State (1966), 'Summary of an ANZUS (Australia, New Zealand, US) Morning Meeting Also Attended by British Representatives in Which They Discuss Military Operations in Indonesia, Malaysia, and Vietnam', 30 June, pp. 2–3, *US Declassified Documents Online*, https://link-gale-com.usnwc.idm.oclc.org/apps/doc/CK2349571335/USDD?u=navalwc&sid=USDD&xid=ed0aae43 accessed 19 February 2020.

Department of State (2019a), 'A Free and Open Indo-Pacific: Advancing a Shared Vision', 4 November, p. 30, www.state.gov/wp-content/uploads/2019/11/Free-and-Open-Indo-Pacific-4Nov2019.pdf accessed 21 February 2020.

Department of State (2019b), 'US–Australia–India–Japan Consultations (The Quad)', Media Note, Office of the Spokesperson, 4 November, www.state.gov/u-s-australia-india-japan-consultations-the-quad-2/ accessed 22 March 2020.

DFAT (2019), 'China–Australia Free Trade Agreement: ChAFTA Outcomes at a Glance', https://dfat.gov.au/trade/agreements/in-force/chafta/fact-sheets/Pages/chafta-outcomes-at-a-glance.aspx accessed 13 December 2019.

DFAT (2020), 'China Country Brief: Bilateral Relations', https://dfat.gov.au/geo/china/Pages/china-country-brief.aspx accessed 14 February 2020.

Dittmer, Lowell and Baogang He (2014), 'Introduction: Australia's Strategic Dilemma', *Asian Survey*, March/April.

Eagleburger, Lawrence (1976), 'Deputy Under-Secretary of State Lawrence Eagleburger Provides Nancy Maginnes Kissinger, Wife of Secretary Of State Henry Kissinger, With the Following Background Information in Preparation For Her Official 3/28–24/11/1976 Visit to Australia', Department of State, 24 March, US Declassified Documents Online, https://link.gale.com/apps/doc/CK2349625042/USDD?u=navalwc&sid=USDD&xid=6f3b33a2 accessed 18 February 2020.

Federal Register (2019), 'DSCA Notification (per AECA requirements) to Congress', 12 September, *Federal Register* (84 F.R. 69365), pp. 69365–69367, www.federalregister.gov/documents/2019/12/18/2019-27277/arms-sales-notification accessed 16 February 2020.

Federal Register (2020), 'DSCA Notification (per AECA requirements) to Congress', 14 January>*Federal Register* (85 F.R. 4301), pp. 4301–4305, www.federalregister.gov/documents/2020/01/24/2020-01135/arms-sales-notification accessed 16 February 2020.

Fredman, Z. (2014), '"The Specter of an Expansionist China": Kennedy Administration Assessments of Chinese Intentions in Vietnam', *Diplomatic History*, 38 (1), 111–136. doi:10.2307/26376537, accessed 3 July 2020.

Global Times (2016), 'How Will President Trump Influence China–US Relations: 9 Major Experts Explain Here', *Global Times*, 9 November.

Greene, Andrew (2017), 'Australian Defence Force Spends Over $10 Billion on US Arms in Four Years', ABC News (Australia), 28 December, www.abc.net.au/news/2017-12-28/us-weapons-spend-tops-billion-dollar/9287170 accessed 10 February 2019.

Harris, Harry B. (2018), 'Statement of Admiral Harry B. Harris, US Navy Commander, US Pacific Command, Before the Senate Armed Services Committee on US Pacific Command Posture', 15 March, www.armed-services.senate.gov/imo/media/doc/Harris_03-15-18.pdf.

Indo-Pacific Strategy Report (2019), *Indo-Pacific Strategy Report*, Washington, DC: Department of Defense.

Johnson, Lyndon B. (1966), 'Draft of President Lyndon B. Johnson's Welcoming Speech in Preparation for Australian Prime Minister Harold Holt's US Visit. Johnson Will Applaud Holt For Australia's Support of the US Policy In Vietnam, White House', US Declassified Documents Online, https://link-gale-com.usnwc.idm.oclc.org/apps/doc/CK2349492768/USDD?u=navalwc&sid=USDD&xid=f317752f accessed 17 February 2020.

Jones, M. (2001). '"Groping Toward Coexistence": US China Policy During the Johnson Years', *Diplomacy & Statecraft*, 12 (3). doi:10.1080/09592290108406219.

Kaidanow, Tina S. (2019), 'Foreign Military Sales: Process and Policy', www.state.gov/foreign-military-sales-process-and-policy/ accessed 16 February 2020.

Keating, Paul (2016), 'Australia Should "Cut The Tag" With American Foreign Policy After Trump Win Says Keating', Australian Broadcasting Corporation, www.youtube.com/watch?v=paPrAG6IY_8 accessed 24 January 2020.

Kubota, Yoko and Liza Lim (2019), 'Beijing Orders Agencies to Swap out Foreign Tech for Chinese Gear', *Wall Street Journal*, 9 December.

Landler, Mark (2012), 'Obama's Journey to Tougher Tack on a Rising China', *New York Times*, 21 September.

Lay, James S. (1961), 'Australia and New Zealand, Long-Range US Policy Interests' in *NSC 6109, Transmittal Note, James S. Lay, Jr., Exec. Secy, to the NSC.*, 16 January, Statement of Policy, 12 p., Eisenhower Library, White House Office, Office of the Special Assistant for National Security Affairs: Records, 1952–1961, Papers Received since 10 January 1961 (6), Box 122, National Security Council, 16 January 1961, US Declassified Documents Online, https://link-gale-com.usnwc.idm.oclc.org/apps/doc/CK2349431285/USDD?u=navalwc&sid=USDD&xid=9c64e87a accessed 17 February 2020.

Le Thu, Huong (2019), 'New Perspectives for the Revived Quad', *The Strategist*, 14 February, www.aspistrategist.org.au/new-perspectives-for-the-revived-quad accessed 17 February 2020.

Liu, Yawei and Justine Zheng Ren (2014), 'An Emerging Consensus on the US Threat: the United States according to PLA officers', *Journal of Contemporary China*, 23 (86).

Lockheed Martin (2020), 'IRST21 Sensor System', www.lockheedmartin.com/en-us/products/irst21-sensor-system.html accessed 16 February 2020.

MacFarquhar, R. (1972), 'Nixon's China Pilgrimage', *The World Today*, 28 (4), 153–162. Retrieved from www.jstor.org/stable/40394616 (accessed 3 July 2020).

Mackerras, Colin (2014), 'China and the Australia–US Relationship: a Historical Perspective', *Asian Survey*, March/April, 54 (2).

McDougall, Derek (2014), 'Australian Strategies in Response to China's Rise: The Relevance of the United States', *Asian Survey*, March/April, 54 (2).

Medcalf, Rory (ed.) (2017), 'Chinese Money and Australia's Security', NSC Policy Options Paper 2, March, https://nsc.crawford.anu.edu.au/department-news/9880/chinese-money-and-australias-security accessed 22 March.

Medcalf, Rory (2016), 'Rules, Balance, and Lifelines: An Australian Perspective on the South China Sea', *Asia Policy*, January, 21.

Melby, John (1968), 'The Cold War – Second Phase: China', *International Journal*, Summer.

Morrison, Scott (2019a), 'Transcript of President Trump and Prime Minister Morrison of Australia before Bilateral Meeting, Oval Office (White House)', 20 September, www.whitehouse.gov/briefings-statements/remarks-president-trump-prime-minister-morrison-australia-bilateral-meeting/ accessed 23 January 2020.

Morrison, Scott (2019b), 'Transcript of Prime Minister Scott Morrison in "Remarks by President Trump and Prime Minister Morrison of Australia in Joint Conference"', 20 September, www.whitehouse.gov/briefings-statements/remarks-president-trump-prime-minister-morrison-australia-joint-press-conference/ accessed 28 February.

Morrison, Scott (2019c), 'Transcript of Prime Minister Scott Morrison in "Remarks by President Trump and Prime Minister Morrison of Australia at State Dinner"', 21 September, www.whitehouse.gov/briefings-statements/remarks-president-trump-prime-minister-morrison-australia-state-dinner/ accessed 28 February 2019.

National Security Council (1953a), 'Basic US Objective Toward Communist China', Study Prepared by the Staff of the National Security Council, 6 April, S/S-NSC files, lot 63 D 351, NWC 148 Series.

National Security Council (1953b), 'Memorandum of Discussion at the 169th Meeting of the National Security Council, Washington, 5 November, in Foreign Relations of the United States, 1952–1954, China and Japan, Volume XIV, Part 1, No. 147', http s://history.state.gov/historicaldocuments/frus1952-54v14p1/d147 accessed 26 February 2020.

National Security Council (1954), *Report by the Secretary of State to the National Security Council*, 28 October, PPS files, lot 65 D 101, 'China', Washington, DC: National Security Council.

National Security Council (n.d.), *Annex To NSC 5713 Regarding US Efforts to Ensure Australia and New Zealand's Cooperation in Providing For a Collective Defense ff Southeast Asia*, Washington, DC: National Security Council, https://link-gale-com. usnwc.idm.oclc.org/apps/doc/CK2349549275/USDD?u=navalwc&sid=USDD&xid= 39e1fcc5 accessed 26 February 2020.

NDS (2018), 'National Defense Strategy', https://dod.defense.gov/Portals/1/Documents/p ubs/2018-National-Defense-Strategy-Summary.pdf accessed 26 February 2020.

Nixon, Richard M. (1967), 'Asia After Viet Nam', *Foreign Affairs*, October, www. foreignaffairs-com.usnwc.idm.oclc.org/articles/asia/1967-10-01/asia-after-viet-nam 2 February 2020.

NSS (2017), 'National Security Strategy', www.whitehouse.gov/wp-content/uploads/ 2017/12/NSS-Final-12-18-2017-0905.pdf accessed 27 January 2020.

Obama, Barack (2011), 'Remarks by President Obama to the Australian Parliament, Parliament House, Canberra, Australia', 17 November, The White House, Office of the Press Secretary, https://obamawhitehouse.archives.gov/the-press-office/2011/11/ 17/remarks-president-obama-australian-parliament accessed 18 December 2019.

O'Rourke, Ronald (2020), 'US–China Strategic Competition in South and East China Seas: Background and Issues for Congress', Congressional Research Service, 6 February, Washington, DC.

Packham, Colin (2020), 'Australia Spy Chief Warns of "Unprecedented" Foreign Espionage Threat', Reuters, 24 February, www.reuters.com/article/US-Australia -security/australia-spy-chief-warns-of-unprecedented-foreign-espionage-threat-idUS KCN20I1CY?il=0 accessed 25 February 2020.

Pence, Mike (2018), 'Remarks by Vice President Pence on the Administration's Policy toward China', 4 October, www.whitehouse.gov/briefings-statements/remarks-vice-p resident-pence-administrations-policy-toward-china/ accessed 26 February 2020.

Pompeo, Michael (2019a), *The Unbreakable Alliance*, Washington, DC: State Department Documents and Publications, 4 August (Nexis Uni).

Pompeo, Michael (2019b), 'A Message from the Secretary', in A Free and Open Indo-Pacific: Advancing a Shared Vision, US Department of State, 4 November.

Quigley, K. (2002), 'A Lost Opportunity: A Reappraisal of the Kennedy Administration's China Policy in 1963'. *Diplomacy & Statecraft*, 13 (5). doi:10.1080/714000332.

Rice, Condoleeza (2000), 'Campaign 2000: Promoting the National Interest', *Foreign Affairs*, January/February.

Rusk, Dean (1990), *As I saw it by Dean Rusk* (New York: W.W. Norton and Company).

Select Committee (1999), 'Overview', Report of the Select Committee on US National Security and Military/Commercial Concerns with the People's Republic of China, 3 January, https://china.usc.edu/sites/default/files/legacy/AppImages/overv.pdf accessed 25 February 2020.

Stillwell, David (2019), 'Nominee to the Assistant Secretary of State for East Asian and Pacific Affairs', 27 March, www.foreign.senate.gov/imo/media/doc/032719_Stil well_Testimony.pdf accessed 25 February 2020.

Thai News Service (2019), 'United States: Secretary of State Michael R. Pompeo and Secretary of Defense Mark Esper, Australian Minister of Foreign Affairs Marise Payne, and Australian Minister of Defense Linda Reynolds at a Press Availability', 5 August, https://advance.lexis.com/api/document?collection=news&id=urn:content Item:5WRB-8YF1-DXMS-81K6-00000-00&context=1516831 accessed 25 February 2020.

Tillerson, Rex. (2017a), 'Defining Our Relationship with India for the Next Century', Center for Strategic and International Studies, 18 October, https://csis-prod.s3.ama zonaws.com/s3fs-public/event/171018_An_Address_by_U.S._Secretary_of_State_Re x_Tillerson.pdf?O0nMCCRjXZiUa5V2cF8_NDiZ14LYRX3m accessed 25 February 2020.

Trump, Donald (2017b), 'Remarks by President Trump at APEC CEO Summit, Da Nang, Vietnam', 10 November, www.whitehouse.gov/briefings-statements/remarks-p resident-trump-apec-ceo-summit-da-nang-vietnam/ accessed 21 February 2020.

Trump, Donald (2018), 'President Trump's Administration is Advancing a Free and Open Indo-Pacific through Investments and Partnerships in Economics, Security, and Governance', White House (Statements and Releases), 18 November.

Trump, Donald (2019a), 'Remarks by President Trump and Prime Minister Morrison of Australia before Bilateral Meeting, Oval Office (White House)', 20 September, www. whitehouse.gov/briefings-statements/remarks-president-trump-prime-minister-morriso n-australia-bilateral-meeting/ accessed 23 January 2020.

Trump, Donald (2019b), 'Remarks by President Trump and Prime Minister Morrison of Australia at Arrival Ceremony, South Lawn (White House)', 20 September, www. whitehouse.gov/briefings-statements/remarks-president-trump-prime-minister-morris on-australia-arrival-ceremony/ accessed 20 September 2019.

Turnbull, Malcolm (2017), 'Speech at Luncheon in honour of His Excellency Li Keqiang, Premier of the State Council of the People's Republic of China', 23 March, transcript ID: 40840, https://pmtranscripts.pmc.gov.au/release/transcrip t-40840 accessed 6 December 2019.

US–Australia Defense Trade Cooperation Treaty (2007), 'Treaty between the Government of Australia and the Government of the United States of America Concerning Defense Trade Cooperation (Sydney, 5 September 2007) and Implementing Arrangement (14 March 2008)', Article 6, www.austlii.edu.au/au/other/dfat/treaties/ ATS/2013/17.html accessed 31 January 2019.

US Embassy (Australia) (2018), 'The History of Mateship', https://usa.embassy.gov.au/ timelines-alliance accessed 13 February 2020.

USINDOPACOM (2020), 'USINDOPACOM, Area of Responsibility', www.pacom.mil/ About-USINDOPACOM/USPACOM-Area-of-Responsibility/ accessed 13 February 2020.

US Navy (2020), 'Fact File', www.navy.mil/navydata/fact_display.asp?cid=2100&tid= 325&ct=2 accessed 16 February 2020.

Walt, Stephen M. (1985), 'Alliance Formation and the Balance of World Power', *International Security*, Spring, 9 (4).

Walt, Stephen M. (1988), 'Testing Theories of Alliance Formation: the Case of Southwest Asia', *International Organization*, Spring, 42 (2).

Walt, Stephen M. (1997), 'Why Alliances Endure or Collapse', *Survival*, Spring, 39 (1).

Ward, Myah (2020), 'Wilbur Ross Says Coronavirus Could Bring Jobs Back To The US From China', *Politico*, 30 January, www.politico.com/news/2020/01/30/wilbur-ross-coronavirus-jobs-109445 accessed 12 February 2020.

White House (2019a), 'Remarks by President Trump and Prime Minister Morrison of Australia at Arrival Ceremony, South Lawn (White House)', 20 September, www.whitehouse.gov/briefings-statements/remarks-president-trump-prime-minister-morrison-australia-arrival-ceremony/ accessed 20 September 2019.

White House (2019b), 'Remarks by President Trump and Prime Minister Morrison of Australia before Bilateral Meeting, Oval Office (White House)', 20 September, www.whitehouse.gov/briefings-statements/remarks-president-trump-prime-minister-morrison-australia-bilateral-meeting/ accessed 23 January 2020.

White House Fact Sheet (2019), 'President Donald J. Trump is Celebrating our Long and Steadfast Friendship with Australia', 20 September, www.whitehouse.gov/briefings-statements/president-donald-j-trump-celebrating-long-steadfast-friendship-australia/ accessed 23 January 2020.

White, Hugh (2012), *The China Choice: Why We Should Share Power*, Oxford: Oxford University Press.

Wiedemann, Kent (1995), 'Prepared testimony of Kent Wiedemann, Deputy Assistant Secretary of State, East Asian and Pacific Affairs, Before the House Ways and Means Committee, Subcommittee on Trade, Federal News Service', 23 May, https://advance-lexis-com.usnwc.idm.oclc.org/api/document?collection=news&id=urn:contentItem:3SJ4-KGM0-0003-12BV-00000-00&context=1516831.

Xia, Yafeng (2006), 'China's Elite Politics and Sino-American Rapprochement, January 1969-February 1972', *Journal of Cold War Studies*, 8 (4).

Yale University (1954), 'Mutual Defense Treaty between the United States and the Republic of China', 2 December, https://avalon.law.yale.edu/20th_century/chin001.asp accessed 28 February 2020.

YouTube (2019), 'The State Visit of the Prime Minister of Australia and Mrs. Morrison', 21 September, www.youtube.com/watch?v=FFcnN6mqJyo accessed 28 February 2019.

4 Security threats and challenges to Australia

Andrew T. H. Tan

Introduction

As a middle power in Asia, Australia's security and the future challenges that it faces are linked to developments in both its regional and global environments. Australia has the fifth largest economy in Asia, with a Gross Domestic Product (GDP) of around US$1,254 billion in 2017. Globally it is ranked 19th in terms of GDP (Statistica n.d.). As former Australian Foreign Minister Gareth Evans mused, referring to Australia, 'middle powers are best described as those states which are not economically or militarily big or strong enough, either in their own regions or the wider world, to impose their policy preferences on anyone else – but which are nonetheless sufficiently capable, credible and motivated to be able to make an impact on international relations' (Evans 2017). While Australia has a moderately strong voice in Asia, it is not a major player globally and the tools that it has to protect its national interests are limited. Its security situation is therefore determined by events and processes that are beyond its control, even though it does have strengths arising from its middle power status which enables it to respond to changing security threats more proactively.

This chapter article assesses Australia's perception of the security threats and challenges to it a result of the complex and changing strategic environment both regionally and globally, and its responses in dealing with the evolving threat landscape. At the time of writing, the global pandemic that broke out in early 2020 has severely impacted Australia, though the implications for the regional and global orders remain unclear.

Australia's strategic challenges

Australia's central strategic challenge has been succinctly summed up by Allan Gyngell: 'as a sparsely settled continent on the edge of Asia, dependent on global markets for its prosperity and on distant allies for its security, Australia has faced as the central question of its foreign policy not whether it should engage actively with the world, but how it should do so' (Gyngell 2005: 99). Thus, according to Gyngell, 'Australians felt that their safety would not be assured by remaining aloof from world events and that the global balance of power mattered to them', and that this world-view has remained central to Australian foreign affairs and security perspectives (Gyngell 2005: 99). Indeed, in his book *Fear of Abandonment*, Allan Gyngell, the director of the Office for National Assessments, Australia's central intelligence assessment agency from 2009 to 2013, argued that it has been the fear of being abandoned by Britain, and later by the United States, that has been an important driver of Australian foreign policy. In this context, what Australia wants to achieve as a country depends on its capacity to understand the world and to respond to it effectively (Gyngell 2017).

In 2008, then Prime Minister Kevin Rudd neatly summed up the key objectives of Australia's national security, which consisted of the 'freedom from attack or the threat of attack', the maintenance of its territorial integrity, political sovereignty and hard-won freedoms, and the capacity to advance economic prosperity for all Australians (Rudd 2008). In fact, Australia has pursued a remarkably consistent national security strategy since achieving Federation in 1901. This has comprised establishing and maintaining alliances with great powers, a military deterrent capability and active diplomacy aimed at shaping the international environment in favour of Australia's interests (O'Neil 2011: 19). In effect, this has meant that Australia has supported Britain and, since 1945, the United States, in maintaining the Western-dominated regional and global order that has served Australia's interests well in terms of preserving its sovereignty and advancing its economic interests. This explains Australia's long and deep involvement in almost all major conflicts involving Britain and the United States, such as the two world wars, the Malayan Emergency, the Korean and Vietnam Wars, the two Gulf Wars, and more recently, Iraq and Afghanistan.

Thus, O'Neil has observed that Australia evinces 'a strong commitment to a rules-based international order' (O'Neil 2011: 20). This 'rules-based order' refers to the post-1945 Western-dominated and US-led regional and international order that followed the end of the Second World War, one which underpinned the relative stability and development that has served US allies such as Australia so well. The problem is that this post-1945 order is now under challenge, from a rising People's Republic of China that has emerged as the United States' main peer competitor, and new non-traditional security challenges that have arisen due to globalization and the emergence of the interlinked global economy, such as global terrorism, cyber-attacks and global pandemics. Indeed, the United States National Intelligence Council has been emphatic that the post-1945 international order is in the process of change and will soon be unrecognizable. This transformation, according to the Council, is 'being fuelled by a globalizing economy, marked by an historic shift of relative wealth and economic power from West to East, and by the increasing weight of new players - especially China and India'. In the aftermath, the United States will still remain the single most important actor but would be less dominant. The transition however, will be fraught with risks, including from non-traditional security challenges. More seriously, 'the rapidly changing international order at a time of growing geopolitical challenges increases the likelihood of discontinuities, shocks, and surprises' (National Intelligence Council 2008: 1). Although written in 2008, just such a discontinuity, shock and surprise did emerge in early 2020 with the devastating global pandemic that has become known as the coronavirus disease 2019 (COVID-19), although it is not entirely clear, at the time of writing, how exactly this would affect the regional and global orders.

The fundamental changes in the international system present serious challenges for Australia, a country that has had a long-established pattern of reliance on a great power ally and on a Western-dominated international system. The challenge is how Australia can break with long-established habits and long-held perspectives to meet the threats arising from the changes to its geo-strategic environment. What are these new challenges? And what should it do to meet the new challenges that it faces?

Known knowns and black swans

To engage effectively with the changing geo-strategic environment requires an accurate reading of current and future strategic trends. Assessing future challenges however, is itself a challenge. While there are observable trends that suggest what the future might look like, there are also discontinuity-based changes which are impossible to predict in advance (O'Neil 2011: 24–32). The observable trend-based markers of change, or 'known knowns' are based on verifiable trends and developments which suggests the future trajectory of the international system. Thus, we know that China has achieved remarkable economic growth in recent decades and that its rise as an economic and military power has given it both confidence and the means to more aggressively assert its national interests on the regional and global stage. There has been ample evidence of this growing assertiveness in recent years, for instance, over the Senkaku islands and the South China Sea. Globally, it is also challenging the United States through its massive 'One Belt, One Road' economic initiative backed by trillions of dollars of Chinese investments, and the setting up of the Asian Infrastructure Investment Bank (AIIB) as an alternative to the US-dominated World Bank (Tan 2016).

Clearly, China's rise will have important implications for Australia, as China will increasingly be able to put pressure on Australia, through its economic links and the influencing operations of its local agents, to dilute its alliance relationship with the United States or even support it in its intensifying strategic competition with the United States (Hamilton 2018). China is Australia's largest trading partner and a key market for Australia's mining resources, agricultural produce and education services. The economic relationship has been buoyant, with bilateral trade reaching A$194.6 billion in 2017–2018, which is 24.4 per cent of Australia's total external trade

(Department of Foreign Affairs and Trade 2019). This potentially gives China increasing leverage over Australia.

Even with 'known knowns', our responses could be affected by historical experience, political and cultural values, personal bias, or simply misperceptions. Indeed, perceptions, beliefs, images of other actors all play a part in misperceptions in foreign affairs decision-making. According to Robert Jervis, the most common forms of misperceptions emanate from the following: perceptions of centralization in the decision-making of other actors, overestimation of one's importance as influence or as target, cognitive dissonance and the influence of desires and fears on perception (Jervis 1976: 319–406). It is in fact 'often impossible to explain crucial decisions and polices without reference to the decision-makers' beliefs about the world and their images of others' (Jervis 1976:78). Thus, in the 'fog of decision-making', decision-makers employ short-cuts to rationality, often without being aware of doing so. These short-cuts, however, 'often produce important kinds of systematic errors, many of which increases conflict' (Jervis 1976: 111).

Unlike trend-based markers of change, discontinuity-based changes are much harder to predict. Dubbed 'black swan' events by Nicholas Taleb, in his seminal book entitled *The Black Swan: The Impact of the Highly Improbable*, history and human experience is replete with examples of assumptions which were subsequently proven to be erroneous. Thus, the assumption that all swans were white became completely up-ended when the first black swan was spotted (Taleb 2007). According to Taleb, drawing an example from Australia's iconic Sydney Opera House, the project was supposed to open in 1963 at a cost of A\$7 million. In fact, it opened in 1973 at a cost of around A\$104 million. Taleb described this as an emblematic example of the 'epistemic arrogance of the human race', as it failed to predict the final actual cost of the project. Thus, Taleb asserts that 'we are demonstrably arrogant about what we think we know'. In what he calls 'the scandal of prediction', we try to predict but almost always miss the big events (Taleb 2007: 138). Eventually some 'outlier' (or 'black swan'), i.e. a completely unforeseen development or event, throws us off-guard and up-ends all our assumptions (Taleb 2007: 158).

Recent examples of unexpected black swan events include: the terrorist attacks in the United States on 11 September 2011 (or 9/11), the election of Donald Trump as President of the United States in 2016, the result of the U.K. referendum in June 2016 which resulted in a vote for the U.K. to leave the European Union (or Brexit) and the Singapore Summit in June 2018 between President Trump and North Korean leader Kim Jong-un – this after months of increasing tension amidst talk of open conflict. While the world did have prior warning through earlier epidemics, such as SARS in 2003, the global pandemic in 2020 is also a black swan event.

Key drivers shaping the security environment

Despite the often problematic nature of prediction, the Australian government's *2016 Defence White Paper* attempted to do just that, albeit based on known trends as can be observed (Department of Defence 2016). According to the White Paper, six key drivers will shape Australia's security environment to 2035:

- roles of US and China, and their relationship;
- challenges to the stability of the rules-based global order;
- the enduring threat of terrorism;
- state fragility (especially within Australia's immediate neighbourhood);
- the pace of military modernization and the development of more capable regional military forces; and
- the emergence of new complex, non-geographic threats, such as cyber threats (Department of Defence 2016: 40–41).

The following sections will evaluate each of these six identified trends.

China's rise and US–China tensions

According to the *2016 Defence White Paper*, the roles of the United States and China in the region, as well as their relationship with each other, will be the most important factors in the security and economic development of the Indo-Pacific region (Department of Defence 2016: 41). It is widely recognized that China's dramatic economic rise and the challenge that it poses to the global dominance of the United States is the biggest international relations issue today. Moreover, the United States and China have the largest and second-largest economies and defence budgets in the world, in addition to being significant nuclear powers. As James Steinberg and Michael O'Hanlon observed, the US–China relationship is 'the most consequential bilateral relationship of our time', with immense implications for global and regional security (Steinberg and O'Hanlon 2014:1). In the United States, the perception that China has emerged as the main economic, technological and military peer competitor to it has unified elite political opinion, despite the partisan and often bitter Republican-Democrat divide in US politics. According to Satoru Mori, 'an ideational mold is emerging in which American political leaders from both sides of the aisle could increasingly justify their China policy within a notional framework that China is undermining American prosperity and security' (Mori 2019).

US policy-makers have taken note that China's economy, measured in Purchasing Power Parity (PPP) terms taking into account price differentials, actually surpassed the United States in 2014 to become the world's largest economy (IMF 2014). In absolute terms, China's economy is in fact on course to overtake that of the United States by 2030 due to its much higher economic growth rates (Kennedy 2018). It is today a trading superstate, with a significant and growing economic presence in every continent in the world, as well as possessing the world's largest foreign exchange reserves estimated at just over US$3,000 billion in February 2019 (Trading Economics n.d.). Globally, it is challenging the United States through its massive 'One Belt, One Road' economic initiative backed by trillions of dollars of Chinese investments, and the setting up of the Asian Infrastructure Investment Bank (AIIB) as an alternative to the US-dominated World Bank (Tan 2016). Moreover, China's policies of forced technology transfer, alleged intellectual property theft and other alleged unfair trade practices is perceived to have reduced the economic competitiveness of US industry (Mori 2019). China today also leads the world in e-commerce and has invested heavily in AI, robotics, renewable energy and other next-generation technologies in an attempt to leapfrog the West technologically. Thus, a senior US official, in an Op-Ed in the *New York Times*, bluntly stated that 'a core threat to the American industrial base comes from China', a view echoed in the United States Defense Industrial Base Report in 2018 (Navarro 2018; Department of Defense 2018). The global pandemic in 2020 which originated from China and has had devastating global economic and health consequences has sharpened mistrust of China amongst Americans, and turbo-charged tensions between the two countries, leading to predictions of a real Cold War after the pandemic is over (Schell 2020).

China's economic growth has had a direct impact on its military spending. Thus, China's estimated military budget was US$19.3 billion in 1989 and US$239.2 billion in 2018 (using 2017 as the base year), compared to just under US$633.5 billion for the United States in 2018 (SIPRI n.d.). While the US still maintains a commanding military lead as well as a global military presence, China's defence interests are mainly focused on the Asia-Pacific, with only one overseas base in Djibouti (CSIS n.d.). Indeed, China's evolving A2 / AD (Anti-access, Area Denial) capabilities are such that a RAND study in 2015 concluded that the current trajectory of China's armed forces suggests that US military dominance will recede in the coming years. This would enable China's armed forces to gain at least temporary local air and naval superiority at the outset of any conflict in East Asia (RAND 2015: xxxi). An Australian study in 2019 concluded as well that 'Chinese counter-intervention systems have undermined America's ability to project power into the Indo-Pacific', and that 'the United States' longstanding ability to uphold a favourable regional balance of power by itself faces mounting and ultimately insurmountable challenges' (Townshend et. al. 2019: 2–6).

The economic and military challenges that China poses raises the risk of regional and even global conflict. As power transition theory has posited, a situation in which rising new powers challenge the prevailing hegemon always leads to open conflict since the currently dominant power would resist such a challenge (Organski 1968). Graham Allison has coined the phrase 'the Thucydides' trap' to explain this historical phenomenon, based on the quote by the ancient Greek writer Thucydides, who observed that 'it was the rise of Athens and the fear that this inspired in Sparta that made war inevitable' (Allison 2017).

The obvious challenge to Australia is the fact that it has come under pressure to choose sides in the intensifying strategic competition between the United States and China. Australia's dilemma is complicated by the fact that China is today Australia's largest trading partner, but Australia remains a close US ally through the ANZUS Treaty of 1952 (Workman 2019; ANZUS Treaty 1952). On the part of the United States, it is clear that Australia remains a key ally in the Indo-Pacific. Indeed, in the face of China's assertiveness over maritime territorial claims in the South China and East China Seas after 2008, the US responded by launching its much-vaunted Asia Pivot or rebalancing strategy, announced with much fanfare by President Obama in his speech to the Australian Parliament in Canberra in 2011. In his speech, Obama acknowledged that the Asia-Pacific was where America's future would lie, vowing that the US would 'play a larger and long-term role in shaping this region and its future, by upholding core principles and in close partnership with allies and friends' (Obama 2011). This has involved the strengthening of alliances in the region, including with Australia, where under the Force Posture Agreement in 2014, the US could station up to 2,500 US Marines for six months each year, and have access to air and naval facilities in Australia for US military aircraft and naval warships (Glenday 2014).

What does China's rise therefore mean for Australia, given the reality of close economic ties? According to the Foreign Policy White Paper of 2017, 'at times, closer engagement will be accompanied by friction arising from our different interests, values and political and legal systems' (Department of Foreign Affairs and Trade 2017: 40). However, the same document also stated, without naming any country, that the Australian government 'is concerned about attempts by foreign governments or their proxies to exert inappropriate influence on and undermine Australia's sovereign institutions and decision-making'. This foreign interference 'aims to shape the actions of decision-makers and public opinion to achieve an outcome favourable to foreign interests' (Department of Foreign Affairs and Trade 2017: 75).

In 2017, an intense debate broke out in Australia when Clive Hamilton, Professor of Public Ethics at Charles Sturt University in Australia, made public his difficulty in finding a publisher for his book on China's influencing operations in Australia, citing the fear by potential publishers of legal action. This sparked lively debate in the Australian parliament, with the parliamentary Joint Committee on Intelligence and Security considering publishing it under parliamentary privilege to protect its author from any potential legal action (ABC 2018a). In any event, Hamilton eventually found a publisher, namely, Hardie Grant, which published *Spycatcher* in 1986, the memoir of the British MI5 principal scientific officer Peter Wright, which the government of Britain attempted to suppress. Hamilton's book thus appeared in

2018 under the somewhat provocative title *Silent Invasion: China's Influence in Australia* (Australian 2018).

Hamilton's book details alleged 'influence operations' in Australia coordinated by the United Front Work Department of the Chinese Communist Party (CCP). The back-cover summary asserts that 'sophisticated influence operations target Australia's elites, and parts of the large Chinese-Australian diaspora have been mobilized to buy access to politicians, limit academic freedom, intimidate critics, collect information for Chinese intelligence agencies, and protest in the streets against Australian government policy'. By working through local agents of influence, China has thus, according to Hamilton, achieved undue influence in major political parties, unions, universities, Chinese media, and business (Hamilton 2018).

Citing a defector from the Chinese embassy in Canberra, Hamilton asserted that China's objectives are: to secure Australia as a secure and reliable base for China's economic growth; drive a wedge into the US–Australia alliance; and attain comprehensive influence over Australia economically, politically, culturally (Hamilton 2018: 2). More seriously, according to Hamilton, China has supported united front organizations in Australia, and penetrated the estimated one million Chinese diaspora in Australia. The majority of these Chinese, Hamilton asserts, are intensely loyal to China, although he issues the caveat that by 'Chinese' he meant Han Chinese, not ethnic Chinese from Southeast Asia or non-Han Chinese such as Tibetans (Hamilton 2018: 280–281).

This builds on the assertions made by others of China's influencing operations abroad, using the worldwide Chinese diaspora to do so. According to New Zealand political scientist James To, Chinese nationals and those of Chinese descent abroad are tapped to provide information or technology for China's development through widespread micro-espionage. According to To, 'many respond positively and voluntarily by appealing to their ethnic pride and sympathies in helping the motherland advance' (Wall Street Journal 2014). In the Australian context, the *Australian Financial Review* reported in 2016 that 'Chinese security services are engaging in the most intense collection of intelligence by a foreign power Australia has ever seen'. More seriously, 'Australia does not have the resources to stop it … the security services are unable to protect all of Australia's secrets' (Patrick 2016). Thus, according to the 2017 Foreign Policy White Paper, rules are being contested through the increased use by some states of 'measures short of war' to pursue political and security objectives. Such measures include 'the use of non-state actors and other proxies, covert and paramilitary operations, economic coercion, cyber attacks, misinformation and media manipulation' (Department of Foreign Affairs and Trade 2017: 24).

In 2017, China lodged a strong diplomatic protest at the perceived anti-China hysteria in Australia, and cancelled bilateral meetings in retaliation (Australian Financial Review 2018). Following the blocking of Huawei from Australia's 5G network, an unofficial ban and go-slow on coal imports from

Australia underlined the threat of economic sanctions from China (ABC 2019). Indeed, China is Australia's largest trading partner, with two-way trade totalling A$194.6 billion in 2017–2018 (Department of Foreign Affairs and Trade 2019). China is also the destination of almost 30per cent of Australia's total experts (Workman 2019). The debate, indeed, the dilemma in Canberra, is therefore this: what is the price that Australia is willing to pay to counter or defy China?

Challenges to the rules-based global order

The second challenge identified by the Defence White Paper 2016 is challenges to the rules-based global order. Thus, the Defence White Paper stressed that 'our security and prosperity depend on a stable Indo-Pacific region and a rules-based global order in which power is not misused, and threats to peace and stability from tensions between countries can be managed through negotiations based on international law' (Department of Defence 2016: 33).

While China is not explicitly named, it is widely understood that this at least partly refers to the challenge that China is posing to the post-1945 Western-led international order and the US-led regional order in the Asia and Indo-Pacific regions. States, especially smaller ones, rely on a stable rules-based global order for security and prosperity since this supports the peaceful resolution of disputes and facilitates free and open trade. However, as the White Paper observed, 'the framework of the rules-based global order is under increasing pressure and has shown signs of fragility'. In particular, 'the balance of military and economic power between countries is changing and newly powerful countries want greater influence and to challenge some of the rules in the global architecture established some 70 years ago' (Department of Defence 2016: 45).

Indeed, the Philippines brought to the The Permanent Court of Arbitration in The Hague its case against China's assertive actions in pursuit of its claims over the South China Sea. The tribunal ruled in 2016 that 'China had violated the Philippines' sovereign rights in its exclusive economic zone by (a) interfering with Philippine fishing and petroleum exploration, (b) constructing artificial islands and (c) failing to prevent Chinese fishermen from fishing in the zone.' More significantly, the tribunal concluded that 'there was no evidence that China had historically exercised exclusive control over the waters or their resources', and thus, the tribunal 'concluded that there was no legal basis for China to claim historic rights to resources within the sea areas falling within the "nine-dash line"' (Permanent Court of Arbitration 2016). China, which claims the entirety of the South China Sea however, rejected the ruling, with its state media declaring that 'the Chinese government and the Chinese people firmly oppose (the ruling) and will neither acknowledge it nor accept it' (Guardian 2016). Smaller states are understandably uneasy with the seeming undermining of international law and possible threats to the freedom of the sea-lines of communications (SLOCs) that traverse the South China

Sea. Thus, Singapore's Prime Minister Lee Hsien Loong observed that both Australia and Singapore shared common interests on the South China Sea issue. According to Lee, 'like Australia, Singapore depends on a peaceful and stable region which supports and promotes free trade and open markets ... we share similar outlooks on the importance of international law and the peaceful settlement of disputes'. He also declared that both countries 'have a vital interest in freedom of navigation and overflight in the South China Sea', and that 'we should continue to uphold these principles' (Straits Times 2018).

Apart from challenging the existing regional order in Asia, China has also used inducements, for example, its One Belt One Road initiative, to consolidate its position in Asia and Africa, thus challenging the US position globally. China's challenge to the existing global order has serious implications. As Martin Jacques asserted in 2010, China's rise is inevitable and would lead to the end of Western dominance in every sphere. More seriously, he asserted that China as a great global power would 'in time require and expect a major reordering of global relationships' (Jacques 2009: 431). In this respect, China is behaving no differently than other great powers historically in attempting to reshape the international system to serve its interests.

China's dramatic rise and its profound challenge on the existing global and regional orders has been accentuated by clear signs that the post-1945 international system dominated by US and Western allies is ending, epitomized by the Global Financial Crisis in 2008, the massive US debt, the Eurozone crisis, and more recently, Donald Trump's 'America First' dictum in prioritizing the narrow economic interests of the United States ahead of fulfilling its responsibilities in sustaining alliances and upholding the current international system. The problem is also accentuated by the fact that the protectionist and isolationist sentiments underpinning 'America First' have deep roots which pre-ceded the emergence of Trump and may outlast his administration (Kagan 2018).

The enduring threat of global terrorism

The third challenge identified by the Defence White Paper 2016 is the enduring threat of global terrorism. Since the terrorist attacks in the United States on 11 September 2001, US-led global counterterrorism efforts have seriously degraded the operational capabilities of Al Qaeda. But the sharp rise in anti-US and anti-Western sentiments in the Middle East as a result of unwise moves, such as the invasion of Iraq in 2003, has sustained the terrorist recruitment of radical Islamist groups. Moreover, the surprising rise of the Islamic State in 2014, when it captured vast swathes of Iraq and Syria, followed by its declaration of a caliphate, galvanized the radical Islamists. Indeed, by late 2015, around 27,000 volunteer fighters from 86 countries around the world had travelled to Syria or Iraq to join the Islamic State (Soufan Group 2015). Worldwide, radical Islamist ideology has spread through social media and other forms of modern communications. This led to the phenomenon of lone wolf attacks in the West by self-radicalized individuals or returning fighters, resulting in a swathe of deadly terrorist attacks in Europe and North America that has been attributed to the Islamic State (Fox News 2017).

In Australia's neighbourhood, namely in nearby Southeast Asia, particularly in Indonesia and Malaysia, an estimated 1,000 people had joined the Islamic State in Syria and Iraq by 2017 with local extremists in Indonesia pledging their support for it (Liow 2017; Emont 2014). Within Australia, the fear of terrorism has risen since the deadly Bali bombings in 2002 that killed 202 people, including 88 Australians (BBC 2012). In more recent times, a string of small-scale terrorist incidences and foiled attacks in Australia attributed to the Islamic State have forced its security agencies to pay careful attention to the very real threat from global terrorism taking place on Australian territory through either self-radicalized individuals or returning fighters from the Middle East (Blackwell 2017). By 2017, an estimated 100 Australians were in Syria and Iraq involved with jihadi groups such as the Islamic State, while around 190 people in Australia were suspected of actively supporting the Islamic State (Zammit 2017). The defeat of the Islamic State in Syria by early 2019, while welcomed, has however only meant that displaced fighters would now turn their attention to further deadly attacks abroad, including in Western countries such as Australia (Wall Street Journal 2019).

Thus, the 2017 Defence White Paper stated that: 'the major threat we are currently facing is from violent extremism perpetrated or motivated by terrorist groups such as Daesh (or Islamic State) and al-Qa'ida', while 'the anti-Western narrative of terrorists means that Australians will continue to be targeted at home and abroad' (Department of Defence 2016: 47). This continued concern over threat emanating from global terrorism has meant that Australia's response has not only included internal counter-terrorism efforts but also external interventions as part of global counter-terrorism efforts. The latter included Australia's contribution of F18 Hornet fighter-bombers from 2014 to 2018 to the US-led combat operations against the Islamic State in Syria and Iraq, as well as deployment of Australian military personnel for training and logistical support in Iraq (Tillett 2018).

The point to note here is that Australia is seen by radical Islamists as an extension of the United States, given its close identification with the US. Australia has indeed supported all US-led global counter-terrorism initiatives since 9–11, including the invasions of both Afghanistan and Iraq, and more recent counter-terrorism efforts in the Middle East aimed at the Islamic State.

State fragility

The fourth challenge identified by the 2016 Defence White Paper is state fragility. This stems from 'the ability of terrorist organizations to organize, train, spread their propaganda and mount operations', which 'is supported by state fragility, weak borders and an increasing number of ungoverned spaces through parts of North Africa, sub-Saharan Africa, the Middle East and Asia including in Libya, Iraq, Syria and elsewhere' (Department of Defence 2016: 48). This, in turn, justifies Australia's support of US-led global counter-terrorism efforts, including in the Middle East.

However, a more pressing concern is Australia's own strategic backyard. As the 2016 Defence White Paper noted, 'we cannot effectively protect Australia if we do not have a secure nearer region, encompassing maritime South East Asia and South Pacific (comprising Papua New Guinea, Timor-Leste and Pacific Island Countries)'. Thus, Australia 'must play a leadership role in our immediate neighbourhood spanning Papua New Guinea, Timor-Leste and Pacific Island Countries in support of our national interests' (Department of Defence 2016: 33). Any instability in Australia's immediate region 'could have strategic consequences for Australia should it lead to increasing influence by actors from outside the region with interests inimical to ours'. It is thus 'crucial that Australia help support the development of national resilience in the region to reduce the likelihood of instability'. This assistance would include defence cooperation, aid, policing and building regional organizations (Department of Defence 2016: 48).

Indeed, China has been making recent inroads into the South Pacific through massive aid and investments, thus threatening to displace Australia as the dominant power in Australia's own strategic backyard (McGregor and Pryke 2018). This has set the stage for Australia and China to compete for influence in the South Pacific, epitomized by the announcement in 2018 by Australia and the United States that they would jointly redevelop the Manus Island naval base in Papua New Guinea (ABC 2018c).

Military modernization in Asia

The fifth challenge identified by the Defence White Paper 2016 is the increasing pace of military modernization in Asia. Indicative of the systemic changes in the global strategic environment as a result of Asia's economic rise, Asia's defence spending overtook Europe in 2012 (IISS 2013: 33). In 2019, Asia (including Australasia) accounted for 24.5 per cent of global military expenditure, compared to 16.6 per cent for Europe (IISS 2020: 21). According to the authoritative Stockholm International Peace Research Institute (SIPRI), defence spending in Asia (including Australasia) rose from US$134 billion in 1988 to US$494 billion in 2018, measured in 2017 constant prices and exchange rates (SIPRI n.d.). The top four defence spenders in Asia in 2018 (measured in 2017 constant US$ million) were: China, at US$239 billion, India at US$66.5 billion, Japan at US$45.3 billion and South Korea at US$41.1 billion. By comparison, Australia spent US $26.8 billion in 2018 (SIPRI n.d.).

What is significant is that the arms spending has led to the acquisition of the latest weapons systems, such as aircraft carriers, submarines, surface warships, main battle tanks, artillery, advanced combat aircraft (including stealth aircraft), electronic warfare aircraft and helicopter gunships. Accompanying this has been the proliferation of missiles, including ballistic and cruise missiles. Analysts have thus argued that an arms race has now broken out in Asia as countries increasingly acquire similar capabilities to match each other (Ball 2010; Tan 2014). These capabilities have meant increasingly capable regional armed forces with the enhanced capacity for power projection. In turn, the comparative advantage enjoyed by the United States and its allies in the region has eroded, thus narrowing the range of foreign policy and defence options for them. As the 2016 Defence White Paper noted, 'the defence capability edge we have enjoyed in the wider region will significantly diminish', as 'technological advances such as quantum computing, innovative manufacturing, hypersonics, directed energy weapons, and unmanned systems are likely to lead to the introduction of new weapons into our region'. In addition, 'the quality and quantity of cruise and short and medium range ballistic missile forces in the Indo-Pacific is rising and relevant technologies are spreading' (Department of Defence 2016: 49–50).

Emergence of new threats

Finally, the sixth challenge identified by the 2016 Defence White Paper is the emergence of complex non-geographic threats, such as in cyberspace and space. Cyber threats from offensive cyber operations, for instance, could have devastating impacts given Australia's heavy reliance on information networks in defence, commerce and government. In 2015, the Australian Signals Directorate detected over 1,200 cyber-attacks targeting government agencies as well as non-government sectors. The White Paper also noted the emergence of anti-satellite capabilities by some states, which could threaten Australia's defence and communications networks. As well, space-based capabilities 'also offer potential state adversaries advanced information gathering opportunities, including imagery gathering' (Department of Defence 2016: 52).

While the White Paper did not mention any country by name, it became clear subsequent to its publication that cyber security issues, especially cyber and other forms of electronic espionage, have been shaping up as a key test for how Australia would deal with China. Indeed, cyber-attacks on the Australian Parliament and its members have focused attention on cyber-espionage and attacks allegedly emanating from China (ABC 2019).

While the 2016 Defence White Paper does not mention other 'complex non-geographic threats', these could emanate from sources as diverse as catastrophic climate change impacts, pandemics, the proliferation of weapons of mass destruction, and generally, black swan events that cannot be predicted in advance, making the preparation of counter-measures difficult. This happened in 2020 with the global pandemic, which has had very serious economic and health consequences for Australia. As well, the strategic implications of the pandemic could be very serious, given that China appeared, at the time of writing, to be the first to recover while the rest of the world, including Europe and the US, struggled to deal with it. This could mean a more influential China in regional and global affairs after the pandemic is over. However, China–Australia relations worsened in 2020 due to Australia's championing of an international enquiry into the origins of the global pandemic, leading to China banning beef imports, an 80 per cent tariff on barley and official discouragement of tourism and students from travelling to Australia (Townshend 2020). In response, Prime Minister Scott Morrison declared that he would not 'trade our values in response to coercion from wherever it comes'. This was followed by moves to reinvigorate the Five Eyes intelligence network comprising the US, the UK, New Zealand, Canada and Australia and to coordinate efforts in building trusted supply chains for vital materials (ABC 2020).

Defence strategic update in 2020

In 2020, Australia published a Defence Strategic Update, which re-assessed the strategic underpinnings of the 2016 Defence White Paper. The Update reaffirmed that the key drivers shaping the development of Australia's future strategic environment remained relevant. However, it also asserted that some have 'accelerated in ways that were not anticipated in 2016', and that additional factors have emerged, in particular, 'the economic and strategic consequences of the COVID19 pandemic' (Department of Defence 2020: 11).

The Update noted that strategic competition between the United States and China will be the principal driver of strategic dynamics in the region, noting as well China's active pursuit of greater regional influence. The Update drew attention to 'grey-zone activities' which it defined as coercive activities, such as 'using para-military forces, militarization of disputed features, exploiting influence, interference operations and the coercive use of trade and economic levers'. In particular, these grey-zone activities will target global supply chains, critical infrastructure and support systems. Many countries in the region are also accelerating their military modernization, with the particular danger that emerging and disruptive technologies would lead to new weapons systems such as autonomous systems and long-range, high-speed weapons. In addition, 'the willingness to use cyber capabilities maliciously are further complicating Australia's environment'. Finally, the Update adjudged that the prospect of high-intensity military conflict in the Indo-Pacific has increased (Department of Defence 2020: 11–20).

In response, the Australian government has decided that defence planning will focus on Australia's immediate region where it has the most direct strategic interest, namely, the Indian Ocean, Southeast Asia and the Southwest Pacific. The Update declared that as access through these sub-regions is critical for Australia's security and trade, 'Australia must be capable of building and exercising influence in support of shared regional security interests' (Department of Defence 2020: 21). Thus, Australia would now adopt three new strategic objectives for defence planning: to shape Australia's strategic environment; to deter actions against Australia's interests; and to respond with credible military force when required (Department of Defence 2020: 25).

Responding to 'known knowns'

Responding to the 'known knowns' as outlined above, as the 2016 Defence White Paper, and the 2020 Defence Strategic Update made clear, cannot be unilateral but must involve international partnerships. In this respect, the Defence White Paper and the Defence Strategic Update both make special mention of the alliance relationship with the United States. As the Defence White Paper stated, 'Australia welcomes and supports the critical role of the United States in ensuring stability in the Indo-Pacific region', noting as well that Australia's relationship with the United States 'is broadly based and we build on that relationship on a day to day basis across many joint endeavours'. More significantly, the Defence White Paper affirmed that 'the levels of security and stability we seek in the Indo-Pacific would not be achievable without the United States'. Thus:

> Australia will continue to work with the United States under the Australia, New Zealand and United States (ANZUS) Treaty to support the United States' strategy of focusing resources and attention towards the Indo-Pacific through its strategic rebalance, which includes strengthening its alliances and ties with countries in the Indo-Pacific.
>
> (Department of Defence 2016: 41–42)

The reaffirmation of the alliance relationship is based on the assumption that the United States would remain the pre-eminent global military power for the immediate to medium-term and that its active presence in the region will underpin its stability (Department of Defence 2016: 41). This assumption was reaffirmed in the 2020 Defence Strategic Update, which declared that 'Australia is a staunch and active ally of the United States, which continues to underwrite the security and stability of the Indo-Pacific' (Department of Defence 2020: 22).

While the 2016 Defence White Paper evaluated a number of security challenges in the context of a complex, diverse and changing threat environment, it is clear that responding to China's rise and the changes in the regional security order weigh heavily on the minds of Australian policy and defence planners. As the 2017 Foreign Policy White Paper pointedly stated, 'we encourage China to exercise its power in a way that enhances stability, reinforces international law and respects the interests of smaller countries and their right to pursue them peacefully' (Department of Foreign Affairs and Trade 2017: 37). The 2020 Defence Strategic Update was more direct regarding the threat that China now posed to Australia, referring to China's 'active pursuit of greater influence in the Indo-Pacific', and challenges emanating from coercive 'grey-zone activities' including economic coercion, cyber-attacks and the use of emerging technologies to field new weapons systems, all of which are obvious references to China (Department of Defence 2020: 12–13).

The assumptions regarding continued US interest and capabilities are however, questionable in the context of China's rapid rise and emergence as the United States' primary economic, technological and military peer competitor. While US global military power remains unparalleled, China's regional ambitions have been bolstered by its increasingly capable armed forces, its economic influence over key US allies in the region, and the fact that, at the time of writing, it appears on course to emerge relatively unscathed from the global pandemic in 2020. Indeed, China is the largest trading partner of Japan, South Korea, Australia and Singapore. Moreover, the Trump administration, in its pursuit of an America First foreign policy that prioritizes US national interests, particularly economic interests, ahead of alliance relationships, has raised concerns in the Indo-Pacific region over whether the US would continue to be willing to uphold the regional order that has existed since 1945, under which US allies have benefitted from the US security umbrella, thus enjoying the stability and economic growth that have sustained their economies and societies for so long.

The issue of US–China strategic competition and what it means for Australia has been taken up by Australian strategic analysts. For instance, Hugh White, a former Australian deputy secretary for defence, noted the 'power shift' in the region and concluded, in contrast to the assumptions of the 2016 Defence White Paper, that 'the most likely outcome is now becoming clear … America will lose, and China will win'. White thus questioned Australia's reliance on the United States and argued that Australia needed to respond realistically to the enormous changes in the regional geo-strategic environment (White 2010; White 2017: 1). This view however, has been countered by former Prime Minister Kevin Rudd in 2018, who essentially concluded that it was too early to say if Trump's US nationalistic position will become permanent and that building a coalition of like-minded democracies in Asia to maintain the 'rules-based order' would be a realistic path for Australia to take (ABC 2018b). In other words, the US has not yet lost and China has not yet won the strategic contest, and there is therefore not yet the need to make momentous foreign policy adjustments.

Thus, the 2017 Foreign Policy White Paper objective of wanting 'a region where our ability to prosecute our interests freely is not constrained by exercise of coercive power', still means sustaining the special relationship with the United States, as 'without sustained US support, the effectiveness and liberal character of the rules-based order will decline' (Department of Foreign Affairs and Trade 2017: 3). The 2020 Defence Strategic Update re-affirmed the centrality of the US alliance (Department of Defence 2020: 22). Significantly, the 2017 Foreign Policy White Paper also noted the need to build 'Indo-Pacific partnerships', observing that countries such as Japan, Indonesia, India and South Korea would also influence the regional order (Department of Foreign Affairs and Trade 2017: 40). Such 'middle power diplomacy' has a characteristic motivation and method, according to former Australian Foreign Minister Gareth Evans, who noted that the characteristic motivation is the 'belief in the utility, and necessity, of acting cooperatively with others in addressing international challenges' while the characteristic diplomatic method is coalition building with like-minded states who share common interests and are prepared to work together (Evans 2017).

The Australian perspective is best summed up by Michael Thawley, a former Australian ambassador to the United States. According to Thawley, referring to the way deterrence works, 'if you are an ally you may not have 100% confidence that the United States is going to defend you … but if the opposition only needs to 5 or 10% confidence that it will and the calculation swings in your favour'. Thus, the biggest contribution Australia can make is to 'run a very healthy economy, a very strong society with strong political institutions, and a very effective defence force' (Greber 2019). Thawley is thus also speaking of the need for a very resilient society which is also what would be able to meet the challenges of unexpected black swan events, such as the COVID-19 global pandemic in 2020.

In sum therefore, the current Australian policy of continuing security reliance on the United States while taking steps to build a multilateral coalition of like-minded states to help bolster the faltering regional order and maintain the status quo in the face of China's attempts to reshape the regional order to better serve its interests looks to be, on balance, a calibrated and correct one. In the 2020 Defence Strategic Update, Australia signalled that it would also make efforts to increase its own defence self-reliance, such as increasing defence spending to 2 per cent of GDP, investing in offensive cyber capabilities, improving the capabilities of its navy, air force and army, acquiring autonomous vehicles and hypersonic weapons, developing its own space capabilities and ensuring 'a robust, resilient and internationally competitive defence industrial base' (Department of Defence 2020: 36–53).

Whether the above will be sufficient to serve Australia in the future as the strategic balance continues to shift, particularly in the wake of the global pandemic in 2020, the dire economic outlook as a result of it, worsening relations between China and Australia as well as a seeming descent into a new Cold War between China and the United States at the time of writing remains to be seen.

References

ABC (2017), 'How Fear of Abandonment Shapes the Way Australia Sees the World', *The World Today*, 3 April, available at www.abc.net.au/worldtoday/content/2016/s4647183.htm accessed 8 April 2020.

ABC (2018a), 'Author Clive Hamilton's Contentious China Book Set for Release', 7 February, available at www.abc.net.au/radionational/programs/breakfast/author-clive-hamiltons-contentious-china-book-set-for-release/9403694 accessed 8 April 2020.

ABC (2018b), 'Interview with Stan Grant on ABC Matter of Fact, 21 June 2018', available at www.youtube.com/watch?v=fiQdOphpD5c accessed 8 April 2020.

ABC (2018c), 'US to Partner with Australia, Papua New Guinea on Manus Island Naval Base', 17 November, available at www.abc.net.au/news/2018-11-17/us-to-partner-with-a ustralia-and-png-on-manus-island-naval-base/10507658 accessed 8 April 2020.

ABC (2019), 'China's Policy on Australian Coal is "As Dark and Impenetrable as Night" and That's How it Wants it', available at www.abc.net.au/news/2019-02-25/ china-policy-on-australian-coal-dark-and-impenetrable/10843148 accessed 8 April 2020.

ABC (2020), 'China Seems Intent on Using its Economic Heft to Intimidate Aus-tralia – But the Government is Eyeing Off a New Plan', 13 June, available at www. abc.net.au/news/2020-06-13/coronavirus-china-australia-foreign-students-threats-fed eral-gov/12350738 accessed 16 June 2020.

Allison, Graham T. (2017), *Destined for War: Can America and China Escape Thucydides's Trap?* Boston, MA: Houghton Mifflin Harcourt.

ANZUS Treaty (1952), 'ANZUS Treaty', available at www.austlii.edu.au/au/other/dfat/ treaties/1952/2.html accessed 8 April 2020.

Australian (2018), 'Clive Hamilton: Poking the Chinese Dragon', 20 February, available at www.theaustralian.com.au/nation/inquirer/clive-hamilton-poking-the-chinese-dra gon/news-story/eef6add51ca1e0919236984b7f0b96be accessed 8 April 2020.

Australian Financial Review (2016), 'Australia is Losing The Battle Against China's Citizen Spies', 3 September, available at www.afr.com/world/asia/australia-is-lo sing-the-battle-against-chinas-citizen-spies-20160831-gr5rfq accessed 8 April 2020.

Australian Financial Review (2018), 'China Puts Malcolm Turnbull's Government into the Deep Freeze', 11 April, available at www.afr.com/news/world/asia/chinas-big-chill-for-australia-20180411-h0ymwb accessed 8 April 2020.

Ball, Desmond (2010), 'Arms Modernization in Asia: An Emerging Complex Arms Race?' in Andrew T. H.Tan (ed.), *The Global Arms Trade*, London: Routledge.

BBC (2012), 'Indonesia's Bali Marks Deadly Bombings 10 Years on', 12 October, available at www.bbc.com/news/world-asia-19906863 accessed 8 April 2020.

Blackwell, Eoin (2017), '13th Foiled Attack In Three Years: A Brief History Of Terror Raids', *Huffington Post*, 31 July, available at www.huffingtonpost.com.au/2017/07/ 30/13th-foiled-attack-in-three-years-a-brief-history-of-terror-rai_a_23057049/ accessed 8 April 2020.

CSIS (n.d.), 'What Does China Really Spend on its Military?' China Power Project, available at https://chinapower.csis.org/military-spending/ accessed 8 April 2020.

Department of Defence (2016), *2016 Defence White Paper*, available at www.defence. gov.au/WhitePaper/Docs/2016-Defence-White-Paper.pdf accessed 8 April 2020.

Department of Defence (2020), *2020 Defence Strategic Update*, available at www.defence. gov.au/StrategicUpdate-2020/docs/2020_Defence_Strategic_Update.pdf accessed 7 July 2020.

Department of Defense (2018), 'Assessing and Strengthening the Manufacturing and Defense Industrial Base and Supply Chain Resiliency of the United States', September, available at https://media.defense.gov/2018/Oct/05/2002048904/-1/-1/1/ ASSESSING-AND-STRENGTHENING-THE-MANUFACTURING-AND-DE FENSE-INDUSTRIAL-BASE-AND-SUPPLY-CHAIN-RESILIENCY.PDF accessed 8 April 2020.

Department of Foreign Affairs and Trade (2017), *2017 Foreign Policy White Paper*, available at www.fpwhitepaper.gov.au/ accessed 8 April 2020.

Department of Foreign Affairs and Trade, Australia (2019), 'Trade and Investment at a Glance 2019', www.dfat.gov.au/about-us/publications/trade-investment/trade-at-a -glance/trade-investment-at-a-glance-2019/Pages/default accessed 8 April 2020.

Emont, Jon (2014), 'The Islamic State Comes To Indonesia', *Foreign Policy*, 17 September, http://foreignpolicy.com/2014/09/17/the-islamic-state-comes-to-indonesia/ accessed 8 April 2020.

Evans, Gareth (2017), 'The Role of Middle Powers in Asia's Future', Jeju Forum for Peace and Prosperity, Jeju, Republic of Korea, 1 June 2017, available at www.geva ns.org/speeches/Speech627.html accessed 8 April 2020.

Fox News (2017), 'Timeline of Recent Terror Attacks Against the West', 1 November, available at www.foxnews.com/world/timeline-of-recent-terror-attacks-against-the- west accessed 8 April 2020.

Glenday, James (2014), 'Tony Abbott and Barack Obama Agree to New Defence Force Posture, Note Different Climate Change Approaches', *ABC News*, 14 June, available at www.abc.net.au/news/2014-06-13/tony-abbott-and-barack-obama-agree- to-new-defence-posture/5520370 accessed 8 April 2020.

Greber, Jason (2019), 'Former Ambassador Turns $2.5trn Fundie', *Australian Financial Review*, 5 April, available at www.afr.com/news/policy/foreign-affairs/form er-ambassador-michael-thawley-isn-t-embarrassed-to-work-in-finance-20190402-p51 9tn accessed 8 April 2020.

Gyngell, Allan (2005), 'Australia's Emerging Global Role', *Current History*, 104 (680).

Gyngell, Allan (2017), 'Speech: Allan Gyngell Outlines Australia's Foreign Policy Challenges', Australian National University, 13 April, available at www.anu.edu.au/ news/all-news/speech-allan-gyngell-outlines-australia%E2%80%99s-foreign-policy-c hallenges accessed 8 April 2020.

Gyngell, Allan (2017), *Fear of Abandonment: Australia in the World Since 1942*, Victoria: Schwartz.

Guardian (2016), 'Beijing Rejects Tribunal's Ruling in South China Sea Case', 12 July, available at www.theguardian.com/world/2016/jul/12/philippines-wins-south-china -sea-case-against-china accessed 8 April 2020.

Hamilton, Clive (2018), *Silent Invasion: China's Influence in Australia*, Melbourne: Hardie Grant.

Henry, Iain (2016), 'The 2016 Defence White Paper's Assessment of Australia's Strategic Environment', *Security Challenges*, 12 (1).

IISS (2013), *The Military Balance 2013*, London: IISS.

IISS (2020), *The Military Balance 2019*, London: IISS.

IMF (2014), 'World Economic Outlook Database', October, available at www.imf.org/ external/pubs/ft/weo/2014/02/weodata/index.aspx accessed 8 April 2020.

Jacques, Martin (2009), *When China Rules the World: The Rise of the Middle Kingdom and the End of the Western World*, London: Allen Lane.

Jervis, Robert (1976), *Perceptions and Misperceptions in International Politics*, Princeton, NJ: Princeton University Press.

Kagan, Robert (2018), 'America First Has Won', *New York Times*, 23 September, available at www.nytimes.com/2018/09/23/opinion/trump-foreign-policy-america -first.html accessed 8 April 2020.

Kennedy, Simon (2018), 'China Will Overtake the US in Less Than 15 Years, HSBC Says', Bloomberg, 25 September, available at www.bloomberg.com/news/articles/ 2018-09-25/hsbc-sees-china-economy-set-to-pass-u-s-as-number-one-by-2030 accessed 8 April 2020.

Liow, Joseph (2017), 'The Counterterrorism Yearbook 2017: Southeast Asia', *The Strategist*, Australian Security Policy Institute, 28 March, available at www.aspistrategist.org.au/counterterrorism-yearbook-2017-southeast-asia/ accessed 8 April 2020.

McGregor, Michael and Jonathan Pryke (2018), 'Australia Versus China in the South Pacific', Commentary, Lowy Institute, 15 November, available at www.lowyinstitute.org/publications/australia-versus-china-south-pacific accessed 8 April 2020.

Medcalf. Rory (2014), 'In Defence of the Indo-Pacific: Australia's New Strategic Map', *Australian Journal of International Affairs*, 68 (4).

Mori, Satoru (2019), 'US–China: A New Consensus for Strategic Competition in Washington', *The Diplomat*, 30 January, available at https://thediplomat.com/2019/01/us-china-a-new-consensus-for-strategic-competition-in-washington/ accessed 8 April 2020.

National Intelligence Council (2008), *Global Trends 2025: A Transformed World*, available at www.files.ethz.ch/isn/94769/2008_11_global_trends_2025.pdf accessed 8 April 2020.

Navarro, Peter (2018), 'America's Military-Industrial Base Is at Risk', *New York Times*, 4 October, available at www.nytimes.com/2018/10/04/opinion/america-military-industrial-base.html accessed 8 April 2020.

O'Neil, Andrew (2011), 'Conceptualising Future Threats to Australia's Security', *Australian Journal of Political Science*, 46 (1).

Obama, Barack (2011), 'Remarks by President Obama to the Australian Parliament', 17 November, https://obamawhitehouse.archives.gov/the-press-office/2011/11/17/remarks-president-obama-australian-parliament accessed 8 April 2020.

Organski, A. F. K. (1968), *World Politics*, New York: Alfred A. Knopf.

Patrick, Aaron (2016), 'Australia is Losing the Battle Against China's Citizen Spies', *Australian Financial Review*, 3 September, available at www.afr.com/news/world/asia/australia-is-losing-the-battle-against-chinas-citizen-spies-20160831-gr5rfq accessed 8 April 2020.

Permanent Court of Arbitration (2016), 'The South China Sea Arbitration (The Republic of The Philippines V. The People's Republic of China), The Hague, 12 July 2016', available at https://pca-cpa.org/wp-content/uploads/sites/6/2016/07/PH-CN-20160712-Press-Release-No-11-English.pdf accessed 8 April 2020.

Ramo, Joshua Cooper (2010), *The Age of the Unthinkable: Why the New World Disorder Constantly Surprises Us and What We Can Do About It*, New York: Little Brown.

RAND (2015), 'An Interactive Look at the US–China Military Scorecard: Forces, Geography and the Evolving Balance of Power, 1996–2017, Santa Monica', www.rand.org/content/dam/rand/pubs/research_reports/RR300/RR392/RAND_RR392.pdf accessed 8 April 2020.

Rudd, Kevin (2008), 'National Security Speech, House of Representatives, Parliament of Australia', 4 December, https://parlinfo.aph.gov.au/parlInfo/search/display/display.w3p;query=Id:%22chamber/hansardr/2008-12-04/0045%22 accessed 4 September 2020.

Schell, Orville (2020), 'The Ugly End of Chimamerica', *Foreign Policy*, 3 April, https://foreignpolicy.com/2020/04/03/chimerica-ugly-end-coronavirus-china-us-trade-relations/ accessed 8 April 2020.

SIPRI (n.d.), 'SIPRI Military Expenditure Database', www.sipri.org/databases/milex accessed 8 April 2020.

Soufan Group (2015), 'Foreign Fighters: An Updated Assessment of the Flow of Foreign Fighters into Syria and Iraq', http://soufangroup.com/wp-content/uploads/2015/12/TSG_ForeignFightersUpdate3.pdf accessed 8 April 2020.

Statistica (n.d.), 'Gross Domestic Product (GDP) Ranking by Country 2017 (in Billion US Dollars)', www.statista.com/statistics/268173/countries-with-the-largest-gross-domestic-product-gdp/ accessed 8 April 2020.

Steinberg, James and Michael E. O'Hanlon (2014), *Strategic Reassurance and Resolve: US–China Relations in the Twenty-First Century*, Princeton, NJ: Princeton University Press.

Straits Times (2018), 'Singapore, Australia Share Common Interests in South China Sea Issue, Says PM Lee', 15 March, available at www.straitstimes.com/politics/singapore-australia-share-common-interests-in-south-china-sea-issue-says-pm-lee accessed 8 April 2020.

Taleb, Nassim Nicholas (2007), *The Black Swan: The Impact of the Highly Improbable*, New York: Random House.

Tan, Andrew T. H. (2014), *The Arms Race in Asia: Trends, Causes and Implications*, London: Routledge.

Tan, Andrew T. H. (2016), 'Challenges in US–China Relations', in Andrew T. H. Tan (ed.), *Handbook of US–China Relations*, Cheltenham: Edward Elgar.

Tillett, Andrew (2018), 'After ISIS: What Now for Australia's Involvement in Iraq?' Australian Financial Review, 2 March, available at www.afr.com/news/politics/after-isis-what-now-for-australias-involvement-in-iraq-20180301-h0wtsg accessed 8 April 2020.

Townshend, Ashley (2020), 'China's Pandemic-Fueled Standoff with Australia', War on the Rocks, 20 May, https://warontherocks.com/2020/05/chinas-pandemic-fueled-standoff-with-australia accessed 4 September 2020.

Townshend, Ashley, Brendan Thomas-Noone and Matilda Steward (2019), *Averting Crisis: American Strategy, Military Spending and Collective Defence in the Indo-Pacific*, Sydney: United States Studies Centre, University of Sydney.

Trading Economics (n.d.), 'China Foreign Exchange Reserves', available at https://tradingeconomics.com/china/foreign-exchange-reserves accessed 8 April 2020.

Wall Street Journal (2014), 'Writing China: James Jiann Hua To, Qiaowu: Extra-Territorial Policies for the Overseas Chinese', 16 August, available at https://blogs.wsj.com/chinarealtime/2014/08/16/writing-china-james-jiann-hua-to-qiaowu-extra-territorial-policies-for-the-overseas-chinese/ accessed 8 April 2020.

Wall Street Journal (2019), 'With End of Islamic State Caliphate, US Shifts to Long New Fight Ahead', 25 March, available at www.wsj.com/articles/with-end-of-islamic-state-caliphate-u-s-shifts-to-long-new-fight-ahead-11553531192 accessed 8 April 2020.

Wesley, Michael (2016), 'Australia's Grand Strategy and the 2016 Defence White Paper', *Security Challenges*, 12 (1).

White, Hugh (2010), 'Power Shift: Australia's Future Between Washington and Beijing', *Quarterly Essay*, 39.

White, Hugh (2017), 'Without America: Australia in the New Asia', *Quarterly Essay*, 68.

Workman, Daniel (2019), 'Australia's Top Trading Partners', *World'sTopExports.com*, 8 February, available at www.worldstopexports.com/australias-top-import-partners/ accessed 8 April 2020.

Zammit, Andrew (2017), 'Australian Jihadism in the Age of the Islamic State', *CTC Sentinel*, March, available at https://ctc.usma.edu/australian-jihadism-in-the-age-of-the-islamic-state/ accessed 8 April 2020.

Part II

The evolution of Australia–US strategic and defence cooperation

5 The common interests that bind the United States and Australia

Bates Gill

Aligned, but the ground is shifting

The Australia–United States relationship presents an odd contradiction. On the one hand, the relationship is grounded in a lengthy history of shared experiences, interests and values. These commonalities begin with their parallel histories as part of the British empire and as settler nations on vast continents. The two countries fought side by side in the First World War and in nearly every other major conflict in which one or the other have been involved since. In recent years, the alliance relationship has deepened in many ways and become more important to Canberra and Washington (Gill and Switzer 2015).

Today, the two countries are deeply intertwined economically: the United States is by far the largest source of inbound investment to Australia and the United States is the number one destination for outbound Australian investment (Holden and Mondschein 2017; Department of Foreign Affairs and Trade 2020). Their governments, businesses and societies mutually benefit from extensive collaborations in defence, foreign relations, technology, science, energy, agriculture, education, athletics and more. In celebrating '100 years of mateship' between the two countries, Australian Prime Minister Scott Morrison stated that 'Australians and Americans understand each other like few other peoples', share 'truths and traditions' and 'see the world through the same lens' (White House 2019).

Polling of Australian and US citizens affirms this view: 97 per cent of Americans see Australia as an ally or friend of the United States, while 94 per cent of Australians view the United States in that way (Jackman et al. 2019: 18–20).

But on the other hand, the strategic interests between Australia and the United States have never fully overlapped and at times diverged considerably (Wesley 2020). Moreover, new pressures have mounted in recent years to challenge some of the long-held fundamentals for Australia–United States relations. These emergent pressures include the rise of the People's Republic of China (PRC) and persistent uncertainties surrounding US global and regional leadership. Additional pressures, such as the COVID-19 pandemic and its impact on globalization, will also present challenges to long-standing core interests of the alliance.

This chapter will examine this conundrum for Australian and US interests. In doing so, it is not possible to cover all areas of overlapping interest between the two, and other chapters in this volume address the specifics of bilateral military-to-military relations, defence-industrial cooperation and alliance management. Instead this chapter will identify, analyse and critique broad Australian and US geopolitical and security interests at the global level, at the Indo-Pacific regional level and at the level of bilateral ties. Recurring themes appear across these levels to affect Australian interests, American interests and the relationship between the two: the growing power of the PRC and the uncertainties of American commitment, especially under the Trump presidency.

Interests in the global order

Shared success in the post-war era

Traditionally, over the course of the post-Second World War era, successive governments in both Australia and the United States formally and repeatedly declared their interest in sustaining the liberal, rules-based international order. Both Australia and the United States, individually and in tandem, invested enormous diplomatic, economic and military resources to building and sustaining a rules-based global order featuring – in principle if not always in practice – peacefully-negotiated rules of the road, collective security institutions, open economic systems; an increasingly free flow of goods, capital, technology, people and ideas; and the promotion of progressive ideals as to democratization, the rule of law, human rights, socioeconomic development and poverty-alleviation.

Led by the United States, this international order brought great benefit to both countries. Australia, as a remote and relatively small country, but one keen to play a role in global affairs, understood it would be more likely to succeed in a system of well-established rules rather than one where might makes right. Australia benefitted in particular from the open international economic system – driven and protected by its closest ally, the United States – especially as the Asian economic miracle took off, beginning with Japan in the 1960s and continuing through China's economic rise of today. Through 2019, Australia enjoyed 29 straight years of recession-free economic expansion and became the world's 14th largest economy (International Monetary Fund 2019). As Allan Gyngell observes about Australia, 'It could enthusiastically support the rules-based order, because it was essentially set by us and our friends' (Gyngell 2018). The same can be said for America.

Over those years, the two countries pursued generally common agendas on the international stage, including with regard to international trade and investment, good governance, development assistance, non-proliferation, peacekeeping, counterterrorism, global health and law of the sea. An analysis of US Department of State data reveals that, over the period from 2000 to 2018, Australia voted with the United States about two-thirds of the time (66.7 per cent) in United Nations General Assembly plenary votes. This is one of the highest records of voting agreement with Washington of any United Nations member state (Department of State 2020).

The Australia–United States Ministerial Consultations (AUSMIN) – which bring together the US Secretaries of State and Defense with the Australian Ministers of Foreign Affairs and Defence – are annual opportunities for the two nations to express their shared strategic interests and common ground on a range of global issues while deepening bilateral defence and security coop-eration. In 2019, for example, the two sides committed to working together across a broad portfolio of shared interests, including: countering interna-tional terrorism, including in Afghanistan, Iraq and Syria; upholding the freedom of maritime navigation and overflight consistent with international law, such as in the South China Sea; maintaining pressure on North Korea to roll back its nuclear and ballistic missile programs; advancing multilateral nuclear arms control involving the United States, Russia and China; promot-ing high-quality infrastructure development initiatives; developing an 'open, interoperable, reliable, free and secure internet'; and building resiliency for critical infrastructure, technologies and minerals (AUSMIN 2019).

Perhaps the most visible expression of their shared interest at the global level is Australia's consistent participation alongside the United States in major military conflicts around the world for over 100 years. Australian troops fought in the First and Second World Wars, in Korea and Vietnam during the Cold War, and in the 1991 Gulf War against Iraq. Australian Prime Minister John Howard invoked the alliance treaty to support the United States following the terrorist attacks on American soil in September 2001 (Howard 2001). Since that time, in pursuit of shared aims with the United States, Australian forces have been deployed to Afghanistan (from 2001 to present), Iraq (2003–2011) and the fight against Islamic State (also known as Daesh) in Iraq and Syria (2014 to present).

As of early 2020, Australia continued to contribute forces toward the international coalition to combat terrorist threats in Iraq and Syria, with approximately 300 personnel deployed in Iraq under Operation OKRA. This operation includes Task Group Taji, located near Baghdad, where Australian Defence Force (ADF) personnel work with New Zealand armed forces to deliver training and capacity building to the Iraqi Security Forces. Operation OKRA also includes a Special Operations Task Group which provides counter-terrorism advice and support to the Iraqi Security Forces. Previously, from 2014 to early 2018, an Australian Air Task Group, consisting of strike aircraft (F/A-18 Hornets), airborne early warning aircraft (E-7A Wedgetail), aerial refuelling aircraft (KC-30A tanker) and supporting maintenance crews (Department of Defence 2020) took part in operations in Iraq and Syria.

As of early 2020, under Operation HIGHROAD, about 200 ADF person-nel – from the Royal Australian Navy, the Australian Army, the Royal Aus-tralian Air Force and Department of Defence civilians – were deployed in Afghanistan. These forces contribute primarily to training and capacity-building for the Afghan National Defence and Security Forces as well as for other Afghan national security institutions, including through the North Atlantic Treaty Organization (NATO)-led training and advisory mission known as Resolute Support, successor to the NATO International Security Assistance Force (ISAF). Australia also contributes a small contingent of special forces personnel to train and assist counterterrorism units in the Afghan security and police forces (Department of Defence 2020).

Shifting interests

By and large, Australia and the United States have been closely aligned on issues of international order over most of the past 75 years. However, those shared views have come under pressure in recent times as some of the funda-mentals of that order have begun to shift. In a frank appraisal of those shifts, the Australian foreign policy white paper of 2017 stated:

> [w]e have entered a period of sharper challenge to the rules and principles that underpin international cooperation. Anti-globalisation, protection-ism, changes in the balance of global power and geopolitical competition are testing the international order.
>
> These challenges present risks to Australia's national interests. Our security and prosperity have been supported by US global leadership, an increasingly open world economy and the development of international institutions and rules.
>
> (Australian Government 2017: 7)

The white paper went on to express concern over US global leadership in parti-cular and its role in upholding the international order. Acknowledging there is 'greater debate and uncertainty in the United States about the costs and benefits of its leadership in parts of the international system', the white paper argued that '[w]ithout sustained US support, the effectiveness and liberal character of the rules-based order will decline' (Australian Government 2017: 7)

The Australian foreign minister, Julie Bishop, elaborated on these views in a speech at Chatham House, in London, in mid-2018. She cited three princi-pal challenges to the rules-based international order. First, she cited such states as Russia, Iran and North Korea which are 'openly defying interna-tional rules and norms'. Second, she also cited the difficulty accommodating a shifting balance of power in the Indo-Pacific region, especially exacerbated by growing US–China rivalry (Bishop 2018).

A third important challenge was the United States. Here the Foreign Min-ister pulled few punches in expressing rising Australian concerns about the trajectory of American leadership under Donald Trump. Pointing to US withdrawal from the Paris Climate Agreement, the Joint Comprehensive Plan of Action (JCPOA, also known as the 'Iran deal'), the Trans-Pacific Partnership and the United Nations Human Rights Council, as well as protectionist trade policies and scepticism toward alliances, she said that the United States now favours a 'more disruptive, often unilateral foreign and trade policy that has heightened anxieties about its commitment to the rules-based order that it established, protected and guaranteed'. For Australia, she concluded, '[o]ur closest ally and the world's most powerful nation is being seen as less predictable and less committed to the international order that it pioneered' (Bishop 2018).

The Foreign Minister's views are reflected in the wider Australian population. The percentage of Australians who expressed confidence that the US president would 'do the right thing in world affairs' dropped from 84 per cent at the end of the Obama administration to 29 per cent after Trump entered office in 2017 (Wike et al. 2017: 4). This figure has not improved much with time: in 2019 only a third (35 per cent) of Australians had confidence in Trump's approach toward the world (Poushter 2020).

The Lowy Poll also shows a similar decline in Australian confidence in the United States and its approach to global affairs. In 2011, 83 per cent of Australians trusted the United States 'somewhat' or 'a great deal' to act responsibly in the world; that number dropped to 61 per cent in the first year of Trump administration and further still to 52 per cent by 2019 (Kassam 2019: 6). Just 25 per cent of Australians in 2019 had 'some' or 'a lot' of confidence that President Trump would 'do the right thing regarding world affairs'; none of the young participants in this poll (223 respondents, aged 18 to 29 years) said they had 'a lot of confidence' in him and two-thirds of them expressed 'no confidence at all' (Kassam 2019: 7). Only 20 per cent of Australians polled in 2019 said they would want to see Trump elected to a second term (Jackman et al. 2019: 70).

These developments have not yet led to fundamental changes in how Australia and America governments publicly express their continuing shared interests in global affairs. By overwhelming majorities, publics in the two countries view one another as allies and friends (Jackman et al. 2019: 18, 20). However, both inside Australian government and within the broader Australian public, concerns are clearly mounting that Australian and American strategic interests at the global level are diverging in many important respects, especially with regard to US leadership, international engagement and commitment to the post-war liberal, rules-based order. As American withdrawal may reflect deeper structural trends in the United States – and is not merely a 'Trump phenomenon' – this divergence in US and Australian interests could persist well into the future, regardless of the White House occupant.

Interests in the Indo-Pacific region

A 'clear, shared focus'

Australian and US strategic interests are most intensively engaged in the Indo-Pacific region. Both countries, individually and as allied partners, have enormous stakes in this part of the world and share a broad interest in sustaining the region's stability and prosperity. For both nations, the Indo-Pacific presents great opportunities and great risks, and they are better off addressing them in concert rather than separately.

The Indo-Pacific region – roughly stretching from the Indian subcontinent to western North America – is home to 50 per cent of the world's population, some of the world's largest militaries, six nuclear-armed states (China, India, North Korea, Pakistan, Russia and the United States) and five US treaty allies. It has become the world's economic centre of gravity, with Asian countries set to generate more than 50 per cent of global gross domestic product (GDP) in purchasing power parity (PPP) terms in 2020; by that measure, China is already the world's largest economy, with countries such as India, Indonesia and Japan also among the world's top ten economies in 2023 (Romei and Reed 2019). The Indo-Pacific is also where the growing geostrategic competition between the United States and China will play out most intensively, with extensive, long-term implications for US–Australia relations and regional stability.

Over the past three decades, both countries have become increasingly dependent on and interconnected with strategic developments in the region. Australia's economic well-being is overwhelmingly linked to partnerships in the region: three-quarters of the country's two-way trade is with Asia-Pacific Economic Cooperation (APEC) members.[1] As early as the mid-1980s, US trade with East Asia and the Pacific surpassed trade with Western Europe (Department of State 1993: 842); according to US government figures released in 2019, the exchange of goods and service between the United States and its APEC partners accounted for nearly 60 per cent of US two-way trade (USTR 2019; BEA 2019). The Obama administration committed to deploying 60 per cent of the US naval fleet to the Indo-Pacific region, and today the Indo-Pacific Command (USINDOPACOM) consists of 375,000 military and civilian personnel, 200 naval vessels (including five aircraft carrier strike groups) and some 2,300 aircraft (Indo-Pacific Command 2020).

The United States and Australia have also signalled their shared commitment to the region through a range of diplomatic and security initiatives. The US 'rebalance' or 'pivot' to Asia was given a high-profile boost by President Obama in a speech before the Australian Parliament in November 2011. In remarks outlining the shared interests of Australia and the United States in the Asia-Pacific, he said:

> [t]his is the future we seek in the Asia Pacific – security, prosperity and dignity for all. ... That's the future we will pursue, in partnership with

allies and friends, and with every element of American power. So let there be no doubt: In the Asia Pacific in the 21st century, the United States of America is all in.

(Obama 2011; see also Clinton 2011)

The Trump administration has also put forward a set of initiatives to expand US commitments to stability and prosperity in the region. These initiatives loosely fall under the concept of a 'Free and Open Indo-Pacific' (FOIP), which President Trump formally announced as US policy in a speech in Vietnam in late 2017 (Trump 2017). The FOIP concept appears to take up where the Obama 'rebalance' left off, while also expanding the geographic scope of US interests in the region to more explicitly encompass India and the Indian Ocean along with East Asia and the Pacific (CRS 2018).

In late 2019, the US Department of State issued a more detailed explanation of FOIP, highlighting its aims of (1) respect for sovereignty and independence of all nations; (2) peaceful resolution of disputes; (3) free, fair and reciprocal trade based on open investment, transparent agreements and connectivity; and (4) adherence to international law, including freedom of navigation and overflight (Department of State 2019: 6). The document states that the US FOIP concept 'aligns closely with closely with Japan's Free and Open Indo-Pacific concept, India's Act East Policy, Australia's Indo-Pacific concept, the Republic of Korea's New Southern Policy and Taiwan's New Southbound Policy' (Department of State 2019: 8).

In outlining initiatives falling within the FOIP concept, the State Department points to a number which directly involve Australia, including: foreign minister-level meetings, begun in 2019, of Australia, India, Japan and the United States under the auspices of the Quadrilateral Consultations (also known as the 'Quad'); the Trilateral Security Dialogue (Australia–Japan–United States) which focuses on such issues as maritime security and counterterrorism; and the economic partnership amongst Australia, Japan, New Zealand and the United States to provide electricity to 70 per cent of the population of Papua New Guinea by 2030 (Department of State 2019).

For its part, the Australian government has taken a number of steps in alignment with US Indo-Pacific initiatives. Prime Minister Scott Morrison has repeatedly expressed his government's strong interest in 'an open, inclusive and prosperous Indo-Pacific' and its strong support for the Quad as a 'key forum for exchanging views on challenges facing the region, including taking forward practical cooperation in maritime, terrorism and cyber issues' (Morrison 2019). In 2018, the Morrison government also announced a significant increase in resources focusing on Australia's Pacific island neighbours – known as the 'Pacific Step-up' – in order to invest in their stability, resiliency, security and prosperity (Department of Foreign Affairs and Trade 2019).

The Australia–US security alliance is seen as a particularly important vehicle through which the two countries can pursue their shared interests in the Indo-Pacific. The 2017 Australian foreign policy white paper put it this way:

> [o]ur alliance with the United States is central to Australia's approach to the Indo-Pacific. Without strong US political, economic and security engagement, power is likely to shift more quickly in the region and it will be more difficult for Australia to achieve the levels of security and stability we seek. To support our objectives in the region, the Government will broaden and deepen our alliance cooperation ....
>
> (Australian Government 2017: 4)

More recently, the AUSMIN consultations stressed the value of the alliance in seeking to achieve shared objectives in the region. Noting that 'our work in the Indo-Pacific region is the clear, shared focus' of US–Australia allied relations, the AUSMIN partners called for an 'increasingly networked structure of alliances and partnerships' to maintain the Indo-Pacific as a 'secure, open, inclusive and rules-based' region and to that end committed to deepening relations with Japan and India. They also committed to strengthening their joint support for Southeast Asian and Pacific Island states, including through maritime security cooperation, economic assistance, infrastructure development and good governance assistance. (AUSMIN 2019).

The China factor

As these examples attest, Australia and the United States share a range of common interests in promoting and sustaining the region's prosperity and stability. However, the two countries do not always see eye-to-eye on how to best realize those interests. American withdrawal from the Trans-Pacific Partnership trade deal – an agreement Australia worked hard to support and ultimately establish – is a case in point. Another is Australia's decision to become a member of the Asia Infrastructure Investment Bank (AIIB) – an initiative launched by China – in spite of Washington's objections (Smyth and Mundy 2015).

Indeed, China rise as a regional and global power looms large in US–Australia relations and is the single-most important factor shaping both convergence and divergence in the alliance's strategic outlook in the Indo-Pacific region. On the one hand, China's growing economic heft, improving military capabilities and expanding diplomatic and political influence present serious challenges to both Australia and the United States. Both countries have been targets of economic pressures, industrial espionage, intellectual property theft, illicit cyber intrusions, military threats and political influence operations emanating from the PRC (Gill and Jakobson 2017: 93–159; USCESRC 2019). The two countries share concerns about China's military build-up, its militarization of features in the South China Sea and its destabilising activities in the Taiwan Strait and East China Sea. With these kinds of challenges in mind, the two countries coordinate with one another in strategic and diplomatic consultations, intelligence-sharing and defence planning. Both countries have responded with tougher measures at home to strengthen societal resilience in the face of PRC pressures and influence-projection.

But on the other hand, Australia and the United States are not in lockstep alignment when it comes to China. A part of this divergence arises from their respective geopolitical relationships with China. The United States, as a global superpower, is far better positioned to confront China than Australia. The United States also has certain security commitments to others in the region which have ongoing sovereignty and territorial disputes with China, such as Japan, the Philippines and Taiwan, which Australia does not. Perhaps most importantly, the United States and China are stuck in an intensifying security dilemma – often framed as a rivalry between the established global power and the rising aspirant to global power – which is not reflective at all of where Australia–China relations are today. As a result, the United States has taken a far tougher approach to China since the latter half of the Obama administration, and especially during the Trump presidency.

Australia must tread more cautiously. A critical factor in that calculus is its economic relationship with China, but that is not the whole story. China is far and away Australia's largest trading partner, a position it has held since 2007. At the end of 2019, fully 38 per cent of Australian exports by value went to China, a record high at the time (Cranston 2019). These exports are driven primarily by Chinese demand for iron ore, coal, liquid natural gas and agricultural products, as well as services such as education and tourism. Some 212,000 PRC students studied in Australia in 2019 – the largest foreign cohort by far – and more than 1.4 million visitors from the PRC came to Australia over the 2018–2019 fiscal year, making it the largest foreign source of Australian tourism. China is also Australia's largest source of imports and has been a fast-growing source of investment; as of 2019 China was among the top ten foreign investors in Australia (Department of Education 2020; Department of Foreign Affairs and Trade 2020a).

The importance of the Australia–China bilateral economic relationship spills over to affect Australia–US relations and the American approach to China. Overall, Australian interests do not favour a deterioration in the US–China economic relations and the rise in protectionism within the world's two largest economies. Moreover, one of the early tentative settlements of US–China trade differences – the 'Phase 1' trade deal achieved in early 2020 – may end up hurting Australian economic interests owing to preferential treatment China will apparently give to US exports in the agriculture and energy sectors (Diss 2020).

There are other factors at play in Australia–China relations beyond the economics. Based on the most recent population census, more than 1.2 million Australian residents claim Chinese heritage, with about half of those born in China; Mandarin Chinese is the second most-widely spoken language in Australia (ABS 2017; ABS 2018). These demographics help drive expanded people-to-people exchanges, deepening collaborations in science and technology research and development, dozens of sister-city relationships, and growing educational, business and cultural partnerships. In 2019, the Australian government established a new National Foundation for Australia–China Relations, funded with A\$44 million for its first five years. The organization aims to work with the public, private and not-for-profit sectors in Australia to 'turbo-charge [the] national effort in engaging China' (Department of Foreign Affairs and Trade 2020b).

These and related developments affect Australian interests vis-à-vis China. Reflecting such realities, the Australian Prime Minister explained the Australian approach to China in this way:

> [w]hile we will be clear-eyed that our political differences will affect aspects of our engagement, we are determined that our relationship not be dominated by areas of disagreement. The decisions we make in relation to China are based solely on our national interests, just as theirs are towards Australia, and these are sometimes hard calls to make. But they are designed always to leave large scope for cooperation on common interests and recognize the importance of China's economic success. This success is good for China, it is good for Australia.
>
> (Morrison 2019a)

Such prudence and pragmatism toward China is found within the broader Australian public as well. According to Pew polling, a majority of Australians, 51 per cent, view China as the world's preeminent economic power, with only 32 per cent saying the United States holds that position. Interestingly, Australia was the only one of the six Indo-Pacific countries polled to hold that understanding of China's economic pre-eminence (Cha 2019). Nearly half of Australians (46 per cent) see the United States in decline relative to China, thus making the alliance less important (Kassam 2019: 10). Importantly, Australians are almost evenly divided on whether to prioritize relations with China or with the United States. Some 50 per cent agreed that priority should be given to maintaining relations with the United States, even if that might threaten ties to China; 44 per cent said building ties to China deserves priority, even at the risk of harming relations with the United States (Kassam 2019: 6).

Yet at the same time, 56 per cent of Australians believe the alliance helps protect their country from Chinese threats (Kassam 2019: 10). There is also evidence that Australian views have begun to show greater concerns about becoming overly-dependent on China, about PRC military activities in Australia's neighbourhood, about China's human rights record and about Beijing's approach to world affairs (Kassam 2019: 8). These mixed and sometimes contradictory views – and the heated debates they generate – will continue to shape Australian views and interests toward China, toward the United States and toward the Indo-Pacific overall. In turn, Canberra and Washington should expect – and will need to work harder to manage – greater tensions in the alliance relationship as they pursue their interests vis-à-vis China and the region.

Interests in the bilateral alliance relationship

'Shoulder to shoulder'

At the bilateral level, the two sides also see considerable value in the relationship, especially in the security sphere. As the junior partner, Australia has a much larger stake in sustaining the alliance and draws enormous benefit from it. Australia's ability to 'punch above its weight' militarily derives in no small measure from its access to American intelligence assets and weapons technology, as well as regular bilateral joint training, exercises and operations, both in peacetime and on the battlefield.

In the largest strategic sense, Australia counts on the United States as an indispensable security guarantor of its vital strategic interests. In the words of the most recent Australian defence White Paper:

> [o]nly the nuclear and conventional military capabilities of the United States can offer effective deterrence against the possibility of nuclear threats against Australia. The presence of United States military forces plays a vital role in ensuring security across the Indo-Pacific and the global strategic and economic weight of the United States will be essential to the continued effective functioning of the rules-based global order.
> … The levels of security and stability we seek in the Indo-Pacific would not be achievable without the United States.
> (Department of Defence 2016: 121, 123)

The United States also benefits from its security partnership with Australia. Most visibly, Australia has proven a reliable and highly effective ally, often bringing critical niche capabilities – such as special forces and advanced air power – in support of American operations such as in Iraq, Afghanistan and Syria. The United States also views very favourably the Australian government's decision – signalled in its 2016 defence white paper – to increase defence spending to 2 per cent of GDP. According to the Australian Minister of Defence as well as outside analysts, the country is on track to reach and possibly surpass that threshold beginning in the 2020/21 fiscal year (Pyne and Reynolds 2019; Hellyer 2019: 6).

The United States benefits as well from Australia's strategic location in the Indo-Pacific. Australia is America's only formal alliance partner bordering the Indian Ocean to the west and lying south of the vital sea lanes around peninsular and archipelagic Southeast Asia. The alliance relationship also allows the United States access to valuable facilities in the southern hemisphere, which have critical implications for US and allied signals intelligence, early warning capabilities and space surveillance. In addition, unlike security partners such as Japan, the Philippines and Taiwan, Australia is not party to territorial and/or sovereignty disputes with China, which can make the alliance less politically complicated vis-à-vis Beijing.

Examples abound of how the two defence establishments translate these shared interests and mutual benefits into operational reality (for more detail, see Chapter 7). The US Force Posture Initiatives – which include the Marine Rotational Force-Darwin and Enhanced Air Cooperation – help the two militaries improve their interoperability and ability to respond to regional crises. The annual six-month rotational deployment of US Marines to Darwin in Australia's Northern Territory has grown from 200 personnel in 2011 to 2,500 in 2019. According to the Australian Department of Defence, the 2019 deployment was 'the most capable to date' and included ground combat, air combat and logistics units. The Enhanced Air Cooperation initiative introduces a range of joint US–Australia exercises and training to support the effective integration of fifth-generation fighters in to the ADF (Department of Defence 2019).

Australia is also one of the leading importers of US military technology. Recent, ongoing and future procurement of US systems include 72 F-35A Joint Strike Fighters, 12 P-8A Poseidon anti-submarine warfare aircraft, EA-18G Growler electronic warfare aircraft, E-7A Wedgetail airborne early warning and control aircraft, MH-60R Seahawk anti-surface and anti-submarine helicopters and 12 to 16 long endurance armed drones. In recent years, Australia has risen to become one of the world's top five importers of weapons, primarily on the back of its procurement from the United States (SIPRI 2020).

Australia and the United States share an interest to sustain and expand American access to a range of facilities on Australian soil. The joint facilities at Pine Gap, deep in Australia's interior, provide valuable intelligence which helps track terrorist movements and communications, monitor foreign military activities, track and target ballistic missiles and verify arms control and non-proliferation commitments in support of Australian and US interests.

In a joint effort between the Australian Defence Force and the US Air Force, a C-band space surveillance radar was relocated from the United States to Western Australia and began operations in 2017 (Department of Defence 2017). In addition, also in Western Australia, a space surveillance telescope, to be owned by the US Air Force but operated by the Australian Defence Force, is to begin operations in 2021; reportedly, the US Air Force is considering other locations in Australia for additional space surveillance facilities (Blenkin 2019). Looking ahead, the Australian Cocos (Keeling) Islands could see an expanded US military presence for long-range surveillance aircraft and armed drones (Bashfield 2019) and – more controversially – some consideration has been given to the possibility of HMAS Stirling, the major naval base on Australia's west coast, opening up to a rotational presence of US surface combatants and submarines (Stewart 2018). Such defence and intelligence cooperation provides Australia with capabilities far beyond those of its regional neighbours and helps the United States build out its own and allied capabilities across the southeast, southwest and southern reaches of the Indo-Pacific region and into the Eurasian landmass.

In short, Canberra and Washington recognize that they are better off working as partners to the greatest extent possible to address the challenges and opportunities they face, particularly in the increasingly vital, dynamic and contested Indo-Pacific region. Such generally positive views in Australia–United States relations are reflected in polling data which finds that 72 per cent of Australians believe the alliance is either 'fairly' or 'very' important for Australia's security and 73 per cent say that the alliance is a 'natural extension of our shared values and ideals' (Kassam 2019: 10).

Bilateral differences

However, while the shared interests in the security relationship are by and large strong and mutually beneficial, the bilateral alliance is not without problems. On many occasions in the past, the strategic interests of the two countries diverged, sometimes considerably, though these seem to be forgotten or overlooked in the interests of alliance solidarity (Curran 2017).

For example, early in alliance history, in 1956, Australia backed the United Kingdom, France and Israel during the Suez Crisis, while the United States opposed their plan to use force against Egypt (Hudson 1989). Also during the 1950s, Australian political leaders and strategists were dissatisfied and sceptical over the level of America commitment to the defence of Southeast Asia and to the viability of the Southeast Asian Treaty Organization (SEATO) to counter a potentially expansionist Chinese threat in the region (Lee 1993; Jones 2004). In 1969, US President Richard Nixon's 'Guam Doctrine', whereby US allies would be expected to do much more for their own defence, came as a 'very unreassuring bombshell' in Canberra (White 2019b). A few years later, Nixon would place Australia as number two on his 'shit list' (after Sweden) for all the criticism coming from the country against America's war in Vietnam (Curran 2017). By 1974, Australia–United States relations had deteriorated to the point that Nixon sought guidance from his national security advisors on how the alliance might be terminated (Curran 2015).

More recently, Australia has also been cautious about how its security alliance with Washington affects relations with China. Some past episodes suggest it is not always clear how Australia will respond if military hostilities were to erupt between the United States and China (or between the United States and others in the region), and much would depend on the circumstances surrounding such a clash. Alexander Downer, when the Australian foreign minister, seemed to suggest in 2004 that Australia would not automatically support a US intervention against China in a war over Taiwan (ABC 2004). The remarks met with a firestorm of criticism, but a decade later, in 2014, the Australian defence minister, David Johnston, appeared to hold a similar view. Asked by a journalist whether the Australia–United States alliance 'commits Australia or not if the United States is in a conflict in our region?', Johnston replied, 'I don't believe it does' (Switzer 2014).

These comments came under fire, but appear to reflect views within the broader Australian public. According to polling released in 2019, less than half of Australians (43 per cent) support Australian military involvement 'if China invaded Taiwan and the US decided to intervene' and 62 per cent would oppose Australian use of force 'if China initiated a military conflict with one of its neighbours over disputed islands or territories' (Kassam 2019: 13).

While such high-profile public utterances by government ministers have not been heard since, these episodes underscore the tensions which can exist in the Australia–United States alliance – or in any alliance – when interests diverge. From the full context of Johnston's remarks and subsequent explanations, he made the point that the circumstances of a given conflict would matter and that, based on the alliance treaty, the security commitment between the two countries is not ironclad.

A strict reading of the alliance treaty supports that point. Article IV states only that 'Each Party recognizes that an armed attack in the Pacific Area on any of the Parties would be dangerous to its own peace and safety and declares that it would act to meet the common danger in accordance with its constitutional processes' (Security Treaty 1951). While the alliance has evolved and become closer over seven decades – and Prime Minister John Howard invoked the treaty its one and only time to come to America's aid following the 2001 terrorist attacks on US soil – the security treaty itself leaves plenty of flexibility for both parties.

Indeed, as one prominent observer of Australian foreign policy writes, the 1951 alliance agreement, or ANZUS Treaty, 'was almost studied in its vagueness' (Wesley 2020: 26). At the time of the alliance's founding, such ambiguity reflected a reluctance on America's part to fully commit to a distant and still-unfamiliar ally. But today Australians have their own concerns about the reliability of the United States. In his later years, the former Prime Minister Malcolm Fraser argued strongly that Australia was too dependent on the United States, Canberra has been too often dragged in to America's fights but could not count on US help in return, Australians need to be wary of getting caught in the affairs of major powers and conduct a more independent foreign policy, and as such the alliance should be abrogated (Fraser 2014). In a similar vein, Hugh White, a well-known professor in strategic studies at Australian National University and former senior official with the Australian Defence Department, has strenuously made that case that American power in Asia is in relative decline and as such Canberra cannot assume the United States will be able to defend Australia from attack (and might not even if it could). As a result, White argues, Canberra needs to seriously think about how it will defend itself without America (White 2017; White 2019a, 2019c).

Such scepticism toward the alliance and relations with the United States are not only held amongst elites. According to recent polling in Australia, only about two-thirds of Australians on the right side of the political spectrum would describe the United States as an 'ally' of Australia. Even fewer on the left – 53 per cent – would say the same (Jackman et al. 2019: 20–21). When asked which country is Australia's 'best friend', only 20 per cent of Australians chose the United States and a large majority (69 per cent) agreed that 'Australia's alliance with the United States makes it more likely Australia will be drawn into a war in Asia that would not be in Australia's interests' (Kassam 2019: 4). In the same poll, some 66 per cent of Australians said that Donald Trump had weakened the alliance (Kassam 2019: 7).

In addition, it appears Donald Trump's presidency has undermined Australian views toward the United States. Following the election of President Trump in 2016, the percentage of Australians who gave the United States a favourable rating dropped by 12 points, from 60 per cent to 48 per cent (Wike et al. 2017: 22). This figure has not improved much since: in 2019 about 50 per cent of Australians expressed a favourable view toward the United States (Poushter 2020).

Overall, a majority of Australians continue to hold generally positive views toward the United States and the alliance, but these numbers have declined in many respects. The two sides cannot take their shared alliance interests for granted, and Canberra and Washington have a lot of work to do to examine these interests carefully and candidly, and respond accordingly.

Conclusions and looking ahead

The relationship between Australia and the United States is firmly-rooted in common histories and shared sacrifice, aligned values, traditions and norms, and a common language. While these attributes are often taken for granted, they nonetheless underpin and sustain a relationship of largely shared geostrategic interests which help bind Australia and the United States together. The two countries work to achieve these shared interests, both individually and in tandem, at global and regional levels and especially within the Indo-Pacific region. Their bilateral security alliance provides an especially strong platform from which to pursue these common interests. Looking ahead, it appears overall that Australian and US interests will continue to overlap substantially with one another.

However, Australian and US interests have never fully aligned across global, regional and bilateral interests. The degree of alignment has waxed and waned over the decades. Like all alliances, the Australia–US partnership wrestles with abandonment and entrapment concerns and has done so since it formally came in to force in 1952.

Today, new pressures are testing the shared interests of the alliance. Australian leaders, and many other allied leaders across the globe, have come to question the long-term strength and commitment of American power to support the post-war liberal order, or to effectively lead in shaping a new order conducive to their collective interests. For Australians, the disastrous US response to the COVID-19 pandemic was just one – albeit critical – example of this tendency, further undermining confidence in their principal ally (Kassam 2020). Many see the Donald Trump presidency signalling a more inward-looking, nationalist bent in American foreign policy which will outlast his time in office, meaning an America less inclined and less able to work with allies and multilateral partners to pursue shared interests.

China's rise and its importance to Australian interests places further pressures on the alliance. Interestingly, these pressures have the effect of driving Australia and America closer together in some ways, while also pulling them apart in others. This drives a fierce and at times divisive debate – both inside Australia and within the US–Australia relationship – about where American, Australian and allied priorities should lie with regard to China. This debate will not resolve easily or soon. In the meantime, when coupled with the uncertainties surrounding American leadership noted above, the China factor will further complicate the ongoing pursuit of shared strategic interests between Australia and the United States.

Lord Palmerston famously said, 'We have no eternal allies, and we have no perpetual enemies. Our interests are eternal and perpetual, and those interests it is our duty to follow'. Australia and the United States share many interests, but this can change. Canberra and Washington should not be complacent, and have much work to do – through greater transparency, more frank consultation, a broadened definition of the alliance and clearer understanding of one another's strategic objectives – to sustain this exceptional partnership in to the 21st century.

Note

1 APEC members are: Australia, Brunei, Canada, Chile, China, Hong Kong, Indonesia, Japan, Malaysia, Mexico, New Zealand, Papua New Guinea, Peru, the Philippines, Russia, Singapore, South Korea, Taiwan, Thailand, United States, and Vietnam.

References

ABC (2004), 'Downer Prepared to Stand Against US Over Taiwan', *The World Today*, 18 August, www.abc.net.au/worldtoday/content/2004/s1179403.htm accessed 20 March 20, 2020.

ABS (2017), 'Census Reveals a Fast Changing, Culturally Diverse Nation', *Australian Bureau of Statistics*, 27 June, www.abs.gov.au/Ausstats/abs@.nsf/dd0ca10eed681f12ca 2570ce0082655d/05dee7dfca9c2e00ca25814800090fb2!OpenDocument accessed 31 March 2020.

ABS (2018), 'ABS Chinese New Year Insights', *Australian Bureau of Statistics*, 16 February, www.abs.gov.au/AUSSTATS/abs@.nsf/mediareleasesbytitle/D8CAE4F74B82 D446CA258235000F2BDE?OpenDocument accessed 31 March 2020.

AUSMIN (2019), 'Joint Statement Australia–US Ministerial Consultations (AUSMIN) 2019', Minister for Foreign Affairs, 4 August, www.foreignminister.gov. au/minister/marise-payne/media-release/joint-statement-australia-us-ministerial-con sultations-ausmin-2019 accessed 16 February 2020.

Australian Government (2017), 'Opportunity, Security, Strength: 2017 Foreign Policy White Paper', Department of Foreign Affairs and Trade, November, www.dfat.gov. au/sites/default/files/2017-foreign-policy-white-paper.pdf accessed 28 March 2020.

Bashfield, Samuel (2019), 'Australia's Cocos Islands Cannot Replace America's Troubled Diego Garcia', *The Diplomat*, 16 April, https://thediplomat.com/2019/04/australia s-cocos-islands-cannot-replace-americas-troubled-diego-garcia/ accessed 20 March 2020.

BEA (2019), 'US International Trade in Goods and Services, December 2018', 6 March, www.bea.gov/news/2019/us-international-trade-goods-and-services-decem ber-2018, accessed 20 March 2020.

Bishop, Julie (2018), 'Keynote Address: The Future of Australia–UK Relations', 19 July, www.foreignminister.gov.au/minister/julie-bishop/speech/keynote-address-futur e-australia-uk-relations accessed 22 March 2020.

Blenkin, Max (2019), 'USAF Considers New SSA Telescope in Australia', 26 Julywww.spaceconnectonline.com.au/operations/3588-usaf-considers-new-ssa-telesco pe-in-australia accessed 16 February 2020.

Cha, Jeremiah (2019), 'People in Asia-Pacific Regard the US More Favorably Than China, But Trump Gets Negative Marks', 25 Februarywww.pewresearch.org/fact-ta nk/2020/02/25/people-in-asia-pacific-regard-the-u-s-more-favorably-than-china-but-t rump-gets-negative-marks/ accessed 15 March 2020.

Clinton, Hillary (2011), 'America's Pacific Century', *Foreign Policy*, 11 October, http s://foreignpolicy.com/2011/10/11/americas-pacific-century/ accessed 20 March 2020.

Cranston, Matthew (2019), 'Australia's Export Share to China Hits Record High 38 Pc', *Australian Financial Review*, 1 October, www.afr.com/policy/economy/australia -s-export-share-to-china-hits-record-high-38pc-20190930-p52w9y accessed 30 March 2020.

CRS (2018), 'The Trump Administration's "Free and Open Indo-Pacific": Issues for Congress, Congressional Research Service', report R45396, 3 Octoberwww.every crsreport.com/files/20181003_R45396_3b75f4bf108ab8d5ab4419b8e98d4edfc80c31e d.pdf accessed 25 March 2020.

Curran, James (2015), *Unholy Fury: Whitlam and Nixon at War*, Melbourne: Melbourne University Press.

Curran, James (2016), 'Fighting with America: Why Saying No To America Won't Rupture The Alliance', Lowy Institute, December, www.lowyinstitute.org/publica tions/fighting-america

Curran, James (2017), 'Australia Needs to Adapt to the New Circumstances of Trump's America', *The Guardian*, 3 February, www.theguardian.com/commentis free/2017/feb/03/australia-needs-to-adapt-to-the-new-circumstances-of-trumps-ameri ca accessed 26 March 2020.

Department of Defence (2016), *2016 Defence White Paper*, 25 February, www.defence. gov.au/WhitePaper/Docs/2016-Defence-White-Paper.pdf accessed 15 March 2020.

Department of Defence (2017), 'Australia's Space Surveillance Radar Reaches Full Operational Capability', 7 March, www.minister.defence.gov.au/minister/marise-pa yne/media-releases/australias-space-surveillance-radar-reaches-full-operational accessed 15 March 2020.

Department of Defence (2019), 'United States Force Posture Initiatives in Australia', www.defence.gov.au/Initiatives/USFPI/Default.asp accessed 20 March 2020.

Department of Defence (2020), 'Global Operations', undated, www.defence.gov.au/Operations/ accessed 25 March 2020.

Department of Education (2020), 'Student Numbers 2019 December Australia', undated, https://internationaleducation.gov.au/research/DataVisualisations/Pages/Student-number.aspx accessed 30 March 2020.

Department of Foreign Affairs and Trade (2019), 'Stepping up Australia's Engagement With Our Pacific Family', September, www.dfat.gov.au/sites/default/files/stepping-up-australias-engagement-with-our-pacific-family.pdf accessed 25 March 2020.

Department of Foreign Affairs and Trade (2020), 'Foreign Investment Statistics', undated, www.dfat.gov.au/trade/resources/investment-statistics/Pages/foreign-investment-statistics accessed 20 February 2020.

Department of Foreign Affairs and Trade (2020a), 'China Country Brief', undated, www.dfat.gov.au/geo/china/Pages/china-country-brief accessed 23 March 2020.

Department of Foreign Affairs and Trade (2020b), 'National Foundation for Australia–China Relations', undated, www.dfat.gov.au/people-to-people/foundations-councils-institutes/nfacr/Pages/request-for-submissions-shaping-the-national-foundation-for-australia-china-relations accessed 29 March 2020.

Department of State (1993), 'Fact Sheet: US Economic Relations with East Asia and the Pacific', *US State Department Dispatch*, vol. 4, no. 48, 29 November..

Department of State (2019), 'A Free and Open Indo-Pacific: Advancing a Shared Vision', 4 November, www.state.gov/wp-content/uploads/2019/11/Free-and-Open-Indo-Pacific-4Nov2019.pdf accessed 30 March 2020.

Department of State (2020), 'Voting Practices in the United Nations [2000–2018]', annual report, www.jewishvirtuallibrary.org/united-nations-member-states-voting-records accessed 28 March 2020.

Diss (2020), 'Donald Trump Claims a Win With the US–China Trade Deal, But Questions Remain', *ABC News*, www.abc.net.au/news/2020-01-16/us-china-trade-deal-could-hurt-australia/11872536 accessed 27 March 2020.

Fraser, Malcolm (2014), *Dangerous Allies*, Melbourne: Melbourne University Press.

Gill, Bates and Tom Switzer (2015), 'The New Special Relationship: The US–Australia Relationship Deepens', *Foreign Affairs*, 19 February, www.foreignaffairs.com/articles/australia/2015-02-19/new-special-relationship accessed 24 March 2020.

Gill, Bates and Linda Jakobson (2017), *China Matters: Getting it Right for Australia*, Carlton, VIC: LaTrobe University Press/Black Inc.

Gyngell, Allan (2018), 'The Rise and Fall of the Liberal International Order', 13 July, www.internationalaffairs.org.au/australianoutlook/the-rise-and-fall-of-the-liberal-international-order/ accessed 15 February 2020.

Hellyer, Marcus (2019), *The Cost of Defence: ASPI Defence Budget Brief 2019–2020*, Australia Strategic Policy Institute, June, www.aspi.org.au/report/cost-defence-aspi-defence-budget-brief-2019-2020 accessed 22 March 2020.

Holden, Richard and Jared Mondschein (2017), 'Indispensable Economic Partners: The US–Australia Investment Relationship', 13 August, www.ussc.edu.au/analysis/indispensable-economic-partners-the-us-australia-investment-relationship accessed 20 February 2020.

Howard, John (2001), 'Application of ANZUS Treaty to Terrorist Attacks on the United States', Office of the Prime Minister Media Release, 14 September, https://pmtranscripts.pmc.gov.au/release/transcript-12169, accessed 17 June 2020.

Hudson, W. J. (1989), *Blind Loyalty: Australia and the Suez Crisis*, Melbourne: Melbourne University Press.

Indo-Pacific Command (2020), 'About USINDOPACOM', undated, available at www.pacom.mil/About-USINDOPACOM/ accessed 25 March 2020.

International Monetary Fund (2019) 'Projected GDP Ranking', International Monetary Fund World Economic Outlook, October, http://statisticstimes.com/economy/projected-world-gdp-ranking.php accessed 29 March 2020.

Jackman, Simon, Shaun Ratcliff, Zoe Meers, Jared Mondschein and Elliott Brennan (2019), *Public Opinion in the Age of Trump: The United States and Australia Compared*, Sydney: United States Studies Centre at the University of Sydney, December, www.ussc.edu.au/analysis/public-opinion-in-the-united-states-and-australia-compared accessed 23 March 2020.

Jones, Matthew (2004), 'The Radford Bombshell: Anglo-Australian-US Relations, Nuclear Weapons and the Defence of South East Asia, 1954–57', *Journal of Strategic Studies*, 27 (4).

Kassam, Natasha (2019), 'Lowy Institute Poll 2019', Lowy Institute, June, www.lowyinsitute.org/sites/default/files/lowyinsitutepoll-2019.pdf accessed 15 February 2020.

Kassam, Natasha (2020), 'COVID Poll: Lowy Institute Polling on Australian Attitudes to the Coronavirus Pandemic', Lowy Institute, 14 May, www.lowyinstitute.org/publications/covidpoll-lowy-institute-polling-australian-attitudes-coronavirus-pandemic#sec42556, accessed 17 June 2020.

Lee, David (1993), 'Australia and Allied Strategy in the Far East, 1952–1957', *Journal of Strategic Studies*, 16 (4).

Morrison, Scott (2019), 'The 2019 Lowy Lecture: Prime Minister Scott Morrison', Lowy Institute, 3 October, www.lowyinstitute.org/publications/2019-lowy-lecture-prime-minister-scott-morrison accessed 23 March 2020.

Morrison, Scott (2019a), '"Where We Live" Asialink Bloomberg Address', 26 June, www.pm.gov.au/media/where-we-live-asialink-bloomberg-address accessed 19 March 2020.

Obama, Barack (2011), 'Remarks by President Obama to the Australian Parliament', White House Office of the Press Secretary, November 17, available at https://obamawhitehouse.archives.gov/the-press-office/2011/11/17/remarks-president-obama-australian-parliament accessed 25 March 2020.

Poushter, Jacob (2020), 'How People Around the World See the US and Donald Trump in 10 Charts', Pew Research Center, 8 January, www.pewresearch.org/fact-tank/2020/01/08/how-people-around-the-world-see-the-u-s-and-donald-trump-in-10-charts/ accessed 27 March 2020.

Pyne, Christopher and Linda Reynolds (2019), 'A Safer Australia – Budget 2019–2020 – Defence Overview', Australian Government Department of Defence, 2 April, www.minister.defence.gov.au/minister/cpyne/media-releases/safer-australia-budget-2019-20-defence-overview accessed 3 February 2020.

Romei, Valentina and John Reed (2019), 'The Asian Century is Set to Begin', *Financial Times*, 26 March, available at www.ft.com/content/520cb6f6-2958-11e9-a5ab-ff8ef2b976c7 accessed 3 February 2020.

Security Treaty (1952), 'Security Treaty between Australia, New Zealand and the United States of America', 29 April, www.austlii.edu.au/au/other/dfat/treaties/1952/2.html accessed 26 March 2020.

SIPRI (2020), 'Trade Registers', Stockholm International Peace Research Institute, http://armstrade.sipri.org/armstrade/page/trade_register.php accessed 26 March 2020.

Smyth, Jamie and Simon Mundy (2015), 'Australia Shifts Stance on China-Led Development Bank', *Financial Times*, March 16, www.ft.com/content/0e7371fc-cba 9-11e4-beca-00144feab7de#axzz3UZL8dED5, accessed 17 June 2020.

Stewart, Cameron (2018), 'Washington Report Floats US Nuclear Attack Subs and Warships in Perth', *The Australian*, 25 April, www.theaustralian.com.au/nation/ defence/washington-report-floats-us-nuclear-attack-subs-and-warships-in-perth/news -story/af5d0e9dd300c8eb96bf74aca790198d accessed 28 February 2020.

Switzer, Tom (2014), 'The Elephant in the Room on US–Australia Relations', *The Drum*, 13 June, www.abc.net.au/news/2014-06-13/switzer-the-elephant-in-the-room -on-us-australia-relations/5522366 accessed 25 March 2020.

Trump, Donald (2017), 'Remarks by President Trump at APEC CEO Summit, Da Nang, Vietnam', The White House, November 10, www.whitehouse.gov/brief ings-statements/remarks-president-trump-apec-ceo-summit-da-nang-vietnam/ accessed 25 March 2020.

USCESRC (2019), *2019 Report to Congress*, US–China Economic and Security Review Commission, November, www.uscc.gov/sites/default/files/2019-11/2019% 20Annual%20Report%20to%20Congress.pdf accessed 23 February 2020.

USTR (2019), 'US–APEC Trade Facts', Office of the United States Trade Repre- sentative, 24 October, https://ustr.gov/trade-agreements/other-initiatives/asia-pacifi c-economic-cooperation-apec/us-apec-trade-facts accessed 15 March 2020.

Wesley, Michael (2020), 'Beijing Calling: How China Is Testing The Alliance', *Australian Foreign Affairs*, February.

White, Hugh (2017), 'Without America: Australia in the New Asia', *Quarterly Essay*, November.

White, Hugh (2019a), 'Standing Alone: Why Australia Can't Rely on America', *The Strategist*, 24 December, www.aspistrategist.org.au/standing-alone-why-australia-ca nt-rely-on-america/ accessed 15 February 2020.

White, Hugh (2019b), 'A Very Unreassuring Bombshell: Richard Nixon and the Guam Doctrine, July 1969', *The Strategist*, www.aspistrategist.org.au/a-very-unreassuring-bom bshell-richard-nixon-and-the-guam-doctrine-july-1969/ accessed 15 February 2020.

White, Hugh (2019c), *How to Defend Australia*, Carlton, VIC: LaTrobe University Press.

White House (2019), 'Remarks by President Trump and Prime Minister Morrison of Australia at Arrival Ceremony', 20 September, www.whitehouse.gov/briefings-sta tements/remarks-president-trump-prime-minister-morrison-australia-arrival-ceremo ny/ accessed 3 February 2020.

Wike, Richard, Bruce Stokes, Jacob Poushter and Janell Fetterolf (2017), 'US Image Suffers as Publics Around World Question Trump's Leadership', Pew Research Center, 26 June, www.pewresearch.org/global/2017/06/26/u-s-image-suffers-as-p ublics-around-world-question-trumps-leadership/ accessed 20 March 2020.

6 The evolution of the US–Australia strategic relationship

Shannon Brandt Ford

Introduction

'Strategic relationship' describes the interaction between two independent states when applying national power in pursuit of their international goals. In cases where the relationship is cooperative, the two states combine national power to achieve sought after strategic outcomes. Here we are talking about each countries' grand strategy, which Hal Brands describes as a 'purposeful and coherent set of ideas about what a nation seeks to accomplish in the world, and how it should go about doing so'. It is, he suggests, the conceptual framework that helps nations determine where they want to go and how they ought to get there; that is, the logic that guides leaders towards the goal of security (Brands 2014: 3). Since the signing of the Australia–New Zealand–United States (ANZUS) Security Treaty in 1951, Australia has aligned itself with the grand strategy of the United States (US). This has provided Australia with the protection of the US's armed forces, the benefits of access to America's extensive intelligence network and its most advanced military technology. A close strategic relationship has allowed Australia privileged access to high-level decision-making in Washington and has given Australia invaluable insight into the most sensitive areas of US strategic thinking. Furthermore, as the strategic relationship between the US and Australia has evolved, it has demonstrated remarkable durability and strength. It has adapted to a variety of challenges over the years. The challenges it has faced include the United States' Guam Doctrine, Australia's 'self-reliance' defence policy, New Zealand's *de facto* exclusion after a dispute with the US over nuclear policy, and the end of the Cold War.

In this chapter, I demonstrate that the US–Australia strategic relationship has evolved from more or less an adversarial position in the 19th century to an Australia largely dependent on the US during the Cold War to the inter-dependent partnership we see today. In the first section, I outline three key features that underpin the strength and durability of the current US–Australia strategic relationship: ideological solidarity, informal institutionalization, and reliability. The present durability of the US–Australia strategic relationship does not mean, however, that a strong partnership was always inevitable. In the second section of the chapter, I briefly examine Australia's strategic starting point in the 19th century as an outpost of the British Empire in the Asia-Pacific region. The Australian colonies' strategic perspectives of the US were largely subsumed by Whitehall's great power competition with Washington. Australia's Federation in 1901, however, allowed the possibility of Australia pursuing its own strategic relations with other countries independently from Britain. The visit of the US Great White Fleet to Sydney Harbour in 1908 was then the starting point for a period of increasing military cooperation between Australia and the US, which culminated in fighting alongside one another to defeat Japan's armed forces in the Pacific Theatre of the Second World War. The failure of Britain's 'Singapore Strategy' and the US's success in defending Australia from Japan's military aggression became an important catalyst in realigning Canberra's strategic relationship with Washington. By 1951, Australia had signed the tripartite ANZUS security agreement, making it an important part of the US 'hub-and-spokes' system of bilateral alliances in the Asia-Pacific. Over the next 20 years, Australia shifted its strategic dependence from Britain to its powerful US friend.

In the chapter's third section, I examine the evolution of the US–Australia strategic relationship from the end of the Vietnam War until the present. The post-Vietnam hangover of the 1970s and the pre-eminence of Australia's policy of defence self-reliance in the 1980s and 1990s provided impetus to lessen its strategic dependence on the US. Although self-reliance never translated into strategic independence for Australia, it paved the way for a more strategically interdependent US–Australia relationship. In the decade that followed the East Timor crisis in 1999, military interventions were the dominant feature of the US–Australia strategic relationship. Australia was focused on demonstrating loyalty to the US in this period. The US–Australia strategic relationship continued to grow throughout the Obama Administration era and into the present day, with interdependence continuing to be a major theme. At the same time, a number of pressing concerns have emerged, especially the long-term impact of the 'Trump effect' and the potential to disagree over policy concerning the People's Republic of China.

A normative alliance

Ideological solidarity

A key feature of the US–Australia strategic relationship is the ideological solidarity that exists between the two countries. According to Stephen Walt, ideological solidarity between two independent states exists when they share common political values and objectives, while continuing to regard themselves as separate political entities. Other things being equal, he suggests, states will usually prefer to ally with governments whose political outlook is similar to their own (Walt 1997: 168). Walt argues that similar regimes may be willing to support each other on the basis that it contributes to promoting what they believe are intrinsic common goods, such as democracy, socialism or Islamic fundamentalism. Ideological solidarity and a commitment to the same strategic goals, he says, can reduce intra-alliance conflicts and help sustain an alliance after its original rationale is gone (Walt 1997: 168). This is true of the US–Australia strategic relationship. The ideological solidarity between Australia and the US is a significant source of its strength. In other words, cultural and normative factors are an integral part of the US–Australia strategic relationship's success. Despite various disagreements and tensions arising between Australia and the United States over specific strategic issues, these have never been more important than the common ideological solidarity of the alliance relationship itself. Australia's relations with the US have an obvious advantage not commonly considered important for a strategic alliance – the similarity and compatibility of language, values, socioeconomic organization and political-legal practices (Albinski 1987: 8).

A broad range of cultural affinities significantly improves understanding and the likelihood of agreement in the relationship. Bill Tow and Henry Albinski suggest that ideological solidarity reinforces ANZUS by creating a sense of 'alliance mutuality' that encourages processes of norm identification, interest adaptability and order-building (Tow and Albinski 2002: 172). This feature led Tow and Albinski to describe ANZUS as a 'normative alliance'. That is, both countries' commitment to liberal democratic political values leads them to similar conclusions in relation to their security interests and ideas about strategy (Tow and Albinski 2002: 170). Inevitably, the choice of a national grand strategy involves a decision about which political values should be pursued. Key strategic questions seek to address the main political ideals that are at stake (Barkawi 1998: 181). The ideological solidarity that is such a prominent feature of the US–Australia strategic relationship has meant that Australia's strategic thinking is more likely to align with US ideas about the purpose of armed force (or the threat to use armed force). John Ikenberry suggests that 'when all is said and done, Americans are less interested in ruling the world than they are in a world of rules' (Ikenberry 2004: 150). Hence, Australia has been supportive of US visions of international order. ANZUS is the type of rules-based institution based on democratic political values with which both the US and Australia are comfortable. Such ideological solidarity is important, but it is not the only factor at work in making a strong strategic relationship between Australia and the US.

Three pillars of institutionalization

A second key feature underpinning the strength and durability of the US–Australia strategic relationship is its institutionalization. Unlike the formal institutionalization seen in many of the US's other strategic relationships, the US–Australia partnership lacks clearly specified formal treaty commitments. This concerns some alliance observers. Stephan Frühling, for instance, describes ANZUS as 'the informal alliance'. He argues that the US–Australia strategic relationship lags behind all other US alliances in 'the development of alliance guidance, command arrangements and policy mechanisms' (Frühling 2018: 202). Frühling wants to 'fill the institutional gap' that he believes exists between formal US–Australia treaty documents and the practices of the strategic relationship. His focus is on mechanisms for strengthening policy dialogue and command-and-control arrangements (Frühling 2018: 210–211).

Yet despite the lack of these types of policies and procedures to translate the ANZUS Treaty into specific strategic practices, three 'pillars' of institutionalization make significant contributions to the strength and durability of the US–Australia strategic relationship. The first of these pillars is the intelligence cooperation between Australia and the US. Des Ball described intelligence cooperation as the 'strategic essence' of the US–Australian alliance relationship. That is, the UKUSA Agreement of 1947–1948 concerning signals intelligence (SIGINT) cooperation and exchange, and the maintenance of the 'joint facilities' in Australia, are the important 'ties that bind' the US to Australia (Ball 2001: 237). Michael Wesley (2016a) also believes that intelligence cooperation sits at the heart of an effective US–Australia strategic relationship. He suggests that, in the absence of 'NATO-like contracts' or 'joint strategic planning', the US–Australia intelligence relationship provides reassurance and risk mitigation. Wesley argues that the best way for the US and Australia to correctly understand one another's thinking on sensitive strategic issues, such as China's rise, is via shared intelligence product. Through this process, both parties end up communicating clearly their assessments and priorities for a variety of strategic situations (Wesley 2016a: 160).

The second pillar of institutionalization binding Australia and the US is the collaboration in defence science and technologies. As mentioned above, the US located in Australia three installations of vital importance to the US's strategic posture. These 'joint facilities' initially consisted of North West Cape, Pine Gap and Nurrungar (Ball 2001: 237). Ball argues that hosting these facilities represents Australia's most meaningful, direct contribution to American security. In return, he suggests, Australia receives access to sophisticated US military technologies (Ball 2001: 238–239). Richard Brabin-Smith concludes that Australia's relationship with the US in capability development and defence science is becoming even closer. But for this to continue, he suggests that Australia must ensure that it is in a position to give as well as to receive (Brabin-Smith 2016: 195). For instance, Australia has bought equity in the US Wideband Global Satellite communications system. Rather than merely paying as a customer for access, Australia funds one of the six satellites of the system's constellation (Brabin-Smith 2016: 184).

The third pillar of institutionalization undergirding the US–Australia relationship are the effective personal relationships at all levels of the strategic partnership. Australia enjoys a privileged level of well-established access to the inner workings of key American political and strategic decision-making. Australia's access in Washington is among the very best of the myriad nations who seek a hearing (Tow and Albinski 2002: 164). At the highest levels, the principal forum for bilateral consultations is the annual Australia–US Ministerial (AUSMIN) meeting, which brings together the Australian Ministers for Foreign Affairs and Defence with the US Secretaries of State and Defense.

But this is merely the tip of the iceberg. Below the surface, a complex array of working-level relationships closely binds Australia and the US. Kim Beazley (a former Australian Defence Minister and Ambassador to the US) has noted that the informal personal relationships forged between Australian and US bureaucrats at the working-level are numerous and perhaps even more significant to the health of the alliance than those at the most senior levels. He suggests that diplomats, intelligence officers and military personnel from Australia and the US 'work with, argue with, and even marry each other constantly', which creates 'an underappreciated sense of common outlook and purpose at the deep-state level' (cited in Beeson and Bloomfield 2019: 346). John Blaxland also makes this point in relation to the extensive military links between the US and Australia. He suggests that US–Australia military ties are strong enough to withstand considerable buffeting from the domestic politics of either country (Blaxland 2016: 140).

A reliable ally

A third feature of the strategic relationship is reliability. The US values Australia's reliability as an ally and, in turn, Canberra's concern is to make decisions that increase the reliability of Washington's commitment to protect Australia. Whether it be John Howard's prescription for Australia to be a '100 per cent ally' or Julia Gillard's reference to the nation being an American 'ally for all the years to come', there has been, suggests James Curran, 'a determination to underline Australia's reliability' (Curran 2016: 117). Australia has committed itself to American strategy over the long haul. In particular, Australia has consistently been a strong advocate of the American regional military presence in the Asia-Pacific region. A key theme of Australian strategic culture has been its tendency to be a pragmatic derivation of the strategic policy of its great power ally. That is, it has taken as its starting point the grand strategic frameworks developed by the British Empire and then the US (Wesley 2016b: 20). Moreover, despite Australia's military being dwarfed by its much more powerful partner, the dependability of Australian support for US strategy has been largely appreciated in Washington. One Obama administration official's comment holds true as an aphorism for Washington's view of Australia's reliability: 'our allies all give us headaches, except Australia. You can always count on Australia' (Curran 2016: 121–122).

Being a reliable ally, however, has not meant that Australia has always agreed with US strategic decision-making. Shannon Tow argues that an effective US–Australia strategic relationship has not meant adopting identical policies. Australian policymakers have not traditionally regarded US strategy as immutable (Tow 2017: 160). US strategic preferences, she suggests, can be changed over time, through argument or actions. But securing US assent has meant convincing US policymakers about the merits of Australia's independent policy (Tow 2017: 160). What this indicates is that alliance reliability is not synonymous with alliance loyalty. *Loyalty* describes an agent's willingness to follow a leader without calculations about the worth of doing so. For instance, Australia is exhibiting loyalty when it follows US strategic decision-making instinctively and without question. In contrast, *reliability* in the context of alliance relationships is a notion requiring the exercise of prudence. In other words, Australia is demonstrating its reliability as an ally when it follows US strategic decision-making for the right reasons. This sense of reliability is more akin trustworthiness than loyalty *per se*. Iain Henry utilizes something like this distinction when he argues that a state does not wish to see loyalty in the behaviour of its ally as much as it wants to see proof that the ally's interests align with its own (Henry 2020: 47). Henry suggests that states are primarily concerned with the observed reliability of an ally rather than questions of whether an ally's behaviour is loyal or disloyal. States want to be confident that their ally's interests align with their own, and therefore the alliance poses no risk of either abandonment or entrapment (Henry 2020: 47).

US belief in Australia's loyalty is consequently a mixed blessing. On the one hand, it grants Australia influence and access. On the other hand, it creates an expectation among American policymakers that is difficult to disappoint (Curran 2016: 122). Moreover, unquestioning loyalty can lend legitimacy to poor US strategic policymaking. One of the great ironies of the Howard government's fulsome and uncritical support of the US, argues Mark Beeson, is that it encouraged policies that were unsustainable, unachievable, highly divisive and ultimately corrosive of US authority. By contrast, he suggests, a more critical and less compliant alliance partner would have benefitted both Australia and the US in the long run (Beeson 2003: 388). According to Brendan Taylor and Bill Tow, Australia has sought to shape and control the alliance so that it maximizes its net benefits. For this reason, Australia has willingly accepted its characterization as a 'dependent' and 'dependable' junior ally to the US (Taylor and Tow 2017: 88). In practice, however, Australia has exercised a remarkable degree of independence within the bounds of the strategic relationship. Washington has afforded Canberra considerable latitude, choosing not to impose significant costs when Australia has explicitly gone against its wishes. For example, when Australia joined the Chinese-led Asian Infrastructure Investment Bank (AIIB) in April 2015 (Taylor and Tow 2017: 88–89). Thus, it should be Canberra's priority to 'disabuse senior US policymakers of the view that Australia's support is simply automatic' (Curran 2016: 119).

From strategic competition to dependence

Anglo-American competition

Although the US–Australia strategic relationship is now strong and dependable, it had inauspicious beginnings. Throughout the 19th century, it was largely subject to Whitehall's great power competition with Washington. The

Australian colonies were generally apprehensive about the US's strategic intent and emerging naval power. The first American interest in Australia was a by-product of interests in Asia. By 1792, American ships trading to China around Cape Horn found that they could profitably call in at Port Jackson with a cargo of stores for the settlers (Bell 1988: 7). The mid-19th century gold strikes also promoted interaction between the US and Australia. At the time of the Eureka Stockade (1854), there were more than 1,000 Americans living in Victoria (Bell 1988: 7). During the Crimean War (1853–1856), the main British enemy was Russia, which was enough of a threat for the NSW colony to construct a stronghold in Sydney Harbour (Fort Denison). Australian colonists also had their concerns about the French (operating from nearby New Caledonia) and the Americans (Bell 1988: 9). In November 1839, for example, two American warships entered Sydney Harbour at night and anchored without being detected until the next morning. This illustrated the potential for a hostile power to control Australia's colonial sea-borne trade or coerce the settlements with the threat of bombardment (Grey 2008: 20).

The first armed conflict that saw Australians fight alongside (and against) Americans was the Civil War (1861–1865). Approximately 100 native-born Australians and New Zealanders fought in the conflict (Crompton 2008). Of particular note are the 42 Australians (from the colony of Victoria) who joined the crew of the Confederate cruiser the *CSS Shenandoah* when it docked in Melbourne in 1865. They sailed 96,500 kilometres around the world and were responsible for destroying 32 Union merchant ships, ransoming six, and capturing more than a thousand prisoners (Smyth 2015: 9). The *Shenandoah* was involved in the final armed conflict of the American Civil War and was the last of the Confederates to surrender, which it eventually did in Liverpool, England on 6 November 1865 (Smyth 2015: 274). The Melbourne recruit George Botriune Canning made history by firing the last shot of the war and by being the last man to die in the service of the Confederacy (Smyth 2015: 269). Since the *Shenandoah* had originally been a British ship, and Victoria was still a British colony at the time, the US Government successfully sued the British Government for £15 million in damages (Bell 1988: 7).

In the 1890s, a surge in French and German colonial activity throughout the Pacific created tension with Britain and anxiety within the Australian colonies. Furthermore, the Spanish-American War of 1898, and the subsequent US annexation of the Philippines, brought the US to the forefront as a major security player in the Pacific (Bell 1988: 10). The US did, in fact, end up developing naval plans to invade Sydney Harbour as a contingency in case it went to war with Britain (Reckner 2001). As early as the 1880s, some colonists were cognisant that close alignment with Britain might increase the dangers to Australia and that the better approach might be to seek a more independent strategic policy (Bell 1988: 9). In the words of one Parliamentarian, 'Let us establish ourselves in a separate community, and not be involved in ... any of England's wars ... The security we should thus have would be of infinite and transcendent benefit to us' (David Buchanan cited in Bell 1988: 10). But such views were unusual and tended to be held by 'radicals.'

The beginnings of cooperation

Australia's Federation in 1901 began the process leading to the gradual emergence of an Australian grand strategy distinct from British policy, which allowed the possibility of strategic cooperation with the US. The seminal event that established the US–Australia strategic relationship was the US Navy's 'Great White Fleet' visit to Sydney, Melbourne, and Albany in 1908. The purpose of sending the fleet of US battleships on tour around the world – their hulls painted white – was to make the statement that the US was a significant maritime power with aspirations in both the Atlantic and the Pacific. The Australian Prime Minister Alfred Deakin had sent US President Theodore Roosevelt an invitation for the ships to visit Australia. The visit was a huge success, with over half a million Sydneysiders turning out to greet the arrival of the sixteen US battleships with escorts (Parkin and Lee 2008: 1). The British Foreign and Colonial office had opposed the idea of the US fleet visit, however, believing that it would signify a more independent Australian mindset. Consequently, they were furious with Deakin for allowing the visit to go ahead (Sheridan 2006: 303).

Another milestone in the US–Australia strategic relationship was the military cooperation between the US and Australia in the final year of the First World War. The US formally joined Britain and its allies in the war against Germany on 7 April 2017. But it was another year before American troops arrived in France in significant numbers (Beaumont 2013: 264). American troops fought under the command of the Australian General John Monash at the successful Battle of Hamel (4 July 1918), which almost didn't go ahead after the US Commander-in-Chief, General John Pershing, initially withdrew the American contingent of ten companies (Beaumont 2013: 264). More significantly, two fresh American divisions (the 27th and 30th from II Corps) were transferred to Monash's command for the final battle involving Australian infantry troops in the War. From 27 September to 5 October 1918, a combined force of Australian, American, and British troops broke the Hindenburg Line and took the French towns of Beaurevoir and Montbrehain (Beaumont 2013: 493).

Of greatest significance to the long-term development of the strategic relationship, however, was the military cooperation required to defeat Japan's armed forces in the Pacific Theatre of the Second World War. By the end of the war, Australians came to regard the US, at least potentially, as their chief protector against a threatening region (McLean 2006: 68). Australia and the US had only formally established diplomatic relations in 1940. The appointment of an Australian Minister to Washington was formally completed when

R.G. Casey presented his credentials to the White House on 5 March (Watt 1967: 124). From early 1942 onwards, Australians fought alongside the US military under the command of General Douglas MacArthur. US–Australia strategic cooperation reached new heights during this time. Military engagement was extensive, involving combined operational planning, logistics, and force preparation between each of the services (army, navy and air force) (Blaxland 2016: 122). A key element of this wartime cooperation was the establishment of an Allied Intelligence Bureau on 6 July 1942. At the heart of this arrangement was the secretive UKUSA agreement that allowed the US, Britain, Australia, Canada, and New Zealand to share sensitive signals intelligence (Wesley 2016a: 149–150).

A 'Pacific pact'

The signing of the ANZUS agreement (1951) signalled the beginning of the era of strategic dependence for the US–Australia relationship. For much of the Cold War, Australia's primary debate regarding the alliance centred on the 'metaphor of dependence'. That is, the notion that Australia was reliant on its 'great and powerful friends' for its security (Carr 2016: 67). Although Australia remained part of the British Commonwealth, its security became increasingly tied to the US (Dean 2016: 238). In what sense was Australia strategically dependent on the US in this period? Dependence is relying on someone or something other than yourself to provide for your basic needs. One party in the relationship cannot or will not provide for itself. Australia's decision-makers concluded that they needed the security offered by the US at the time and they had little of material substance to offer in return. There was no real expectation that Australia would be able to make a reciprocal contribution to America's security.

Australia's timely support to the US in the Korean War played a key role in the realization of ANZUS. The burden of controlling Japan had been eagerly assumed by the US in August 1945. But nations such as Australia felt let down by the general lack of consultations in relation to US strategic intentions for Northeast Asia (Buckley 2002: 26). Furthermore, Canberra had experienced little success in advocating for a 'Pacific Pact', akin to NATO in Europe, involving the US (Lowe 2001: 189). The war in Korea, however, quickly changed the strategic landscape. After war broke out on 25 June 1950, when the Communist north invaded the south, Australia was one of the first member states to volunteer forces to the US-dominated United Nations Command. Australian officials believed that agreeing to US requests for troops would favourably influence negotiations for a security treaty with the US. By 2 July, Royal Australian Air Force aircraft from Squadron 77, which were based in Japan under the operational command of the 5th US Air Force, were attacking the advancing North Korean forces. The Australian government also agreed to send a battalion of ground troops in response to a request by the United Nations (Siracusa 2005: 98). Following China's entry into the

War on 25 October, the US was in need of reliable allies. Australian Minister for External Affairs Percy Spender's public comments steadfastly supporting the US approach in Korea convinced the US Joint Chiefs of Staff that the State Department needed to pursue a Pacific Pact with Australia (Siracusa 2005: 100). An important reason for Australia then sending a second battalion to Korea was to underline its reliability as a strategic partner to the US.

The ANZUS Treaty was signed in San Francisco 1 September 1951 and came into force 29 April 1952 (Siracusa 2005: 102). Its aim was to reassure Australia (and New Zealand) that the US would use its military to intervene if either country was attacked. What was seen as a vital necessity by Australia was something to be accepted 'with a resigned shrug' by the Americans. In essence, it was a lopsided arrangement, hardly more than 'a protectorate or one-way guarantee' (Bell 1988: 199). The terms used in the ANZUS Treaty were also vague. Unlike the North Atlantic Treaty, which states unambiguously that an attack on one of its allies will trigger an automatic US response, the ANZUS Treaty merely declares that it would 'act to meet the common danger in accordance with its constitutional processes' (Wesley 2016a: 146). Since the actual commitment to reciprocity within the treaty was unclear, Australia was motivated to follow US strategic initiatives in the attempt to lower whatever fixed costs ANZUS might have in American eyes (Leaver 1997: 72–73). Moreover, the vast asymmetry of military capabilities between Australia and the US led to 'the behavioural pattern characteristic of that between patrons and their clients' (Watt 1967: 124).

Australia strongly supported US national grand strategy in the region throughout the Cold War. The US's increasing support for an alliance with Australia was part of a broader transformation of Washington's East Asian policy in 1949–1950 (McLean 1990: 66). Differences existed between Washington and Canberra over the strategic planning for the defence of Southeast Asia (see: Jones 2004; Lee 1993; Lee 1992). But the onset of the Cold War in Asia prompted US officials to reflect more on the benefits to be gained from a Pacific alliance system that included Australia and New Zealand. It would, they concluded, help protect US interests by strengthening ties with friendly countries and reducing the burden on American resources (McLean 1990: 67). The result was the US-led system of bilateral security ties that included Japan, South Korea, Taiwan, and Australia. Dubbed the 'hub-and-spokes' system by US Secretary of State John Foster Dulles, this network of bilateral arrangements still represents the most important and enduring element of the security architecture for the region (Cha 2010). The region underwent dramatic transformation over decades of war, political upheaval, democratization, and economic boom and crisis. Yet despite the turmoil, this most basic reality of the post-war regional order remained remarkably fixed and enduring (Ikenberry 2004: 353).

Strategic interdependence

Australian self-reliance

The early 1970s through to the mid-1990s began a more strategically *inter-dependent* trajectory for the US–Australia relationship. There was 'a greater propensity for Australian governments of both political persuasions to state candidly their disagreement with US strategic policies' (Curran 2016: 118). In agreeing to the ANZUS treaty, Washington had wanted the strategic benefits of Australia's unique geographical position in the South Western Pacific. Hosting what became known as the 'joint facilities' was the most effective contribution Australia made to the Western alliance at the time (Bell 1996: 27). There was considerable political controversy surrounding these American bases in Australia, many of which had deterrence or warning functions associated with US nuclear forces. The concern was that US bases likely made Australia a target in any nuclear exchange (McCaffrie and Rahman 2014: 89). Nevertheless, the value that Washington put on these facilities meant that the US–Australia strategic relationship became considerably less unequal. Whereas American reliance on its Australian installations increased over time, the scenario where Australia was most dependent on the US – a conventional war of aggression by a hostile regional power – became less likely (Bell 1988: 199). As a result, the bargaining power that was initially weighted almost entirely in Washington's favour, gradually shifted towards Canberra. That is to say, a 'one-sided dependence had in effect transmuted itself into interdependence of a relatively symmetrical sort' (Bell 1988: 199–200).

Part of the reason for this shift was Australia's defence policy of self-reliance. The seeds for a more self-reliant Australian approach to its security were sown in the shadows of the Vietnam War (1962–1975). The Menzies government had embarked upon its Vietnam commitment in order to bind the US more closely to Australia. The goal of supporting the US was to bring reciprocal support when Australia most needed it (Edwards 1997: 28). In 1969, however, the Nixon Doctrine had made clear the US expectation that its Asian allies should shoulder more of the burden for their own defence (Frühling 2018: 206). General anti-US sentiments in Australia had also been fuelled by the war in Vietnam and the Moratorium Movement (Bloomfield and Nossal 2010). Although defence matters and the alliance were not a high priority for the new Labor Whitlam Government (1972–1975), self-reliance was debated and then formally articulated under the subsequent Fraser Government in the first Defence White Paper *Australian Defence* in 1976 (Brabin-Smith 2016: 180). Self-reliance was at its most influential as government policy, however, in the mid-1980s when the newly appointed Labor Defence minister, Kim Beazley, commissioned Paul Dibb to undertake a review of 'the content, priorities and rationale' for Australian defence planning. The 1986 'Dibb Report' was recognized across the political spectrum as a 'revolution in Australian defence', for in advocating a 'strategy of denial', it turned its back on the strategic tradition of 'forward defence', which started with the proposition that Australia was essentially indefensible through its own resources (Leaver 1997: 70). It recommended a concentration on the defence of Australia's 'area of direct military interest'. It argued that, with limited resources, a country such as Australia should avoid using the Australian Defence Force to fight wars outside its region (Dibb 1986). This meant restricting defence planning to the Australian mainland and its contiguous waters, the South Pacific islands, and Southeast Asia. The subsequent 1987 Defence White Paper *The Defence of Australia* mostly accepted Dibb's propositions and conclusions.

Australia's policy of defence self-reliance did not equate to strategic independence, however. Strategic independence would indicate that Australia had isolated itself from outside support and become completely self-sufficient (Brabin-Smith 2016: 181). The policy of self-reliance never intended to achieve such a result. Rather, it was always understood as 'self-reliance in alliance'. The focus on self-reliance in defence planning was to ensure that Australia had sufficient military capability for independence in operations that were likely to be of lesser consequence to the US, especially in Australia's near region (Frühling 2016: 18). Ultimately, it represented a significant evolution in the US–Australian strategic relationship because it opened the door to interdependence. An *interdependent* relationship is one where each of the parties relies to a significant degree on the resources of the other party to fulfil its needs. Australia's strategic role and influence in this period became increasingly intertwined with American power and capabilities. A doctrine of strategic interdependence now started to play a significant role in Australian security policy (Lyon and Tow 2003: 34).

The decade of military interventionism

Military interventions were the dominant feature of the US–Australia strategic relationship for the decade following the East Timor crisis. This was the era where a key focus for Australian grand strategy was demonstrating loyalty to the US; disparagingly described by some at the time as playing the role of 'deputy sheriff'. The strategic goal of Canberra's military commitments in this period was to bind the US more closely to Australia's security interests. Australia had a consistent record of fighting alongside US forces in every major conflict since the First World War. A major reason for Australia's consistent willingness to fight in these wars was a concern to improve the reliability of its great power ally. That is to say, Australia's strategic goal has been to ensure that, initially London and then later Washington, 'would remember Australia's sacrifices abroad and come to its aid if needed' (Green, Dean, Taylor and Cooper 2015: 8).

Thus, Australian Prime Minister John Howard was bitterly disappointed after Washington refused his request for US ground troops to address the political crisis in East Timor. When it came to power in 1996, a foreign policy priority for the Australian Howard Government was to 'reinvigorate' the

ANZUS alliance (Tow 2001: 162). In July 1996, it presented the Sydney Statement at the annual Australia–US Ministerial (AUSMIN) consultations. This was a joint security initiative outlining closer defence links between Australia and the US (Wesley 2007: 10). Then, in 1999, a vote for independence in East Timor led to a series of massacres by Indonesian-backed militia groups. After a public outcry in Australia, the Howard Government reluctantly responded by pushing for a UN-mandated military intervention and by taking the lead in pulling together the international coalition. A number of South East Asian and European countries agreed to contribute military personnel to the International Force East Timor (INTERFET). But Howard was particularly disappointed in President Clinton's unwillingness to send US ground troops, suggesting that 'it was a poor repayment of past loyalties and support' (Curran 2016: 64). Consequently, some prominent alliance commentators have used this incident as evidence for the US's lack of reliability when it comes to supporting Australia's strategic concerns (Beeson 2003: 396; Curran 2016: 65–66; Frühling 2016: 18).

Far from being a failure of the US–Australia relationship, however, the East Timor crisis instead highlighted the effectiveness of strategic interdependence. There was no shortage of countries offering ground troops for INTERFET. What the US provided instead were the crucial strategic elements that Australia most needed to make the intervention a success. First, it applied economic and political pressure on the Indonesian government, causing it to back down and accept the international intervention (Blaxland 2016: 128). Second, it provided valuable logistical capabilities and intelligence support lacked by the international coalition (Blaxland 2016: 128–129). Third, the US maintained a significant offshore military presence via a Marine Amphibious Ready Group supported by a Navy Aegis cruiser. This deterred rogue elements of the Indonesian military or Indonesian-backed militia groups from attempting to confront INTERFET directly, particularly in the tense initial days of the deployment (Blaxland 2016: 129).

Furthermore, leadership of the East Timor intervention demonstrated Australia's worth to the US as a reliable ally in the region. A foreign policy priority of the Bush Administration, when it was voted into office in early 2001, was 'to renew strong and intimate relationships with allies who share American values and can thus share the burden of promoting peace, prosperity, and freedom' (Rice 2000: 47). Australia's performance in East Timor was held up by Washington as a model of how an ally should behave in a regional crisis (Edwards 2005: 46). Canberra was also seen to have acted decisively by intervening in the civil war in the Solomon Islands and against North Korea's rogue behaviour when it intercepted the *Pong Su* in 2003. US policy-makers looked on these initiatives favourably, especially when compared to the inability of its European allies to resolve successive Balkan crises (Wesley 2007: 113–114).

In 2001, Australian Prime Minister John Howard was quick to invoke the ANZUS Treaty, for the first time in its history, in response to the 9/11 terrorist attacks on the US. This led to Australian military commitments to Afghanistan (from 2002) and Iraq (2003 and 2014) in support of President George W. Bush's War on Terror (Dean 2016: 241). Alan Bloomfield (2015) suggests that these Middle Eastern military commitments conformed to a 'Move Fast, Commit Little' pattern. By committing quickly, he suggests, Canberra hoped to gain a 'first mover advantage' that would reap tangible benefits from the alliance. But the substance of what it offered was limited, especially when compared to other contributors. In Afghanistan, for instance, Australia initially contributed 150 Special Forces troops followed by 950 troops in 2006. The number rose to 1,550 troops by 2009 with the contingent largely based in the comparatively quiet Oruzgan province. In comparison, US troop numbers peaked at 101,000, the UK's peaked at 7,700 and Canada's peaked at 2,300. Similarly, Australia's contribution for the invasion of Iraq (2,048 troops) was much smaller than the US (148,000 troops) or the UK (46,000 troops), with these Australian troops withdrawn by mid-2003 (Bloomfield 2015: 26). Australia certainly reaped many benefits from Howard's approach to the US–Australia strategic relationship. Greg Sheridan (2006) concluded that Howard ended up receiving most of what he wanted from the alliance at very little cost. This was

> an enhanced intelligence relationship; enhanced defence cooperation; greater Australian influence in Washington's decision-making; a free trade agreement; increased US involvement in the region, especially in Indonesia; the greater prestige in Asia that comes from being close to and able to influence Washington; and the enhanced prestige for his government with Australian voters.
>
> (Sheridan 2006: 13)

Unfortunately, however, Australia also developed a reputation in Washington for talking a 'good war'. That is to say, Australia's 'uncritical support comes with words, but not necessarily in the numbers of Australian boots that the Pentagon would like to see on the ground' (Curran 2016: 122).

From Obama to Trump

The US–Australia strategic relationship continued to grow throughout the Obama Administration era and into the present day, with interdependence continuing to be a major theme. At the same time, pressing concerns about China's rise and the impact of the Trump Administration on the effectiveness of US strategy have also emerged. Under the leadership of US President Barack Obama (2008–16), the alliance went from strength to strength 'deepening institutionally and broadening into new areas of cooperation such as cyber security, ballistic missile defence, space cooperation and new measures to combat terrorism' (Taylor and Tow 2017: 81–82). In November 2011, Obama and Australian Prime Minister Julia Gillard jointly announced in

Canberra the Force Posture Initiative, an arrangement where 2,500 US marines would be based in Darwin on a six-month rotational basis, and plans for the US Air Force to make greater use of facilities in northern Australia (Gyngell 2017: 311). This was part of Obama's 'pivot to Asia' strategy. An Obama-commissioned review of global strategy and force disposition had concluded that the US defence posture was unbalanced. Too much of the US's overseas force presence was based in Europe and the Middle East during a time when US predominance in Asia was being tested by China's rising power. Hence, in 2011, Obama revealed a shift in US policy towards the Asia-Pacific region (Gyngell 2017: 310).

Another important change was Australia's inclusion of the Indian Ocean in the framing of its strategic environment. The term 'Indo-Pacific' was increasingly being used in official language, with its first official appearance in the *2013 Defence White Paper* and then again in the *2016 Defence White Paper.* In contrast to the more familiar 'Asia-Pacific', which predominantly focused on the area north of Australia, the Indo-Pacific strategic concept was an attempt to elevate the importance of the maritime environments on either side of Australia and the critical sea lines of communication from the Middle East through Southeast Asia to North Asia (Gyngell 2017: 315). The change in emphasis was also motivated by a desire to give more attention to India. The thought being that an increasingly powerful India would make a valuable addition to the US's regional alliances by acting as a counterweight to China's rise (Gyngell 2017: 315). It is far from certain, however, that India is willing to play such a role for the US. Such an alliance with India, suggest Nick Bisley and Andrew Phillips, risks entangling Washington in the long-running Sino-Indian rivalry. The US would then take on a substantial strategic burden without the 'compensating benefit of securing India as a reliable junior ally prepared to uncomplainingly support US hegemony' (Bisley and Phillips 2013: 105).

As the US–Australia strategic relationship moves into the future, a pressing concern is the potential for disagreement on how to approach the rise of China. The US is undoubtedly Australia's most important strategic ally, but China is its largest trading partner. Hence, Australia's goal is for the two powers to find ways to avoid serious conflict. Hugh White stirred up some controversy, however, when he suggested that in order to pursue such conflict avoidance, Australia should push the US to relinquish regional primacy and agree to share power with China. He suggested that Australia should urge the US to treat China as an equal on key strategic issues, such as nuclear strategy and Taiwan (White, 2011: 91). Potentially diverging views on the rise of China has caused a small but growing number of scholars and policy-makers in the US to question Australia's future reliability as an ally (Mahnken 2016: 42). The irony of this, note Michael Green et al. (2015: 8), is that 'for much of Australia's history, its leaders have been nervous about abandonment by its primary ally' and yet now it is 'Australians who worry about entrapment by Washington and Americans that worry about abandonment by Canberra'.

US policy-makers worry about losing Canberra's steadfast support in its strategic rivalry with Beijing. In contrast, Canberra's fear is being pulled into an armed conflict between China and the US.

The other major challenge for the US–Australia strategic relationship is US President Donald Trump's 'transactional' and chaotic approach to making foreign policy decisions. Trump's attacks on various US allies have cast doubt on Washington's willingness to continue supporting the strategic goals that are in Australia's interests. This 'Trump Effect' has sparked a debate in Australia about the trustworthiness of the relationship (Beeson and Bloomfield 2019: 341). Mark Beeson and Alan Bloomfield argue that deep and broad institutionalization has reinforced a natural cultural affinity that imparts powerful path dependency effects on the relationship (Beeson and Bloomfield 2019: 353). The hope is that such features, that have made the US–Australia strategic relationship strong and helped it endure over time, are sufficient to mitigate any long-term harm caused by the Trump Effect. The Trump Administration's mishandling of the coronavirus disease 2019 (COVID-19) pandemic, however, has been an alarming indicator to the international community that US power is potentially declining rapidly, more so than anyone could have anticipated.

Conclusion

The US–Australia strategic relationship today is an *interdependent* partnership that has experienced a number of historical phases in its evolution. First of all, in the 'Imperial Rivalry' era, Australia's views were synonymous with Britain's imperial grand strategy. The US was simply one of a number of great power rivals to Britain. The visit of the US Great White Fleet to Sydney Harbour in 1908, however, signalled the beginning of the 'Military Cooperation' phase. This culminated in the joint effort to defeat Japan's armed forces in the Pacific Theatre of the Second World War. Next, the 'Strategic Dependence' phase began when the ANZUS security agreement was signed, making Australia an important part of the US 'hub-and-spokes' system of regional bilateral alliances. Over the next 20 years, Australia shifted its strategic dependence from Britain to the US. In the wake of the Vietnam War, the strategic relationship entered the 'Self-Reliance' phase. This paved the way for a more strategically interdependent US–Australia relationship. Then, the decade that followed the East Timor crisis was the 'Military Interventions' phase, where Australia was focused on demonstrating loyalty to the US. Most recently, the relationship reached the 'Strategic Interdependence' phase as it continued to flourish throughout the Obama Administration era and into the present day.

Strategic interdependence means that the US–Australia relationship is not merely a one-sided affair. It also means that Australia has something of substance to offer the strategic relationship. Part of the reason that the relationship is strong is because of a shared language, similar social values, and compatible political-legal systems. Moreover, the relationship has been thoroughly institutionalized via intelligence cooperation, defence science collaboration, and extensive personal relationships. But what the US really seems to value is Australia's reliability as an ally. Australia best demonstrates its reliability as an ally, however, when it follows US strategic decision-making *for the right reasons*. This sense of reliability is more akin to trustworthiness than it is to loyalty. History demonstrates that Australia has not always agreed with the US. But agreeing does not matter so much when Australia has established a track record of consistently applying sound reasoning to its strategic decisions and making substantive contributions to jointly sought-after strategic outcomes.

References

Albinski, H. S. (1987), *ANZUS, the United States, and Pacific Security*, Lanham, MD: University Press of America.

Ball, D. (2001), 'The Strategic Essence,' *Australian Journal of International Affairs*, 55 (2).

Barkawi, T. (1998), 'Strategy as a Vocation: Weber, Morgenthau and Modern Strategic Studies', *Review of International Studies*, 24 (2).

Beaumont, J. (2013), *Broken Nation: Australians in the Great War*, Crows Nest: Allen and Unwin.

Beeson, M. (2003), 'Australia's Relationship With The United States: The Case For Greater Independence', *Australian Journal Of Political Science*, 38 (3).

Beeson, M., and Bloomfield, A. (2019), 'The Trump Effect Downunder: US Allies, Australian Strategic Culture, and the Politics of Path Dependence', *Contemporary Security Policy*, 40 (3).

Bell, C. (1996), *The Cold War in Retrospect: Diplomacy, Strategy and Regional Impact*, Canberra: Strategic and Defence Studies Centre.

Bell, C. (1988), *Dependent Ally: A Study in Australian Foreign Policy*, Melbourne: Oxford University Press.

Bisley, N., and Phillips, A. (2013), 'Rebalance to Where?: US Strategic Geography in Asia', *Survival*, 55 (5).

Blaxland, J. (2016), 'US–Australian Military Cooperation in Asia', in P. Dean, S. Frühling and B. Taylor (eds), *Australia's American Alliance*, Carlton: Melbourne University Press.

Bloomfield, A. (2015), 'First Mover Advantage? Australia's "Move Fast, Commit Little" Grand Strategic Followership Pattern', Conference Paper, British International Studies Association.

Bloomfield, A. and Nossal, K. R. (2010), 'End of an Era? Anti-Americanism in the Australian Labor Party', *Australian Journal of Politics & History*, 56 (4).

Brabin-Smith, R. (2016), 'Capability Development and Defence Research', in P. Dean, S. Frühling, and B. Taylor (eds), *Australia's American Alliance*, Carlton: Melbourne University Press.

Brands, H. (2014), *What Good Is Grand Strategy?: Power and Purpose in American Statecraft from Harry S. Truman to George W. Bush*, Ithaca, NY: Cornell University Press.

Buckley, R. (2002), *The United States in the Asia-Pacific Since 1945*, Cambridge: Cambridge University Press.

Carr, A. (2016), 'ANZUS and Australia's Role in World Affairs', in P. Dean, S. Frühling, and B. Taylor (eds), *Australia's American Alliance*, Carlton: Melbourne University Press.

Cha, V. D. (2010), 'Powerplay: Origins of the US Alliance System in Asia', *International Security*, 34 (3).

Crompton, B. (2008), 'Civil War Participants Born in Australia and New Zealand', https://web.archive.org/web/20090217060350/http://users.bigpond.com/bcrompton/A usborn.htm accessed 26 April 2020.

Curran, J. (2016), *Fighting with America: Why Saying 'No' to the US Wouldn't Rupture the Alliance*, Sydney: Penguin.

Dean, P. J. (2016), 'The Alliance, Australia's Strategic Culture and Way of War', in P. Dean, S. Frühling, and B. Taylor (eds), *Australia's American Alliance*, Carlton: Melbourne University Press.

Dibb, P. (1986), *Review of Australia's Defence Capabilities*, Canberra: Australian Government Publishing Service.

Edwards, P. (2005), *Permanent Friends?: Historical Reflections on the Australian-American Alliance*, Sydney: Lowy Institute of International Policy.

Edwards, P. (1997), *A Nation at War: Australian Politics, Society and Diplomacy During the Vietnam War 1965–1975*, St Leonards, NSW: Allen & Unwin.

Frühling, S. (2018), 'Is ANZUS Really an Alliance? Aligning the US and Australia', *Survival*, 60 (5).

Frühling, S. (2016), 'Wrestling with Commitment: Geography, Alliance Institutions and the ANZUS Treaty', in P. Dean, S. Frühling, and B. Taylor (eds), *Australia's American Alliance*, Carlton: Melbourne University Press.

Green, M., Dean, P. J., Taylor, B., and Cooper, Z. (2015), *The ANZUS Alliance in an Ascending Asia*, Canberra: Strategic and Defence Studies Centre.

Grey, J. (2008), *A Military History of Australia* (3rd ed.), Cambridge: Cambridge University Press.

Gyngell, A. (2017), *Fear of Abandonment: Australia in the World since 1942*, Carlton: LaTrobe University Press.

Henry, I. D. (2020), 'What Allies Want: Reconsidering Loyalty, Reliability, and Alliance Interdependence', *International Security*, 44 (4).

Ikenberry, G. J. (2005), 'Power and Liberal Order: America's Postwar World Order in Transition', *International Relations of the Asia-Pacific*, 5 (2).

Ikenberry, G. J. (2004), 'American Hegemony and East Asian Order', *Australian Journal of International Affairs*, 58 (3).

Jones, M. (2004), 'The Radford Bombshell: Anglo-Australian-US Relations, Nuclear Weapons and the Defence of South East Asia, 1954–57', *Journal of Strategic Studies*, 27 (4).

Leaver, R. (1997), 'Patterns of Dependence in Post-War Australian Foreign Policy', in R. Leaver and D. Cox (eds), *Middling, Meddling, Muddling: Issues in Australian Foreign Policy*, Sydney: Allen & Unwin.

Lee, D. (1993), 'Australia and Allied Strategy in the Far East, 1952–1957', *Journal of Strategic Studies*, 16 (4).

Lee, D. (1992), '*Australia, the British Commonwealth and the United States, 1950–1953*', *Journal of Imperial and Commonwealth History*, 20 (3).

Lowe, D. (2001), 'Percy Spender's Quest', *Australian Journal of International Affairs*, 55 (2).

Lyon, R., and Tow, W. T. (2003), *The Future of the Australian–US Security Relationship*, Carlisle Barracks, PA: Army War College.

Mahnken, T. G. (2016), 'The Australia–US Alliance in American Strategic Policy', in P. Dean, S. Frühling, and B. Taylor (eds), *Australia's American Alliance*, Carlton: Melbourne University Press.

McCaffrie, J., and Rahman, C. (2014), 'The US Strategic Relationship with Australia', in C. Lord and A. S. Erikson (eds), *Rebalancing US Forces: Basing and Forward Presence in the Asia-Pacific*, Annapolis, MD: Naval Institute Press.

McLean, D. (1990), 'ANZUS Origins: A Reassessment', *Australian Historical Studies*, 24 (94).

McLean, D. (2006), 'From British Colony to American Satellite? Australia and the USA During the Cold War', *Australian Journal of Politics and History*, 52 (1).

Parkin, R., and Lee, D. (2008), *Great White Fleet to Coral Sea: Naval Strategy and the Development of Australian-United States Relations, 1900–1945*, Barton, ACT: Department of Foreign Affairs and Trade.

Reckner, J. R. (2001), '"A Sea of Troubles": the Great White Fleet's 1908 War Plans for Australia and New Zealand', in D. Stevens and J. Reeve (eds), *Southern Trident: Strategy, History and the Rise of Australian Naval Power*, Crows Nest, NSW: Allen and Unwin.

Rice, C. (2000), 'Promoting the National Interest', *Foreign Affairs*, 79 (1).

Sheridan, G. (2006), *The Partnership: The Inside Story of the US–Australian Alliance Under Bush and Howard*, Sydney: New South Publishing.

Siracusa, J. M. (2005), 'The ANZUS Treaty Revisited', *Security Challenges*, 1 (1).

Smyth, T. (2015), *Australian Confederates*, North Sydney: Random House Australia.

Taylor, B., and Tow, W. T. (2017), 'Crusaders and Pragmatists: Australia Debates the American Alliance', in M. Wesley (ed.), *Global Allies: Comparing US Alliances in the 21st Century*, Canberra: ANU Press.

Tow, S. (2017), *Independent Ally: Australia in an Age of Power Transition*, Melbourne: Melbourne University Publishing.

Tow, W. T. (2001), *Asia-Pacific Strategic Relations: Seeking Convergent Security*, Cambridge: Cambridge University Press.

Tow, W. T., & Albinski, H. (2002), 'ANZUS – Alive and Well After Fifty Years', *Australian Journal of Politics & History*, 48 (2).

Walt, S. M. (1997), 'Why Alliances Endure or Collapse', *Survival*, 39 (1).

Watt, A. (1967), *The Evolution of Australian Foreign Policy: 1938–1965*, London: Cambridge University Press.

Wesley, M. (2016a), 'The Alliance as an Intelligence Partnership', in P. Dean, S. Frühling, and B. Taylor (eds), *Australia's American Alliance*, Carlton: Melbourne University Press.

Wesley, M. (2016b), 'Australia's Grand Strategy and the 2016 Defence White Paper', *Security Challenges*, 12 (1).

Wesley, M. (2007), *The Howard Paradox: Australian Diplomacy in Asia 1996–2006*, Sydney: ABC Books.

White, H. (2011), 'Power Shift: Rethinking Australia's Place in the Asian Century', *Australian Journal of International Affairs*, 65 (1).

7 Defence cooperation between Australia and the United States

Alan Bloomfield

Australia and the United States engage in a lot of defence cooperation: both typically support each other's broad strategic goals; their troops regularly fight (and train) together; Australia hosts key US communications and surveillance facilities, plus the two states generally cooperate closely in intelligence matters; and Australia sources a very high proportion – typically more than half by Australian dollar (A$) value – of its defence equipment from the US. Moreover, the broad trend of late is one of ever-closer bilateral defence ties, and there is a good reason to believe that this trend will continue and likely also intensify. That reason, of course, is the rise of People's Republic of China. Despite some divergence related to somewhat dissimilar economic interests, Canberra and Washington seem to hold broadly similar views about the likely strategic implications of, and the appropriate defence-policy responses to, China's rise.

Readers should also note, first, that the focus of analysis in this chapter is on the near-past, mainly the decade between 2010 and 2020, because other chapters in this volume survey the deeper history of the Australia–US relationship. Second, the perspective taken is primarily an Australian one, reflecting the expertise (and citizenship) of the author.

The strategic realm

There are significant differences between the 'raw power' capabilities of each state. The United States remains the single-most-powerful state in the world, with an economy about 14 times larger than Australia's, a population about 13 times bigger, and defence spending about 18 times higher. Put simply, the US is the global hegemon with interests all over the world and ample capabilities to pursue them, while Australia is a middle power which pursues a narrower range of interests, focused mainly on the Indo-Pacific.

Yet their grand strategies are quite complementary because both are *status quo* powers in the sense Morgenthau used the phrase ('The policy of the status quo aims at the maintenance of the [current] distribution of power'; Morgenthau 1978: 46). This is readily apparent in Australia's 2016 defence white paper; it was said fifty-six times that Australia would act to buttress the so-called 'rules-based order' which was largely created after 1945 by the United States (Kagan 2012). The single-most illuminating paragraph is the following one:

> The United States will remain the pre-eminent global military power over the next two decades. It will continue to be Australia's most important strategic partner through our long-standing alliance, and the active presence of the United States will continue to underpin the stability of our region. The global strategic and economic weight of the United States will be essential to the continued stability of the rules-based global order on which Australia relies for our security and prosperity. The world will continue to look to the United States for leadership in global security affairs and to lead military coalitions that support international security and the rules-based global order.
>
> (Australian Government 2016: 41)

There is, of course, an elephant in the room: China is now Australia's single-largest trading partner, accounting for over one-quarter of total bilateral trade. And in a reversal of the dynamic which prevails in the US–China economic relationship, Australia typically enjoys a healthy surplus; in 2019 this stood at A$52 billion ($123bn exports to versus $71bn imports from China: Australian Government 2019a: 17, 32). Further, few Australian companies manufacture in China, meaning the allegations of Chinese technology-theft which increasingly strain other Western states' ties to China are a less-pressing issue for Australia.

These matters are why Hugh White, probably Australia's most influential contemporary strategic thinker, presented his 'China Choice' thesis in 2010. His premise was simple:

> There is a problem with Australia's vision of its future. On the one hand, we assume that China will just keep growing indefinitely, buying more and more … On the other hand, we expect America to remain the strongest power in Asia, the region's natural leader and Australia's ultimate protector. We will have a very nice future if both these things happen. The problem is that they cannot both happen at once.
>
> (White 2010: 1)

White's thesis that Australia faces a 'hard', 'inevitable' choice has been critiqued from numerous angles (He 2014: 248–251; Taylor and Tow 2017) and repudiated by senior politicians from both major parties (Bloomfield 2016: 260). There is some evidence that in the mid-2000s China felt it might be able to 'peel off' some US allies – including Australia – using economic enticements, but a decade later Beijing had abandoned the idea (Lui and Hao 2014: 357). Nick Bisley concluded in 2013 that Australia had already chosen to stay closely aligned with the United States strategically. His conclusion was grounded in a rationalist cost-benefit analysis of the ANZUS alliance for Australia. The main benefits were: 'the USA would come to Australia's aid in the event that it was attacked'; 'privileged access to US military hardware and training'; 'access to US intelligence networks and technology'; and 'access to Washington'. The main costs were: 'provision of geographic advantages', meaning Australia hosts US defence facilities which may become targets if the US fought a high-intensity war against another great power; 'burden-sharing', or contributing to US military operations even when Australia's vital interests were not at stake; and 'diplomatic and political support' of US policies which might be unpopular at home and/or may damage some of Australia's other foreign relations (Bisley 2013: 405–408). Bisley ultimately concluded that the benefits considerably outweigh the costs, and while there have always been dissenting voices (Teichmann 1966; Cheeseman 1993; Beeson 2003; Fraser 2014), over the long-term most surveys of this type have reached similar conclusions to Bisley's.

For the 'view from Washington' – ironically, delivered by an Australian – Thomas Wilkins created a '"ledger" of national "assets" and "liabilities"' which 'inverts the usual preoccupation of Australian analyses of why the country values the US alliance to emphasise more why and how the United States values Australia' (Wilkins 2019: 12). The first asset was 'loyalty', meaning Australia can be trusted to consistently support most US foreign policies. The second was 'military contribution': notably, of America's major overseas military operations since 1945 the only two which Australia did not participate in were the 1983 invasion of Grenada and the 2011 Libyan intervention (which Australia lobbied strongly for, and voted for, in the Security Council). The third asset was 'defence/economic collaboration'; Wilkins noted that in the mid-2010s Australia was spending about A\$13 million per day on American weapons. The fourth was 'regional networking', by which Australia draws other states and regional organizations in Asia – especially Singapore, Indonesia and ASEAN – closer to Washington 'by proxy'. The fifth was 'convergent threat perceptions', meaning that 'the allies co-operat[e] against challengers to the liberal international order'. The sixth and final asset was 'ideological-compatibility' (of which more is said below).

Against these six assets Wilkins only found three liabilities: 'power-asymmetry', meaning Canberra is just one of many smaller allies competing for Washington's attention; 'path dependency-sunk costs', meaning Washington may sometimes ignore Australia's concerns, and/or just assume Australia will back it without consulting Canberra first; and 'complex economic interdependence', especially vis-à-vis Australia's trade interests with China (Wilkins 2019: 14–22). While Wilkins noted that more work was needed to determine the relative weighting of each factor (and how they interact), he concluded that 'assets have far outweighed liabilities', meaning Australia is clearly a valuable ally from America's perspective (Wilkins 2019: 30).

Others invoke constructivist logic to explain the strong relationship. Constructivists assert that ultimately states' interests 'flow from' their identities

(Wendt 1999: ch. 3), meaning culturally similar states tend to have similar interests, which can underpin a so-called 'security community' marked by 'trust and collective identity formation' (Adler and Barnett 1998: 29–31). It is commonly accepted that Australia and the US are members of the 'Anglosphere' security community. Defence cooperation between these states is both too intense and too stable to be explained solely with reference to rationalist understandings of interests. Instead, the strong, consistent strategic cooperation in varied contexts over many decades is ultimately 'a function of ... collective/shared identity' (Vucetic 2011: 263), meaning that one state's 'core interests [become] encapsulated in their counterpart's own interests, and vice versa' (Hardin, quoted in Wesley 2016: 147).

This sort of logic is regularly enunciated by policy-makers from both major Australian political parties. For example, when asked about Australia–US ties in 1997, former Liberal Party Prime Minister John Howard said 'it is common values that in the end bind us together more tightly than anything else' (Howard 1997). More recently – and with direct reference to White's 'hard/inevitable choice' thesis – former Labor Party Foreign Minister Bob Carr said 'we'll go with American values if we've got to choose' because 'Australians will always prefer American values' (Carr 2014: 98, 294).

Of course, similar values/identity alone and the similar interests which such generate (if you accept the constructivist position, as this author does) do not guarantee close alliance relations, they must be 'buttressed by' or perhaps 'expressed in' institutional arrangements too. This author recently argued (Beeson and Bloomfield 2019: 344–347) that the so-called 'Trump Effect' (i.e. negative consequences of US President Donald Trump's foreign policies) was not nearly strong enough to undermine the alliance given the relationship's 'institutional density', including:

- Strong formal-treaty links (the 1951 ANZUS treaty, plus the 1963 'status of forces' treaty) which are operationalized in over 1000 currently active/relevant Memoranda of Understanding (MoUs).
- Strong economic links, structured by the 2004 Australia–US Free trade Agreement, whereby the US is Australia's third biggest trade partner ($69 billion two-way, with a surplus in America's favour of A$27 billion in 2019: Australian Government 2019a, 17 and 32). The US is also the largest investor in Australia (A$894 billion, 24% of total FDI in 2019: 42)
- The annual AUSMIN talks between each state's defence and foreign ministers/secretaries, plus dense person-to-person links at the 'deep-state' level.
- So-called 'Track 2' academic, business, sporting, social (etc.) linkages.
- Very strong, consistent, Australian public opinion in favour of the alliance (support averages 77% across the 15 Lowy Polls since the first in 2005; see Kassam 2019: 11).

The broader argument advanced in that article was that Australian strategic culture has been marked by a strong, enduring preference for closely aligning with an Anglo great power, first Britain and then the United States (Beeson and Bloomfield 2019: 347–349). Strategic cultures typically exhibit powerful path-dependent tendencies (Beeson and Bloomfield 2019: 339–340), and more importantly, there are currently no other states which could replace the US as Australia's 'great and powerful friend', and no reason to expect that situation to change soon (Beeson and Bloomfield 2019: 349–352). For Australia to choose a strictly independent strategic posture would involve the most radical strategic cultural change ever, and it would probably take an unprecedently severe exogenous shock – like the US losing a high-intensity conflict with China and being driven out of Australia's region – before such happened (Beeson and Bloomfield 2019: 352–353).

Stephan Frühling, however, recently asked 'Is ANZUS really an Alliance?' (Frühling 2018) given there is no equivalent to Article V of the NATO treaty ('an armed attack against one or more … shall be considered an attack against them all'). Instead, Article III of ANZUS states 'The Parties will *consult* together' (emphasis added) if one is attacked, and Article IV says 'Each Party … would act to meet the common danger *in accordance with its constitutional processes*'(emphasis added), which provides firm legal grounds for one party to 'dodge' the other's request for military assistance. There is also no integrated command arrangement, like that for NATO or the US–South Korea alliance (Frühling 2018: 202), or even broadly stated war-plans to respond to various contingencies like those in the US–Japan Defense Guidelines (Frühling 2018: 201).

Frühling's points are well-taken, and of course from Australia's perspective the twin alliance dilemmas Glenn Snyder (1984: 466–468) identified – 'entrapment' in an ally's wars or 'abandonment' by an ally when threatened – have long been considered potential problems for Australia (respectively: Beeson 2003; Gyngell 2017). Indeed, the Americans are not worry-free either. Two Americans, Michael Green and Zack Cooper, have argued that Australia's economic interests with China – and Washington's appreciation of such – means 'it is Australia which [now] worries about entrapment … and Americans who worry about abandonment' (Green et al. 2015: 8).

Nevertheless, while we should not entirely dismiss concerns like these, entrapment and/or abandonment are potential problems which *all* allies have vis-à-vis each other (Snyder 1984). Further, the wording of the key ANZUS articles is virtually identical to that in the US–Philippines, US–South Korea, and US–Japan treaties, and is 'stronger' than many others (i.e. the US–Pakistan Mutual Defence Association Agreement; see Wesley 2016: 146). Comparatively speaking, the Australia–US strategic relationship seems very strong, perhaps the third-strongest behind Israel–US and United Kingdom–US. Accordingly, it seems very likely that the Australia–US alliance relationship will remain a very close one well into the foreseeable future.

Joint operations and training

This section considers the allies' joint operations, starting with combat operations in the past decade, then the 'war-gaming' both states' armed forces undertook together recently.

The decade began with the Australian forces which had been deployed to Iraq between 2003 and 2009 already withdrawn. They would return, however, when Islamic State (IS) emerged in 2014. The speed, if not the scale, of Australia's contribution to *Operation Okra* (i.e. the Australian Defence Force's (ADF) label for the anti-IS campaign) is indicative of the loyalty which Wilkins noted was probably Australia's greatest alliance-asset (Wilkins 2019: 15).

Canberra does have an interest in Middle Eastern stability – it sources some petroleum from the region and is concerned about Islamic terrorism – yet it certainly has far fewer, and less-pressing, interests than Washington. Nevertheless, a week before the US announced it would re-commit its forces to Iraq to combat IS, then-Prime Minister Tony Abbott telegraphed that Australia would too, if requested (Sheridan 2014). Less than 24 hours after Washington formally requested Australian assistance (on 31 August 2014) Abbott agreed. On 3 September Royal Australian Air Force (RAAF) planes air-dropped weapons to Kurdish forces in northern Iraq, and on 14 September a 600-strong ADF contingent arrived in the Middle East. This consisted of 400 RAAF personnel with 6 F/A-18F *Super Hornets*, plus an AEW&C plane and an in-flight refuelling 'tanker', plus 200 Australian Army troops to train Iraqi forces (300 more followed in March 2015). The RAAF jets began air strikes against IS targets on 17 September 2014, and by the end of operations in January 2018 2,700 sorties had been flown. Importantly, when commenting on the possibility that the US may call for Australian Army combat units to be deployed in May 2015, Abbott said:

> The US is obviously the leading Western country ... [W]e don't expect [it] to do what needs to be done in the defence of decency right around the world on its own, and that is why Australia has been more than ready to be an utterly reliable partner ... As always, we stand ready ... to do what we can to help.
>
> (Nicholson and Owens 2015)

Ultimately the US did not commit ground forces, so neither did Australia. Yet the virtually automatic, highly accommodating reaction by America's 'utterly reliable partner' is consistent with long-standing dynamics in the bilateral relationship.

ADF personnel also spent the whole decade in Afghanistan. Australian special forces took part the 2001 invasion, and were withdrawn in November 2002. But 950 ADF personnel redeployed in 2006 when *Operation Slipper* began, with the number rising to 1,550 in 2009, and these units fought regularly in the restive Oruzgan Province. *Slipper* continued until 31 December

2014; by then 41 Australians had been killed in combat. But some ADF personnel remained, transitioning into *Operation Highroad*, a NATO-led training-only operation, which continues today (numbers deployed have varied between about 200 and 400).

Finally, when IS-affiliates began fighting openly against Philippines military and police units in Marawi in May 2017, Australia committed 100 ADF personnel, including a special forces training unit and two *Orion* surveillance planes. The request for assistance came from Manila, not Washington, but the ADF personnel worked closely with in-theatre US forces (Cox 2018).

It is worth noting, however, the *absence* of one type of joint Australian–US operation which could have taken place; Australia has not participated in a 'freedom of navigation operation' alongside the US Navy in the South China Sea (on the *surface*: see below). The US Navy periodically sails within 12 nautical miles of the 'islands' that China has created in the South China Sea to dispute Beijing's claims to virtually the entire South China Sea.

This matter has stimulated controversy in Australia. Taylor and Tow have identified two camps: 'Crusaders' typically 'argue that Canberra should "double down" on the American alliance ... [to] see[] off the Chinese challenge to the US-led security order in Asia'. Crusaders thus call for Canberra to dispatch Royal Australian Navy (RAN) vessels to participate in the US Navy patrols (Taylor and Tow 2017: 77–78). Yet the 'Pragmatists' – persons 'who contend that Canberra needs to establish a greater degree of autonomy from Washington' – disagree, arguing that to carry out (surface) operations of this sort would draw unnecessary, adverse Chinese anger (Taylor and Tow 2017: 85–86). Australia has, however, been conducting *overflights* of the Chinese 'islands'. The RAAF confirmed in 2016 that the planes' crews are 'nearly always challenged' by Chinese forces over radio, and then-Defence Minister Marise Payne bluntly stated 'Australian vessels and aircraft will continue to exercise rights under international law to freedom of navigation and freedom of overflight, including in the South China Sea' (Tiezzi 2016). *Operation Gateway* RAAF surveillance flights over the north-east Indian Ocean and over the South China Sea have been ongoing since 1985 in accordance with Australia's Five Power Defence Pact obligations. Accordingly, Australia can say 'it's just business as usual' while simultaneously challenging China's illegal claims.

Regarding training, in 2019 the seventh iteration of the biennial *Operation Talisman Sabre* took place in Australia's north. This was a very large war game involving 34,000 troops, mainly Australian and American, but with contingents from Canada, Japan, the United Kingdom and New Zealand too. The centrepiece was a simulated amphibious assault to 'liberate' an island in Shoalwater Bay in northern Queensland. Another large biennial exercise which Australia participates in alongside US forces is RIMPAC. The last iteration took place in 2018, and Australia sent four RAN surface vessels, a submarine, a *Poseidon* surveillance plane and an Army battalion (1,600 personnel in total). The RAAF also holds biennial *Pitch Black* exercises with the

US Air Force and other friendly states. The latest iteration took place in 2018 in Australia's Northern Territory, and involved 141 aircraft and about 4,000 personnel. In addition, in 2011 the RAN frigate HMAS *Darwin* sailed 'alongside' the US Navy Carrier Strike Group centred around USS *George Washington*, and in 2013 HMAS *Sydney* was fully integrated and 'under orders' from the American Flag Admiral. The RAN was keen to gain first-hand knowledge of America's *Aegis* combat-control system given it would be fitted to the *Hobart*-class destroyers then being built for the RAN (Blaxland 2016: 135).

Further, since 2012 a 'Marine Rotational Force' has spent time in and around Darwin, in Australia's far-north. This has steadily increased in size – it reached the projected 2,500 personnel in 2019 (i.e. a full Marine Expeditionary Unit: MEU) – and they stayed for just over 6-months in 2019, taking part in *Talisman Sabre* plus four other 'live-fire' exercises (*Koolendong, Southern Jackaroo, Diamond Storm* and *Carabaroo*) involving battalion-sized units, plus dozens of other smaller-unit exercises (Australian Government 2019b).

There are two further matters to address. First, in the past decade the ADF has worked regularly alongside US forces to deliver disaster relief in the region; in Japan in 2011, the Philippines in 2013, and in Fiji in 2016. Second, defence personnel from both nations are regularly 'exchanged and embedded' in the other's armed forces. The numbers vary, but an (undated) page on Australia's Washington Embassy website says:

> Australia has approximately 580 Defence personnel in the United States, spread across 31 states, and the District of Columbia. The majority are embedded into the US military – effectively filling the role as if they were a member of the American military – in US units or work alongside US partners on combined project teams on issues including operational planning and intelligence, capability development, military education, and legal support.
>
> (Australian Government n.d. a)

Australians have also recently begun to hold very senior roles in US command structures. For example, in 2013 Major-General Rick Burr was appointed as Deputy Commanding General: Operations, in US Army Pacific Command. After two years he was succeeded by Major-General Greg Bilton, and since then it has become customary for a senior Australian Army officer to serve in this post (the incumbent is Major-General Chris Field). Senior ADF officers – from the RAAF and RAN – have held similar senior positions in the US Air Force and the US Navy command structures during RIMPAC exercises too (Green et al. 2015: 16).

'Foreign' bases and intelligence cooperation

Canberra insists there are 'no foreign bases' in Australia. But this is only technically true given that the 'Joint' Facilities which 'host' US personnel in Australia have only a limited – although typically not a 'token' – Australian presence. These are discussed in more detail below; we consider access-arrangements at ordinary ADF bases first.

US forces are typically granted access to ADF bases upon request (and in accordance with specific MoUs). For example, during a large exercise like *Talisman Sabre*, US forces are housed at the ADF bases closest to where the exercise takes place. Notably, as part of the regular Marine Rotational Force visits to Darwin (see above), US Air Force units have begun visiting nearby RAAF *Tindal* airfield more often (Taylor and Tow 2017: 82). Robertson Barracks in Darwin was also expanded significantly to house the MEU when it rotates through, and it also hosts a small permanent American command, communications and logistics centre which, put colloquially, 'holds the fort' during the six months when the MEU is absent (Australian Government n.d. b).

Since the Marines began rotating through Darwin there has been speculation that substantial upgrades might be made to the RAN's HMAS *Stirling*, near Perth in Western Australia, to enable it to re-provision US Navy submarines (and maybe aircraft carriers too). Similar rumours have circulated about the US Air Force possibly operating Unmanned Aerial Vehicles (UAVs) out of the Cocos/Keeling Islands; the 2019 decision to widen the (mainly civilian-use) airport's runway to accommodate RAAF *Poseidon* aircraft, meaning large American *Triton* UAVs could operate from there too, fuelled those rumours (Levick 2019; but some remain sceptical: see Jennings 2016: 59).

Finally, reports emerged in mid-2019 that '$US211.5 million (A$305.9 million) has been allocated for new "Navy Military Construction" in Darwin', by the US Congress (Greene 2019). Later, in December, the Australian Defence Department confirmed that A$715 million had been allocated to upgrade the RAN base HMAS *Coonawarra* in Darwin (Robson 2019). Neither government has confirmed exactly what these funds will be spent on, but Washington was upset when the Northern Territory Government leased Darwin's container port to Chinese company Landbridge in 2015 (Taylor and Tow 2017: 82). Larger US Navy vessels unable to dock at *Coonawarra*'s piers have occasionally tied up at the container port, so American officials were concerned about 'being watched' by Chinese nationals working in the port's administrative buildings. The geography of Darwin harbour means it would be more difficult for foreign agents to surreptitiously surveil *Coonawarra*.

Turning now to the Joint Facilities, they are mainly US-run, so readers should think about them in this way: Canberra is fully aware of what their broad capabilities and purposes are, but typically knows little about the day-to-day operational decisions informed by data gathered by them. For example, US forces do not seek permission from Australia to carry out particular drone strikes after gathering targeting data through Pine Gap (Tanter 2013: 119–122). One can therefore quibble with the 2016 defence white paper's claim that the 'policy of full knowledge and concurrence ensur[es] that all activities at the Joint Facilities are consistent with Australia's interests' (Australian Government 2016: 122). Nevertheless, the Joint Facilities' importance to Washington means they have for decades been regarded by Australian strategists as 'the jewel in the crown' (Jennings 2019) of the Australia–US strategic relationship.

Three Joint Facilities are currently of particular importance. The first is the Kojarena base near Geraldton in Western Australia, which is 'the Australian anchor' of the UKUSA global satellite communications system. Further, Australia joined the American-led Wideband Global SATCOM communications system by contributing almost A$1 billion dollars – the cost of one of the ten satellites (so far: an eleventh will be launched in 2023) – which gives Canberra dedicated-access to the system (Tanter 2013: 95–97).

The second is the Naval Communication Station Harold E. Holt, located near Exmouth, also in Western Australia. It was initially built in the 1960s so the US Navy could communicate with its nuclear-armed ballistic missile submarines in the Indian Ocean using Very Low Frequency (VLF) transmissions. Interestingly, in the 1990s the development of the *Trident* SLBM system meant this base became less important because America could deploy its 'boomers' in the Pacific. Australia therefore took over the base in 1999. But a decade later the US Navy decided that it needed to operate from there to communicate with its attack submarines; the Indian Ocean region had risen in importance given the ongoing Middle Eastern operations and more Chinese naval activity too (Bloomfield 2018). The RAN also communicates with its *Collins*-class submarines through one of the four main communications channels. Finally, in 2020 the newest edition to the base – an optical telescope in the US Air Force's Space Surveillance Telescope system – will be installed. The RAAF will also use this system when it becomes operational (Tanter 2013: 100–102; Beattie 2019).

The final and most-important Joint Facility is Pine Gap, near Alice Springs in the Northern Territory. Somewhat ironically, the secrecy associated with Pine Gap has generated much public interest and, inevitably, conspiracy theories. For example, there is (allegedly) 'a secret room no Australian can enter', and (allegedly) a CIA officer stationed there played a key role in the 1975 dismissal of Prime Minister Gough Whitlam by Australia's Governor-General. Indeed, a conspiratorially-themed Netflix TV series, *Pine Gap*, aired in 2019.

Pine Gap houses two main systems. The first relies on a varying number of antennas (33 in 2016: Ball et al. 2016) which uplink to numerous US and allied, especially British, satellites, radar systems – terrestrially located, on naval vessels, on surveillance planes, etc. – and terrestrial microwave transmitters (like the VLF system mentioned above). There is also a substantial data *analysis* centre, meaning that if the other two similar facilities (in Colorado in the US and Menwith Hill in the UK) were destroyed, Pine Gap could potentially take over and run the entire the United States' global sur-veillance and communications system. The second system located at Pine gap is a Remote Ground Station which controls and receives data from infra-red satellites which can detect missile launches, aircraft engines, terrestrial explo-sions and fires, etc. (Tanter 2013: 108–110). The ADF also uses these systems under strictly secret, so poorly understood, sharing arrangements.

We cannot explore all the implications for Australia of hosting such an important American facility as Pine Gap: readers should refer to Desmond Ball's work, especially *A Suitable Piece of Real Estate* (1980; summarized in Tanter 2013: 116–139). Consider, for example, how culpable is Australia in legally and/or morally questionable drone strikes against targets in states the US is not technically 'at war with', like Yemen or Pakistan? But the single-biggest controversy for decades has been whether Pine Gap would be a nuclear target. We now know the Soviets planned to strike it in many war-fighting scenarios, given its importance to the US (Dibb 2005). More recently, a 'secret appendix' to the 2009 defence white paper reportedly acknowledged that in 'a conflict with the United States, China would attempt to destroy Pine Gap' (Uren 2009: 128). At the risk of over-simplification, Ball concluded that it was in Australia's interests to host the Joint Facilities, especially Pine Gap. First, by enhancing the military capabilities of Australia's primary ally, Aus-tralia's security was enhanced; in particular, Australia benefited from Amer-ica's extended deterrence posture, or 'nuclear umbrella'. Second, the infra-red detection-system enhances international nuclear and ballistic missile non-proliferation efforts.

Finally, we turn to intelligence sharing. We have already seen that Australia has access to 'a lot' – but certainly not 'all' – the signals intelligence data gathered by the Joint Facilities. The precise details of such are hard to dis-cern, partly because the arrangements are classified Ultra Top Secret, and partly because they are continuously changing. But Australia and the United States share a lot of other intelligence too.

First, their units routinely share operational military intelligence in combat zones, and Australians embedded in US units (and vice versa) typically did not have to pass through the other army's security clearance processes if 'home' clearance remained valid (Stephen Barton, personal conversation with the author, Perth, 17 March 2020), except in exceptional circumstances (pre-sumably the Australian Major-Generals serving in senior US roles – see above – were vetted more thoroughly).

Second, most bilateral intelligence-sharing is governed by 'Five Eyes', which Australia joined in 1956 (for a detailed history, see Pfluke 2019). Five Eyes is often presented as key evidence for the Anglosphere being a mature security community (Vucetic 2011: 2). The key norm informing its operation is that intelligence gathered by one member must not be shared by another member with any other state without the gatherer's express permission, and typically the three other members will be consulted too. These practices create and sustain very deep levels of trust (Pfluke 2019:305; O'Neil 2017: 537). It is difficult to provide details about its operations other than to say it primarily shares signals intelligence through the ECHELON system, which automatically intercepts commercial/private satellite signals and then 'sweeps' them for 'key words' using sophisticated software. But plenty of human intelligence is shared too, and Five Eyes has reportedly been the institutional vehicle for sharing oceanographic data, geospatial data, co-ordinating counter-intelligence operations, and even the conduct of belligerent covert missions against enemies (O'Neil 2017: 533–536). Each member has primary responsibility for a geographic region, mainly for gathering SIGINT: Australia monitors its Southeast Asian neighbours, especially Indonesia, and southern China. Five Eyes has also become the basis for intelligence sharing arrangements with other 'friendly' states, although this tends to happen on a temporary, *ad hoc* basis.

Unsurprisingly, the US gathers most of the data given, as Loch Johnson says, it has 'the largest and most expensive intelligence apparatus in the world, indeed, in the history of humankind' (quoted in O'Neil 2017: 529). Interestingly, since 2004 talk has emerged of a 'Three Eyes' sub-grouping after former US President George W. Bush directed the CIA to relax the 'Noforn' (i.e. 'no foreign eyes') designation vis-à-vis Australia and the UK after they supported America's invasion of Iraq (which reportedly upset the Canadians, see Wesley 2016: 158). Accordingly, some Australian strategists believe that intelligence sharing is the single-most valuable aspect of the alliance from Australia's perspective given Canberra receives enormously more intelligence than it could gather on its own (Bisley 2013: 406; Ball 2001: 235). For example, Alan Dupont reports that the two-way flow of data is about 90 per cent in Australia's favour (Dupont 2007: 56). There are, of course, those who have argued that membership in Five Eyes damages Australian interests; see O'Neil (2017: 536–539) for an excellent overview of the debate. But this author is not impressed by the nay-sayers' arguments.

Defence equipment

Australia spent A$36.6 billion on defence (US$23.7 bn in May 2020) in the 2018–2019 financial year. This represents 1.91% of GDP and a 1.35% increase on the previous year. In 2015 Canberra announced defence spending would rise steadily to 2% of GDP in 2020–21. Spending has been going up, but there have been 'pipeline problems' actually spending all the money allocated to capital-acquisition projects (Watt 2018), so it probably won't reach 2% until the mid-2020s. Spending in 2018–19 was broken down 31% on capital investment – mostly new equipment (i.e. some is spent on upgrading ADF bases) – 33% on personnel costs, and 35% on operations, including foreign deployments (Hellyer 2018:6).

The United States is Australia's primary source of defence equipment, with the 2016 defence white paper confirming that 'Around 60 percent of our acquisition spending is on equipment from the United States'. The main reason is stated in the next sentence: 'The cost to Australia of developing these high-end capabilities would be beyond Australia's capacity', with the next-most important reason mentioned immediately, namely, the ADF should 'maintain high levels of interoperability … [which] allows our forces to integrate [with US forces] when they are working together' (Australian Government 2016: 122).

Accordingly, Australia sources most of the RAAF's aircraft from US manufacturers. In particular, all combat aircraft are American, most airlift aircraft are American, and only the 7 tankers and most of the trainers are sourced from Europe. Three Australian-made planes are on order, and if they perform well (they are 'experimental') more will likely be ordered, and possibly produced for export, including to the US (Insinna 2020). But these *Loyal Wingman* UAVs will be built by Boeing Australia which is, of course, a subsidiary of America's Boeing Company. To give readers an appreciation of the RAAF's combat capabilities, it is currently replacing its ageing 'classic' F/A-18 *Hornets* with F-35 *Lightning IIs*; it is expected that all 72 will arrive by 2023. The RAAF also operates 11 EA-18G *Growlers* and 24 F/A-18F *Super Hornets*, and these fast-jets operate closely with six *Wedgetail* AEW&C planes and the seven tankers. Finally, the RAAF is currently replacing its *Orion* maritime surveillance planes with 15 *Poseidons* and seven *Triton* UAVs, and it operates 30 transport aircraft (RAAF n.d.).

The situation is different when it comes to naval shipbuilding. The domestic capacity to build naval vessels has swung wildly in the past century, with 'spurts' of building followed by so-called 'valleys of death' without building, resulting in vital skills being lost and shipyards deteriorating. At times vessels were procured from overseas shipyards, including American yards, but that raised its own problems (especially currency fluctuations: see Australian Government 2006: ch. 3). Accordingly, in 2017 an ambitious Naval Shipbuilding Plan (Australian Government 2017) was released. The RAN's future vessels will be Australian-built at a cost of A$89 billion (in 2017 dollars) over about 25 years.

At least three reasons for Canberra committing to this expensive project can be advanced. First, the idea is to build continuously to avoid another 'valley of death' and, consequently, to keep unit-costs down and build-quality high. Interestingly, the Plan directly references a RAND report which noted the cost-premium of producing vessels in Australia, compared to America, was 30–40% (Birkler et al. 2015: xxxv). The Australian government's Plan somewhat disingenuously implied that this was due solely to the stop-start nature of naval shipbuilding historically (Australian Government 2017: 14), but RAND claims numerous factors cause it (Birkler et al. 2015: ch. 5). Second, Canberra wants to create a 'motivated, innovative, cost-competitive and sustainable Australian industrial base' (Australian Government 2017: 18). This is *prima facie* a reasonable aspiration, but RAND found that while new shipyards usually benefited local economies, 'it is unrealistic to expect that shipbuilders will produce significant favourable spin-offs' in the wider economy (xxxviii), and a recent version of the Australian Strategic Policy Institute's excellent annual *Cost of Defence* report agreed (Hellyer 2018: 62–67). Accordingly, the third reason – unstated in the government's Plan – is arguably classic 'pork-barrelling'; the recent end of car-manufacturing has damaged South Australia's economy and some commentators assume the fact most shipbuilding will take place there is not coincidental (McDonald 2017).

Importantly, Australia remains highly reliant on American contractors for the combat systems and weapons current (and future) RAN vessels require. For example, the *Harpoon, Hellfire, Evolved Sea Sparrow* and SM-2 missiles are all sourced from US defence contractors. The radar, communications and fire-control systems are also typically US equipment; as noted above, the *Hobart*-class destroyers are fitted with the *Aegis* system, and the RAN's web-page explaining what an *Aegis* system is lists 24 sub-systems, all of which are standard US Navy systems (RAN: n.d.). Importantly, while French companies will build (in Australia) the next generation of RAN submarines, these will be fitted with 'upgraded versions of the AN/BYG-1 combat system' (Australian Government 2016: 91) to ensure 'a high degree of interoperability with the United States' (Australian Government 2016: 90).

Readers will likely be interested to know what Australia could potentially contribute to US-led maritime operations. The RAN's largest ships are two 27,000-ton *Canberra*-class Landing Helicopter Docks (i.e. amphibious warfare vessels). The RAN also now operates three 7,000-ton *Hobart*-class Air Warfare Destroyers. The core of the surface fleet is eight 3,600-ton *ANZAC*-class frigates; the first was commissioned in 1996, but they are being or will be given a mid-life overhaul to ensure they last until the nine 'Future Frigates' begin to appear 'from the late 2020s' (a design has not yet been finalized: Australian Government 2016: 93). 6 *Collins*-class submarines are still operating. They will be replaced by 12 new so-called 'Shortfin Barracudas' which will 'begin to enter service in the early 2030s' (Australian Government 2016: 91), although concerns are already rising about the project's viability (Greene 2020). The RAN also operates 13 *Armidale*-class patrol boats, 4 *Huon*-class mine-sweepers, 1 Landing Ship Dock (HMAS *Choules*), 1 replenishment ship (HMAS *Sirius*) and 6 oceanographic survey ships.

Turning to the Australian Army, it is typically less-reliant on US equipment than the other services. For example, most of its small arms and some of its vehicles are produced locally. The 257 ASLAVs (the core of the Army's mobile-strike capability) are Australian made, as are the 1,052 Bushmaster PMVs, and the 1100 on-order Hawkei light-PMVs will be built in Australia too. But the 5,000+ 4WDs and light trucks the Army operates are German-made. The Army's American equipment includes: 59 M1 Abrams tanks, about 400 M113 APCs, 30 helicopters, dozens of battle-field UAVs, and most of the light-vehicle-mounted weapons (grenade launchers, anti-tank missiles, etc.).

Again, readers will likely be interested in the Australian Army's combat capacity. Its 30,810 personnel in 2019 made up about 40% of the total 76,167 ADF 'regulars', although there are also 18,000 Army Reserves. 1st Division comprises 6 regular brigades and 2nd Division contains 6 more reserve brigades of varying size depending on which state they are located in. The regular brigades are typically 'operational' units and the reserve brigades are more geared to administration and training, meaning reserve units will train regularly alongside regular units, but the core of a deployed Battle Group will typically be composed of regular units mostly from a single regular brigade (which also exercises command). Reserve units might be deployed 'whole' into such formations, but it is actually more common for individual reservists to be rotated through regular units on operations to 'pad them out' (Stephen Barton, personal conversation with the author, Perth, 17 March 2020). Australian Army units are relatively light – with relatively little heavy armour or artillery – but they are highly mobile and relatively high-technology because they are designed to be integrated into joint operations with the other services (and, of course, with American and other allied units).

Finally, the ADF has worked hard since 2010 to improve its joint operations capabilities by improving its command, control, computing, communications, intelligence, surveillance and reconnaissance (C4ISR) capacity. It has done so mainly by purchasing US equipment for all three services – the *Wedgetails*, the *Aegis* systems, field-communications sets for the Army, etc. – and then training regularly with US forces, as described above (Davies and Davis 2016).

Conclusion

As this chapter makes clear, the defence relationship between Australia and the United States is a very close one. The two states have been formal allies since 1951, the bilateral relationship is strongly institutionalized, and the fact they are members of the Anglosphere security community – and especially Five Eyes – provides additional support. The trend since the turn of the millennium has been one of steadily closer defence ties, in large part because the two allies share similar threat perceptions. In the 2000s both states felt threatened by the global jihadi challenge, but more recently it has been China's rise – and the broadly similar attitudes in both capitals towards such – which has provided the basis for closer engagement.

Another event – the global coronavirus pandemic – arguably enhanced this trend in the first half of 2020. It was too early, at the time of writing, to assess the full impact of this global epidemic, but one thing is already clear: Australia–China ties have deteriorated significantly. The cause was Prime Minister Scott Morrison's call in April 2020 for an 'independent international review' with powers 'akin to weapons inspectors' to investigate when, where and how the virus spread, given the persistent rumours that Beijing systematically engaged in a cover-up during the pandemic's early stages (Yuan 2020). Beijing responded with furious rhetoric towards Canberra and then took steps to seriously damage the Australian barley, beef and tourism industries. The Communist Party-controlled *Global Times* also warned bluntly that 'Australia has become a close collaborator of the US in its anti-China strategy' and that '[i]f Australia wants to retain the gain from its economic ties with China, it must make a real change to its current stance on China' (Walden 2020). US–China ties have also been badly strained by mutual recriminations and accusations concerning who should be held responsible for the damage caused by the epidemic (Auslin 2020).

Both Australia's and America's bilateral relations with China therefore deteriorated in the first half of 2020. This author believes that overt threats of the type printed in the *Global Times* actually achieve the opposite of what is presumably their intent, namely, they drive the culturally Anglo, liberal-democratic states closer together by reinforcing the broadly similar threat perceptions Washington and Canberra already have towards China. We are some way from the allies deciding to pursue a full-blown containment effort similar to that directed towards the Soviet Union during the Cold War, but it is nevertheless clear that both Canberra and Washington are balancing against Beijing across a broad spectrum of policy areas, and co-ordinating while doing so. Accordingly, US–Australia defence cooperation seems likely to intensify steadily in the short- to medium-term given there is little prospect of Beijing abandoning its grand strategic ambitions to dominate the Indo-Pacific.

References

Adler, Emanuel, and Michael Barnett (1998), *Security Communities*, Cambridge: Cambridge University Press.

Auslin, Michael R. (2020), 'The Coronacrisis will Simply Exacerbate the Geo-Strategic Competition Between Beijing and Washington', Hoover Institute, 23 April, www.hoover.org/research/coronacrisis-will-simply-exacerbate-geo-strategic-competition-between-beijing-and.

Australian Government (2006), 'Inquiry into Naval Shipbuilding in Australia', www.aph.gov.au/Parliamentary_Business/Committees/Senate/Foreign_Affairs_Defence_and_Trade/Completed_inquiries/2004-07/shipping/index accessed 16 July 2020.

Australian Government (2016), *Defence White Paper 2016*, Canberra: Commonwealth of Australia.

Australian Government (2017), *Naval Shipbuilding Plan*, Canberra: Commonwealth of Australia.

Australian Government (2019a), *Trade and Investment at a Glance*, Canberra: Department of Foreign Affairs and Trade.

Australian Government (2019b), 'Marine Rotational Force – Darwin', www.defence.gov.au/Initiatives/USFPI/Marines.asp accessed 16 July 2020.

Australian Government (n.d. a), 'Australia–US Defence Relationship', https://usa.embassy.gov.au/defence-cooperation accessed 16 July 2020.

Australian Government (n.d. b), 'United States Force Posture Initiatives – Infrastructure', www.defence.gov.au/Initiatives/USFPI/Infrastructure.asp accessed 16 July 2020.

Ball, Desmond (1980), *A Suitable Piece of Real Estate: American Installations in Australia*, Sydney: Hale & Iremonger.

Ball, Desmond (2001), 'The Strategic Essence', *Australian Journal of International Affairs* 55 (2).

Ball, Desmond, Bill Robinson, and Richard Tanter (2016), 'The Antennas of Pine Gap', *NAPSNet Special Reports*, February 21, https://nautilus.org/napsnet/napsnet-special-reports/the-antennas-of-pine-gap accessed 16 July 2020.

Beattie, Shannon (2019), 'Exmouth Telescope Facility Takes Next Step', *Pilbara News*, 23 May.

Beeson, Mark (2003), 'Australia's Relationship with the United States: The Case for Greater Independence', *Australian Journal of Political Science*, 38 (3).

Beeson, Mark, & Alan Bloomfield (2019), 'The Trump Effect Downunder: US Allies, Australian Strategic Culture, and the Politics of Path Dependence', *Contemporary Security Policy* 40 (3).

Birkler, John, *et al.* (2015), *Australia's Naval Shipbuilding Enterprise: Preparing for the 21st Century*, Santa Monica, CA: RAND Corporation.

Bisley, Nick (2013), '"An Ally for All the Years to Come": why Australia is not a conflicted US Ally', *Australian Journal of International Affairs*, 67 (4).

Blaxland, John (2016), 'US–Australian Military Co-operation in Asia', in Peter J. Dean, Stephan Frühling & Brendan Taylor (eds), *Australia's American Alliance*, Carlton: Melbourne University Press.

Bloomfield, Alan (2016), 'To Balance or to Bandwagon? Adjusting to China's Rise During Australia's Rudd–Gillard Era', *Pacific Review*, 29 (2).

Bloomfield, Alan (2018), 'The US in the Indian Ocean', in Andrew T. H. Tan (ed.), *Handbook on the United States in Asia*, Cheltenham: Edward Elgar.

Carr, Bob (2014), *Diary of a Foreign Minister*, Sydney: NewSouth Publishing.

Cheeseman, Graeme (1993), *The Search for Self-Reliance: Australian Defence Since Vietnam*, Melbourne: Longman Cheshire.

Cox, Samuel J. (2018), 'Australian Assistance to the Philippines: Beyond the Here and Now', *The Strategist*, 18 May.

Davies, Andrew & Malcolm Davis (2016), 'ADF Capability Snapshot 2016: C4ISR', *ASPI Strategic Insights*, June.

Dibb, Paul (2005), 'America Has Always Kept Us in the Loop', *The Australian*, 10 September.

Dupont, Alan (2007), 'The Virtues of the US Alliance', *Sydney Papers* 19 (4).

Fraser, Malcolm (2014), *Dangerous Allies*, Melbourne: Melbourne University Press.

Frühling, Stephan (2018), 'Is ANZUS Really an Alliance? Aligning the US and Australia', *Survival*, 60 (5).

Green, Michael J., Peter J. Dean, Brendan Taylor & Zack Cooper (2015), 'The ANZUS Alliance in an Ascending Asia', *Centre of Gravity Series*, 23.

Greene, Andrew (2019), 'America's $300 million Push to Expand Naval Facilities in Northern Australia', *ABC News*, 29 July.

Greene, Andrew (2020), 'French Submarine Program "Dangerously Off-track" Warns Report Urging Australia to Consider Nuclear Alternative', *ABC News*, 11 March.

Gyngell, Allan (2017), *Fear of Abandonment: Australia in the World Since 1942*, Carlton: LaTrobe University Press.

He, Baogang (2014), 'Collaborative and Conflictive Trilateralism: Perspectives from Australia, China, and America', *Asian Survey*, 54 (2).

Hellyer, Marcus (2018), *The Cost of Defence: ASPI Defence Budget Brief 2018–19*, Canberra: Australian Strategic Policy Institute.

Howard, John (1997), *Speech*, Asialink Centre: The 5th Annual Sir Edward 'Weary' Dunlop Lecture, Melbourne, 11 November.

Insinna, Valeria (2020), 'Boeing Rolls out Australia's First "Loyal Wingman" Combat Drone', *DefenceNews*, 4 May.

Jennings, Peter (2016), 'The 2016 Defence White Paper and the ANZUS Alliance', *Security Challenges*, 12:1.

Jennings, Peter (2019), 'The Joint Facilities: Still the Jewel in the Crown', *ASPI – The Strategist*, 21 February.

Kagan, Robert. (2012), *The World that America Made*, New York: Alfred A. Knopf.

Kassam, Natasha (2019), 'Lowy Institute Poll 2019', June, www.lowyinstitute.org/p ublications/lowy-institute-poll-2019 accessed 16 July 2020.

Levick, Ewen (2019), 'Cocos Runway to be Widened as Defence Looks North', *Australian Defence Magazine*, 18 April.

Lui, Weihua, and Yufan Hao (2014), 'Australia in China's Grand Strategy', *Asian Survey*, 54 (2).

McDonald, Hamish (2017), 'Australian Naval Program Sums up Dilemmas for 'Middle Power' Nations', *Nikkei Asian Review*, 2 June.

Morgenthau, Hans (1978), *Politics Among Nations: The Struggle for Power and Peace*, 5th ed., New York: Alfred A. Knopf.

Nicholson, Brendan, & Jared Owens (2015), 'Tony Abbott Leaves the Door Open to Increased Military Commitment', *The Australian*, 26 May.

O'Neil, Andrew (2017), 'Australia and the "Five Eyes" Intelligence Network: The Perils of an Asymmetric Alliance', *Australian Journal of International Affairs*, 71 (5).

Pfluke, Corey (2019). 'A History of the Five Eyes Alliance: Possibility for Reform and Additions', *Comparative Strategy*, 38 (4).

RAAF (n.d.), 'Aircraft', www.airforce.gov.au/technology/aircraft accessed 16 July 2020.

RAN (n.d.), 'Semaphore: The Navy's New Aegis', www.navy.gov.au/media-room/p ublications/semaphore-navys-new-aegis accessed 16 July 2020.

Robson, Seth (2019), 'Australia Investing $715 million in Northern Port that Hosts US Navy Warships', *Stars & Stripes*, 12 December.

Sheridan, Greg (2014), 'RAAF May Join US Air Strikes on Islamic State', *The Australian*, 25 August 2014.

Snyder, Glenn H. (1984), 'The Security Dilemma in Alliance Politics', *World Politics*, 36 (4).

Tanter, Richard (2013), 'The "Joint Facilities" Today', *ARENA Journal*, 39/40.

Taylor, Brendan and William T. Tow (2017), 'Crusaders and Pragmatists: Australia Debates the American Alliance', in Michael Wesley (ed.), *Comparing US Alliances in the 21st Century*, Canberra: ANU Press.

Teichmann, Max (1966) 'Australia – Armed and Neutral?', *Victorian Fabian Society*, 13.

Tiezzi, Shannon (2016), '"Nearly All" Australian Patrols in South China Sea Are Challenged by China', *The Diplomat*, 5 February.

Uren, David (2009), *The Kingdom and the Quarry: China, Australia, Fear and Greed*, Melbourne: Black Inc.

Vucetic, Srdjan (2011), 'Bound to Follow? The Anglosphere and US-Led Coalitions of the Willing, 1950–2001', *European Journal of International Relations*, 17 (1).

Walden, Max (2020), 'Australia Says China Travel Warning "Unhelpful" Amid Escalating Diplomatic Row', *ABC News*, 8 June.

Watt, David (2018), 'Defence Budget Overview', www.aph.gov.au/About_Parliament/ Parliamentary_Departments/Parliamentary_Library/pubs/rp/BudgetReview201819/ DefenceB accessed 16 July 2020.

Wendt, Alexander (1999), *Social Theory of International Politics*, Cambridge: Cambridge University Press.

Wesley, Michael (2016), 'The Alliance as an Intelligence Partnership', in Peter J. Dean, Stephan Frühling & Brendan Taylor (eds), *Australia's American Alliance*, Carlton: Melbourne University Press.

White, Hugh (2010), 'Power Shift: Australia's future between Washington and Beijing', *Quarterly Essay*, 39.

Wilkins, Thomas (2019), 'Re-assessing Australia's Intra-alliance Bargaining Power in the Age of Trump', *Security Challenges*, 15 (1).

Yuan, Shawn (2020), 'Inside the Early Days of China's Coronavirus Coverup', *Wired*, 5 May.

8 China–US–Australia

Redefining the strategic triangle

Adam Lockyer, Scott D. McDonald and Yves-Heng Lim

The Asia-Pacific region has undergone dramatic changes over the past thirty years. At the most elementary level, the relative erosion of United States (US) power and the rise of the People's Republic of China (PRC) have deeply changed the structure of the regional system, putting an early end to the unipolar moment. As US dominance progressively erodes and the strategic landscape changes, patterns of relations between the different actors of the regional system have altered – sometimes significantly. Bilateral relations between China, the US and Australia have not been immune as shifts in the balance of power and evolving interests generate new dynamics among the three players.

This chapter argues that US–China–Australia relations can be understood as a strategic triangle. While the notion of the strategic triangle is commonly used to describe any situation involving three actors, it is used here more restrictively. As first explained by Lowell Dittmer (1981), it implies that any bilateral relations in the triangle cannot be fully explained without reference to the third player in the triangle. In the context of US–China–Australia relations, the application of the concept of the strategic triangle must be treated carefully. Obviously, the logic of US–China relations is primarily driven by factors well beyond Australia's control. The application of the concept remains nonetheless useful because it helps explain the two other edges of the triangle: relations between Canberra and Washington are increasingly difficult to explain without reference to Beijing, and Sino-Australian relations are similarly difficult to explain without reference to the US.

The first section briefly outlines the concept of the strategic triangle and the particular dynamics that drive this type of structure. The following section applies the concept to the US–Australia–China triangle, examining the status and implications of each of the three legs. The final section integrates these discussions by drawing conclusions regarding the actions each of the three powers can take to strengthen the triangular relationship and the stability of the environment in which it exists.

The logic of strategic triangles

The concept of the strategic triangle has gained considerable currency in the post-Cold War Indo-Pacific region. A cursory look at the literature shows that it has been used to explain the dynamics of relations in the US–China–Japan (Dreyer 2012; Liu and Wang 2013), the China–Japan-Russia (Dittmer 2005), the US–China–Pakistan (Smith 2013), the China–India–Pakistan (Chellaney 2002), the Russia–China–India (Pant 2006) triads, but also the US–China–Philippines triad (Heydarian 2017) and the US–China–New Zealand triad (Steff and Dodd-Parr 2019). Lowell Dittmer, to whom we owe the modern formalization of the concept, recently applied it to the Australia–China–US triad (Dittmer 2012; Dittmer and He 2014). This section briefly outlines the specificity of security dynamics in a strategic triangle.

The triangular structure

While the idea of triangular games makes intuitive sense, Lowell Dittmer (1981) formalized the concept of 'strategic triangle' in the international relations literature. From a broad perspective, strategic triangles matter because they cannot be simply reduced to a superposition of three independent bilateral relations; the triangular structure of a game entails the emergence of particular patterns of interaction among the different players.

For Dittmer (1981: 489), a strategic triangle emerges when '[t]he relationship of each player in a bilateral relationship to a third player – the distinctively triangular variable in the equation – may affect either the value or the symmetry of the first relationship'. Bilateral relations in a triangular configuration cannot be understood in isolation. In other words, the relationship between any pair of players cannot be understood without reference to the third player in the triangle. While, as explained below, it is likely that players in a triangle will be acutely aware of security interdependences created by the existence of a strategic triangle and will most likely adjust their respective strategy accordingly, this awareness is not entirely necessary for a strategic triangle to emerge. The existence of a strategic triangle implies a high degree of security interdependence between the different players and the tightening or loosening of the relationship between two players necessarily has consequences for the third player, whether these consequences were intended or not. In this sense, strategic triangles can be understood through the notion of externality that has been used by David Lake (1997) to explain the emergence of regional security complexes. Any change in one of the bilateral relations has necessarily spillover effects on the two other bilateral sides of the triangle.

Depending on the position of each bilateral relation along the amity-enmity continuum, Dittmer (1981, 2012) distinguishes between four different types of strategic triangles. At the two extremes of the spectrum 'unit-veto triangles' and '*ménage à trois*' are characterized, respectively, by the existence of hostile-only and friendly – only relations among the three players. The two other possible forms are 'stable marriages' – in which one of the pairs of states is characterized by friendly relations while having unfriendly relations with the third player, and 'romantic triangles' – in which one of the players has positive relations with the two others while the later have unfriendly relations. Depending on which of the players have developed friendly and unfriendly relations, there are in fact three configurations for stable marriages (depending on which pair has developed stable positive relations) and romantic triangles (depending on which player is in the position of the 'pivot player'; Dittmer 1981: 489).

Triangles and strategies

The above description of different types of strategic triangles should not lead to the conclusion that triangles become static entities once defined. Quite the contrary, strategic triangles are likely to be particularly dynamic power configurations as each state can attempt to manipulate their relations with the two other players to consolidate or improve its relative position. The acuteness of positional competition in triangles stems from the very structure of the game. As highlighted by Lowell Dittmer (2012: 665), while from a system perspective, a *ménage à trois* is arguably the preferable option, the preferred role for an individual actor is, in rank order: pivot player in a romantic triangle, partner in a marriage, partner in a *ménage* and pariah facing a marriage.

In this sense, none of the triangular configurations appears stable because each of them includes at least one player that can – and will presumably endeavour to – improve its position. A state facing a stable marriage between the two other players has little choice but to try weakening, and ideally breaking, the bond that exists between its opponents. The two wings of a romantic triangle are in a position in which abandonment by the pivot would result in a sharp decrease of their security. In this configuration, the two 'wing players' have incentives to improve their bilateral relations while trying to undermine the relations between the pivot and the other wing. Each state in a unit-veto system can improve its position by building positive relations with at least one of the other players, and in a *ménage à trois*, each state can improve its position by trying to weaken the relations between the two other players.

In some circumstances, changes of alignments might occur relatively mechanically. Interestingly, the image of strategic triangles is compatible with several paradigms, though the logic of re-alignments tends to differ depending the overarching theoretical framework in which the strategic triangle is interpreted. Triangles can be considered in a liberal context (Oneal et al. 1996; Russett 1998), in which one would likely expect realignments when the degree of economic interdependence between two players changes, when new international organizations emerge, or when one of the players sees its domestic political regime change. By contrast, in a neorealist world (Waltz 1979, 2000), changes in the distribution of power that lead one of the states to obtain a dominant position in the system creates incentives for the two other players to align with each other in order to balance against their most powerful counterpart. In the more fine-grained framework established by Walt (1987), changes in the balance of power, offensive capabilities, or intentions of one of the players is likely to lead to realignments.

Patterns of interactions in a strategic triangle are, however, likely to be only partly shaped by structural factors, and players will usually have some margin of manoeuvre to try to reshape the triangle in a way that is more favourable to their interests. The emergence of a romantic triangle in the 1970s with the US as the pivot and the Soviet Union and China as the wings appears, for instance, at least as much the consequence of a deliberate policy as it is the result of structural changes in the international system (Dittmer 1981). Put simply, under certain circumstances, states might be able to provoke some degree of realignment by offering another player a 'better deal' than the third party. While necessarily costly, the 'deal' is potentially attractive for the initiator because the benefits it might derive from potential realignments – which include a closer relation with the coveted partner but also the weakening of the relation between the partner and the third player – remain superior to the 'gross cost' of the deal. A relatively unfavourable trade deal might for instance still prove attractive for an isolated player if it allows it to weaken the relation between the target partner and the third, more hostile party. In the same way, shelving a point of dispute might also be costly in terms of prestige, but the trade-off might be valuable if it removes one of the obstacles to cooperation against the third player.

In its initial form, the strategic triangle model tends to treat all of bilateral relationships binarily – they are either friendly or hostile. In his original work on the concept, Dittmer (1981) tends to suggest that changes of triangular configurations are marked by watershed events – such as the major degradation of USSR–PRC relations that led to the 1969 border clash and the spectacular US–PRC realignment initiated by US President Richard Nixon and National Security Adviser, Henry Kissinger. However, contemporary international society is characterized by a range of interests that individual countries share and disagree about. Across the scope of multiple issues, states may align in a variety of different ways. This implies that the 'positive' and 'negative' types of relations identified by Dittmer (1981) are best conceived as the extreme ends of a continuum. To ignore the possibility of varied triangular relationships across various issues not only risks mischaracterizing the relationship at any given time, but it also misses a deeper understanding of when states are likely to conflict, as well as when opportunities may be available for cooperative solutions based on shared interests.

Dynamics and prospect for changes in the US–China–Australia triangle

Strategic triangles intuitively conjure up the image of a struggle between the most powerful actors of the system and, in short, tripolarity (Schweller 1993, 1998). They suggest the existence of a rough equivalence in power among the players – the 'A = B = C' configuration in Schweller's (1993: 78–79) typology of tripolar systems. The notion of strategic triangles is, however, applicable well beyond situations of equality among the players, and in his initial statement of the concept Dittmer (1981) suggests that power asymmetries can be an inherent component of triangular dynamics. The applicability of the triangular model depends, in this sense, not on the strict existence of parity – or near-parity – in power among the three players, but on whether or not a change of alignments would significantly impact the security of one of the players. Lowell Dittmer emphasizes that there are some limits to the application of the strategic triangle model to the US–China–Australia triangle. Put simply, the power gap between China and the US on the one hand and Australia on the other hand suggests that 'Australia does not qualify *stricto sensu* as a strategic triangle in that its defection would not be critical to the balance' (Dittmer 2012: 664). From an Australian perspective, the triangular model remains nonetheless useful to grasp Canberra's position and options. From their perspective, and relations with the two other powers, a form of triangular game has translated in an increasingly difficult balancing act between Australia's two 'wings', as changes in Australia–China relations have significant repercussions on US–Australia relations – and vice versa – while changes in the relationship between Washington and Beijing have obvious major consequences for Canberra. This section explores changes and potential redefinitions of the US–China–Australia triangle.

The US–Australia stable marriage

For a significant part of the post-Cold War era, the US–China–Australian triangle has presented the features of a stable marriage between Washington and Canberra. Inherited from the Cold War era, the US–Australia alliance, as codified in the ANZUS Treaty, has continued to constitute the cornerstone of Canberra's relation with Washington. The alliance benefited from a new impetus with the victory of the Liberal-National Coalition in the 1996 election (Kelton 2007). John Howard gave priority to bolstering alliance ties with Washington, and by July 1996, the 'Sydney Statement' affirmed that 'the relationship will remain central to the security of both countries, because it reflects fundamental shared interests and objectives' and committed the two partners to the promotion of a regional environment that 'promotes democracy, economic development and prosperity, and strategic stability' (Department of Foreign Affairs and Trade 1996). The increased closeness of the alliance was further epitomized by the Howard government's commitment in 1998 of '110 SAS troops, 120 intelligence and medical specialists and two RAAF Boeing 707s, to the proposed US led, but UN backed, force to ensure Iraq complied with its UNSCOM agreements' (Kelton 2007: 12). The millennium ended on a more ambiguous note in the East Timor crisis, in which 'the United States became involved […] only reluctantly, late and in a disappointingly limited way' (Lockyer 2012, 2017: 63). The episode was, however, not entirely negative for the alliance and 'Australia's performance in East Timor was held up by Washington as a model of how an ally should behave in a regional crisis' (Edwards 2005: 46) – leading to the rise of the much-debated 'Howard doctrine' and questions about Canberra's new status as a 'deputy sheriff' in the region (Leaver 2001; Edwards 2005; Holland and McDonald 2010).

The 9/11 attacks and the subsequent War on Terror created the conditions for even tighter relations between Washington and Canberra (Dibb 2007; Kelton 2007), thus consolidating the stable marriage around a new major issue. John Howard was present in Washington when the attacks took place, and by 14 September 2001 the Prime Minister had invoked article IV of the ANZUS Treaty for the first time in history (Howard 2001). This resulted in the commitment of 1,000 troops, as well as combat and support aircraft and thee frigates to Operation Enduring Freedom starting in October 2001 (Kelton 2007). The alignment of strategic concerns under the new War on Terror deepened further after the Bali bombings perpetrated by members of the Jemaah Islamiyah killed 88 Australians in October 2002 (Kelton 2007; Holland and McDonald 2010). The bombing brought home a sense of acute vulnerability at a time when US relations with all its allies revolved around the question of Iraq and the possible use of force. Australia strongly supported a UN resolution allowing the use of force against Baghdad and John Howard (2003) bitterly criticized the French opposition to the use of military force when Jacques Chirac announced that France would veto such a resolution. Canberra remained at the forefront of the coalition of the willing; '[b]y early February 2003, nearly 2,000 Australian troops, a squadron of F/A-18 aircraft, three naval vessels and C-130 Hercules transport aircraft were either pre-positioned in, or en route to, the Gulf in support of American military pressure against Iraq' (Tow 2004: 273) and, one month later, Australia was one of the three US allies – together with the United Kingdom and Poland – to commit troops to the first phase of the invasion of Iraq (Carney 2011). After the end of major combat operations, Australian forces were redirected to reconstruction efforts with over 800 Defence personnel providing vital support 'through a range of tasks including training volunteers for the new Iraqi army, providing air traffic control services and searching for WMD as part of the Iraq Survey Group' (Department of Defence 2003). Australia would be one of the last US allies to maintain troops in Iraq until it progressively withdrew its forces between June 2008 and July 2009 (Carney 2011), after participation in the Iraq operation had become a bone of contention in the domestic debate (Isakhan 2014). However, though these operations were ultimately contentious, the debate over Australian involvement in Iraq did not erode the pivotal importance of the alliance for the successive governments (Bisley 2013).

Despite internal disagreement on the advisability of the ongoing campaign in Iraq, the stable marriage between Australian and the US is served by a clear convergence of interest between Canberra and Washington. As summarized by Nick Bisley (2013: 405–406), the alliance provides Canberra with a security guarantee through Article 4 of the ANZUS Treaty, 'privileged access to US military hardware and training' that allows Australia to maintain a qualitative edge in its region, 'access to US intelligence networks and technology' and, more broadly, 'access to Washington'. However, as the weaker partner in an alliance, Australia faces the traditional risks of abandonment and entrapment. Although the alliance brings many benefits, some fear 'it commits Australia to policies that reflect America's global geopolitical priorities, but which may not be in keeping with Australian interests' (Beeson 2003: 395).

For the US, the alliance provides an important southern anchor in the system of alliances that have helped keep the Indo-Pacific stable and prosperous since the end of the Second World War (Department of Defense 2019: 3). In an effort to bolster the value of that position, in 2014 the allies signed the Force Posture Agreement, governing two Force Posture Initiatives – Enhanced Air Cooperation and Marine Rotational Forces-Darwin – which promote a combined capability to respond to crises and contingencies, strengthen interoperability and further engagement with regional partners (Department of Defense 2019: 27). Integral to this concept is the underlying conviction that Australia shares a set of values and interests that has underwritten a partnership begun on the battlefields of the First World War, and reinforced by economic and security arrangements (White House 2017: 46). This sentiment is more than platitudes regarding a long relationship; rather it represents an understanding that Australia and the US can work together for a shared vision of the future. In order to leverage and improve the effectiveness of this partnership in building a cooperative security architecture for the region, the US is actively leveraging a 'partner-centric approach' to engagement with the Pacific Island states (Department of Defense 2019: 41). This concept is evident in the manner Marine Rotational Forces-Darwin and the Australian Defence Force are working together with other regional countries as part of Australia's Indo-Pacific Endeavor (Department of Defense 2019: 27). However, in the US fears remain that Australia could be swayed by extensive economic investment from the PRC, fears heightened by recent revelations regarding attempts to influence and undermine the Australian government through the purchase of Australian politicians (Cave and Tarabay 2019).

In sum, this marriage is grounded in common values and operates in pursuit of common interests. Despite periodic missteps it has endured and is likely to continue. In fact, disagreements from time to time make the relationship stronger when the partners are open and honest with one another (Chapter 11, this volume). Both partners have fears over the future of the relationship, but neither thinks it is in imminent danger of collapse, or would desire a future without the relationship. It is a marriage that has many more anniversaries to celebrate.

Weakening the marriage: China–Australia relations

As the outsider power in a stable marriage, China has naturally attempted to reshape the US–China–Australia strategic triangle. To a certain extent, China's dissatisfaction with the close alignment between Washington and

Canberra is part of a much wider problem Beijing has with the existing alliance structure in the Asia-Pacific region. During the last decade Beijing has proven consistently inimical to the network of alliances the US maintains in the region, denouncing it as the remnant of the Cold War security architecture and seeing it largely as an obstacle to its own rise (Liff 2017). In this context, it is hardly surprising that Beijing has resorted to 'wedging' strategies (Crawford 2008, 2011; Izumikawa 2013; Chai 2020) to weaken the existing strategic bond between Australia and the US, and give the triangle a shape that is more conducive to its interests.

The objectives that can be achieved by a wedging strategy fall in four different categories when considering the target's position (Crawford 2011). At one end of the spectrum, the most ambitious change is 'realignment' (Crawford 2011: 164) when the target state is invited to fully switch allegiance. At the opposite end, a state might simply aim for 'disalignment' and 'see[k] to weaken a target's cooperation within an opposing bloc, without trying to convert the target into a neutral or an ally' (Crawford 2011: 165). 'Dealignment' and 'realignment' constitute two intermediate forms centred on securing the neutrality of the target state. When implementing a wedging strategy, a state has a broad choice between 'rewarding' the target state in order to provoke defection, or 'coercing' it by threatening to impose costs if defection does not occur (Crawford 2011, Izumikawa 2013).

Over the last decades, China has arguably attempted to employ wedging tactics to draw Canberra away from Washington. Chai (2020) has demonstrated for instance that Beijing has successfully employed a mix of reward and coercion tactics to drive a wedge between the two allies on issues such as the South China Sea – where Beijing opposed any Australian involvement in US-led Freedom of Navigation Operations. Beyond this important but still limited success, the evolution of China–Australia relations provides Beijing opportunities to implement wedging strategies at a broader level.

Australia has benefited mightily from the economic ascent of China. For Australia, China's rise has translated into a spectacular change of trade patterns. China ranked ninth among Australia's largest trade partners in 1990, behind the Republic of Korea, Singapore and Taiwan (Department of Foreign Affairs and Trade 2019). At the turn of the decade, China ranked third behind the United States and Japan. By 2005, China had overtaken the United States and by 2009 it ranked first among Australia's trade partners. When measured in monetary value, the growth of China–Australia trade has been, by any standard, staggering. Trade between China and Australia represented less than AUD 5 billion[1] in 1990. By 2010, it had mushroomed to more than AUD 100 billion, before doubling to more than AUD 200 billion in 2018 (Department of Foreign Affairs and Trade 2019).

This remarkable growth has translated to increased linkages between the Australian and PRC economies. Trade with China represented around 5 percent of Australia's total trade in 1990. In 2018, almost one third of Australia's foreign trade was conducted with China (Department of Foreign Affairs and

Trade 2019), and no less than 37.4 percent of Australian exports were directed to China (including Hong Kong). Some major sectors have become particularly reliant on the Chinese market. Worth AUD 63.3 billion, exports of iron ore and concentrate represented 18.4 percent of Australian total exports by value in 2018. That same year, more than 81 percent of these exports we directed to China (Department of Foreign Affairs and Trade 2019). Among Australia's other main exports, a little more than one fifth of Australia's coal exports, almost one third of its petroleum gases exports and around one quarter of its agricultural exports were also sent to China (Department of Foreign Affairs and Trade 2019).

Australia's massive ties to the Chinese market create a perceived political vulnerability for Canberra. Over the last decades, Beijing has repeatedly expressed its political discontent by using economic leverage: in 2010, China imposed an embargo on rare earth exports to Japan after a collision between a Chinese trawler and a Japanese Coast Guard ship around the Senkaku/Diaoyu Islands, used restrictive measures against salmon imports from Norway after Liu Xiaobo won the Nobel Peace Prize and in 2012 it imposed restrictions on banana imports from the Philippines at the height of the Scarborough Shoal crisis (Reilly 2012; Hornung 2014; Lai 2018; Kolstad 2019). How vulnerable is the Australian economy to economic coercion by Beijing remains a debated question (Armstrong and Drysdale 2019; Grattan 2019), but the asymmetry of size between the two economies and the increasing level of perceived dependence of critical export sectors arguably create the position of vulnerability described more than half a century ago by Albert Hirschman (1945, see also Abdelal and Kirshner 1999; Kirshner 2009). As argued by Hirschman (1945: 28), 'the "danger of losing a market" if political conditions deteriorate makes for as much concern as the danger of losing supplies' and the disruption of an established trade pattern could force very costly and painful adjustments in the sectors of the economy where exports to the particular market are concentrated.

This is, however, not to say that economic statecraft provides a surefire lever for China. While a complete assessment of Beijing's economic statecraft is well beyond the scope of this chapter (Reilley 2012, 2013; Norris 2016), there are significant uncertainties about the potential results of a Chinese attempt to economically coerce Australia. First, in an increasingly interconnected world, economic readjustments can occur rapidly. In 2014, for instance, Russia attempted to ban US chicken imports in retaliation for US sanctions to punish Russian involvement in Ukraine. While there were many factors why this failed to influence the US, one was the ready availability of other buyers on the international market (Passy 2014). Second, economic sanctions tend to provide a temporary source of pain that is overlooked in defence of national security interests that are deemed more important in the long run (Pape 1997). Third, economic sanctions tend also to be a one-shot measure: once the target has adapted and patterns of economic interaction have changed, the coercer loses a large part – if not all – of its leverage. More broadly, China's economic statecraft might be constrained by the limited fungibility of its economic power. In his recent study, Robert Scott Ross (2019: 318) concludes that while 'China is approaching approximate international economic parity with the US in the international political economy', its 'influence in the international political economy does not have consequential strategic implications, either for the East Asian strategic order or for US security interests'. Thus, despite the quantity of exports consumed by the PRC, its influence on Australian decision-making may not be as large as some fear. As Ross (2019: 317) observes, 'despite Australia's significant dependence on natural resource exports to China, Australia not only expanded defense cooperation with the US, but also adopted "unfriendly" policies toward China'.

While Beijing's ability to move Canberra into disalignment or realignment through economic coercion is uncertain, its ability to do so through a 'rewarding' strategy (Crawford 2011) appears even more limited. The problem can be framed in terms of what power transition theory (PTT) terms 'satisfaction' (Lemke and Reed 1996; Tammen et al. 2000) with the status quo and a possible China-led alternative system in the Indo-Pacific region. As mentioned above and in other chapters of this book, Australia has benefited from the existing Indo-Pacific order defined and dominated by the United States. While variations exist in the criteria used by PTT to determine satisfaction, Australia presents two of the major characteristics of state satisfied with the US-led status quo: broad similarities in terms of regime and participation in an alliance (Kim 1996; Lemke and Reed 1996).

In this context, while from an economic perspective Australia has benefited mightily from China's rise, it is difficult to see what kind of China-led order could benefit Australia more than the current status quo, even when taking into account a possibly the mild 'compensation' strategy by Beijing, which 'may involve adjustments to its peripheral territorial claims or spheres of influence, ties to partners and allies, economic relations and privileges, policies and positions of influence in international organizations, or a willingness to negotiate other issue-specific agreements or regimes' (Crawford 2011: 170). Over the last decade, some of Beijing's policies have in fact aggravated Canberra's concerns about the shape of a China-led Indo-Pacific order. The rise of preservation of a 'rules-based order' (Department of Defence 2016) to the forefront of Canberra's defence policy is, in large part, a response to Beijing's rising assertiveness, especially in maritime East Asia. In parallel, Beijing's growing influence in Australia has generated significant pushback and the stricter foreign influence laws passed in 2018 by the Australian Parliament that were clearly aimed at China (Gill and Schreer 2018; Munro 2018).

The lack of attractiveness of a China-led regional order and the level of uncertainty surrounding the potential results of economic coercion mean that China's ability to implement the type of wedging strategy necessary to separate Australia from the United States has, to date, been limited. This is not to say that the configuration of the triangle is impervious to change. As mentioned above, Beijing has made no mystery of its hostility toward the US alliance system in the Indo-Pacific region and contemporary dynamics might make Australia more prone to reassess its alignment choices under certain conditions. For instance, the continuous expansion of China's share in Australian exports means sanctions could inflict more economic pain in the future and potentially change Australia's cost–benefit calculations. It is more difficult to see how China could improve its rewarding strategy. However, resurgent strains of neo-isolationism in US domestic politics could work to Beijing's advantage, as the attractiveness of rewards is ultimately relative and could be bolstered by uncertainties about Washington's willingness and ability to provide leadership (Haas 2017). Thus, the interplay between US and PRC strategic directions could here again modify Australia's cost-benefit calculations.

A 'grand bargain': US–PRC relations and Australia

At the time of writing, China–US relations have arguably reached a post-Cold War nadir. Beijing and Washington engaged in a tit-for-tat game of escalating tariffs that has come to impact the majority of their bilateral trade over two years (Williams and Hammond 2019). Meanwhile, Chinese forces continued to behave provocatively towards their US counterparts in the South China Sea, leading to dangerous encounters (Ali 2017; Wong 2018) and the Trump administration ratcheted up the rhetoric, officially labelling China a 'strategic competitor [that] us[es] predatory economics to intimidate its neighbors while militarizing features in the South China Sea' (Department of Defense 2018: 1). Finally, just as trade issues appeared to be resolving, the outbreak and spread of the coronavirus has led to a highly acrimonious blame game (Pomfret 2020), which has expanded to the point of undermining the integrity of international organizations, such as the World Health Organization, which is defending the PRC and being attacked by the US (Forgey and Oprysko 2020; Nebehay 2020).

There might be reasons to believe current levels of distrust and hostility are here to stay, as a number of scholars and former decision-makers acknowledge the failure of Washington's engagement policy (Pillsbury 2015; Blackwill 2018; Campbell and Ratner 2018). But the current nadir might also be only temporary. The history of PRC–US relations has undergone major ups and downs – periods of flirtation interspersed with hostility. The realist balance of power logic employed by Henry Kissinger combined with Mao Zedong's own brand of Chinese Realpolitik made power-based accommodation attractive vis-à-vis Soviet Russia. Sino-US relations unravelled after the Tiananmen Massacre, but were soon rebuilt around the hope that an engagement policy could lead to the integration of China into the liberal international order, a policy pursued by four successive administrations from both political parties (McDonald 2019: 29–31). Though Xi Jinping's foreign policy and Donald Trump's reaction to it have cooled relations again, a future recognition of common interests could lead to a more amicable environment.

In the aftermath of the 2008 global financial crisis, the possibility of convergence, though perhaps not a 'stable marriage', between Washington and Beijing led to the emergence of concepts like a Sino-US G-2 or a 'grand bargain' between the two superpowers (Bergsten 2008; Glaser 2015). However, the intervening years have seemed to solidify differences, rather than expand areas of cooperation. While the personalities in Beijing and Washington have likely played a role, the two powers face a fundamental disagreement regarding their vision for the region. This divergence is founded in each state's concept of their national interests. As McDonald notes, US policy has attempted to engage and cooperate with the PRC across all administrations since the end of the Cold War, 'predicated on an assumption that long-term interests were aligned and that engagement with the PRC would ultimately change it into a more liberal state domestically and another "stakeholder" in the US-influenced liberal international order' (McDonald 2019: 32). Meanwhile, the PRC's interest in maintaining rule by the Communist Party causes it to view the US interest in promoting its own values as a direct attack on the regime (General Office of the Chinese Communist Party 2013; Jiang 2018: 36). Combined with a strategic tradition that views nature as a constant process of cyclic becoming and unbecoming, it is not surprising that the PRC views the relationship in terms of competition (Luo 2017: 44–45). Near term accommodation, therefore, is not likely, especially since the most recent *US National Security Strategy*, also now views the relationship in these terms (White House 2017: 3).

From the Australian point of the triangle, overcoming these differences and improving Sino-US relations to the point of transforming the China–US–Australia triangle into something approaching a *ménage à trois* appears highly desirable. Such a transformation would most notably lessen the likelihood that Canberra could be drawn into a crisis or armed confrontation involving the two superpowers and, more broadly, eliminate the fear of having at some point to pick a side. But the rise of cordial relations between Washington and Beijing is not without risks for Canberra. Put simply the creation of a US–China condominium would create the same type of issues as those arising from 'concerts', when great powers negotiate a new status quo with relatively little regard for the interests or feeling of other, weaker actors (Acharya 1999). However, Australia also benefits from its current important roles in both the US vision of regional security and the PRC's economy.

Conclusion: time to start dating

While the above analysis suggests the US–Australia leg of the triangle is the strongest and friendliest, each relationship has areas of cooperation and disagreement. In order to increase their security and redefine regional relations, Australia and the US should leverage their strengths to both court and cajole the PRC into a security architecture that demonstrates the value of Dittmer's *ménage à trois*. In short, Australia and the US should develop means of shaping the security environment so that the PRC no longer deems over-turning it to be in its interest, both because it is of value and because the Australian–US marriage is unassailable.

Australia, recognizing that its security lies in a stable Southeast Asia and Oceania should continue to encourage both powers to engage the region in a constructive and cooperative way. To do so, Australia can continue to lever-age its security relationship, and the growing reliance of the US on regional partners, to provide a positive influence on the development of the US's envisioned regional security architecture. In short, it can use its regional knowledge and geographic position to shape the regional security architecture in a manner that incorporates the US in accordance with its vision. Mean-while, Australia can leverage its more cordial relationship with the PRC to encourage inclusion, much as it has done with Kowari, an annual trilateral military exercise Australia has engineered with the PRC and US (Howe 2019).

If Australia is to leverage its position to bring the PRC and US closer together, it must first envision the context that will make this relationship possible. What are the characteristics of a regional security environment that would be attractive to Australia, the PRC and the US, thus laying the groundwork for a more balanced triangle, if not a *ménage à trois*? To establish such an accommodation, the regional architecture must accommodate the interests of all parties and minimize areas of competition.

First, Australia should encourage the trend towards an Association of Southeast Asian Nations (ASEAN)-centred security architecture. Though its consensus-based decisions model has its challenges, the organization is viewed as an honest-broker by most parties. Moreover, its slow, deliberative process is actually a value for maintaining stability and avoiding rash changes. While this does disrupt the PRC's desire for deference from the region, it does not actually threaten their regime. Moreover, it accommodates US interests in a stable region that is not dominated by any particular regional hegemon.

Second, Australia should be more vocal in expressing its disagreement with both the US and the PRC Though this may at first seem counterintuitive, it is by speaking up that Australia identifies that it can be neither neglected nor bullied, and that it has something valuable to add to the triangular relation-ship. Both the US and the PRC currently need and want their relationship with Australia. Though it may see itself as the weaker power in terms of military and economic size, its position within the region and the international economy provide it leverage if it chooses to use it.

Third, to make the triangle more equal, Australia must look beyond the triangle. The Indo-Pacific can no longer be dominated by great powers. The states of the region are more aware and more interconnected than ever before. They have a say, and a power in numbers. Australia, should leverage this innate multi-polarity and expand its presence in the region, especially where it can do so on a bilateral or multilateral basis. Identifying issue areas where it can build multilateral coalitions will build a regional sense of cooperative solutions to the region's problems. Wherever possible, these initiatives should be linked to one of the many ASEAN Forums. Additionally, both the US and the PRC should be brought into these coalitions so they work with Australia, as well as having their outsized influence moderated by collaborative systems.

Of course, for a relationship to work, all parties must make an effort. From the US perspective, the primary threats posed by the PRC are its attempts to disrupt the international system and desire to remove the US from the region. As the US has no desire to leave the region, but does seek to reduce its cost of engagement, its manner of participation should be cooperative, while demonstrating the value of the US to the region – including the PRC. In this regard, Australia remains a natural and attractive partner. Working with Australia, the US can present an international face to the region and promote community building. However, three decades of failed engagement have built doubt in the US regarding the PRC's willingness to play a constructive role. To overcome this obstacle to regional cooperation, the US should specifically *not* focus on the PRC, but on building a regional architecture that will support US interests by nurturing a region that is both secure and prosperous. Therefore, it should work with Australia to strengthen and support ASEAN as the fulcrum of regional stability, and encourage its independence from all powers, including the US. By focusing on a positive regional security architecture, rather than a Chinese bogeyman, the US can shift the regional narrative from negatively countering the PRC to positively enabling regional security, freedom and prosperity. The long-term goal is to establish a regional architecture that remains amicable to the US, led by ASEAN and open to all who are willing to cooperate and trade. This effort will build an environment that will shape the manner in which all states, including the PRC, engage with each other and create the conditions for a better bilateral US–PRC relationship.

Finally, the PRC must also play a role in establishing a stable international order. This may be the most difficult portion of the puzzle, because unlike the US and Australia, it views the ideas of the other parties as an existential threat to its system of government. While initiatives such as One Belt, One Road do not necessarily conflict with a stable, open international order, the PRC's attempts to control the actions of states through debt and threats must be stopped. For this to occur, the PRC needs to realize that it benefits more from a region of dynamic states, than through obedient vassals. This will not happen overnight and not through engagement for the sake of engagement; rather the PRC must be presented with the reality that the region is moving forward as a collection of sovereign states that cooperate on the basis of shared interests, rather than a Sino-centric order. Thus, Beijing will be faced with a choice between politics of the past and isolation, or cooperating in the Indo-Pacific of the future.

The Indo-Pacific region will continue to be a mix of multilateral relationships. There may be triangles and quads or even circles and roads, but ultimately states strive for security and individuals for prosperity. The Australia–US–PRC triangle may never be perfectly equilateral, but both the Australia–PRC and US–PRC legs can be strengthened through the construction of a regional architecture that maintains a stable environment where states do not feel insecure and individuals are free to prosper. The future shape of the triangle can be more equal, but it requires effort by all three parties to strengthen both those ties, and the environment it exists within.

Note

1 The figures include Hong Kong.

References

Abdelal, Rawi and Johnathan Kirshner (1999), 'Strategy, Economic Relations, and the Definition of National Interests', *Security Studies*, 9 (1–2).

Acharya, Amitav (1999), 'A Concert of Asia?' *Survival*, 41 (3).

Ali, Idrees (2017), 'Chinese Jets Intercept US Surveillance Plane: US Officials', Reuters, 24 July, www.reuters.com/article/us-usa-china-military/chinese-jets-intercept-u-s-surveillance-plane-u-s-officials-idUSKBN1A91QE accessed 27 April 2020.

Armstrong, Shiro and Peter Drysdale (2019), 'China Coal Trade Too Big For Beijing to Meddle With... or Australia to Get Alarmed About', *East Asia Forum*, 25 February, www.eastasiaforum.org/2019/02/25/china-coal-trade-too-big-for-beijing-to-meddle-withor-australia-to-get-alarmed-about accessed 27 April 2020.

Beeson, Mark (2003), 'Australia's Relationship with the United States: The Case for Greater Independence', *Australian Journal of Political Science*, 37 (3).

Bergsten, C. Fred (2008), 'A Partnership of Equals: How Washington Should Respond to China's Economic Challenge', *Foreign Affairs*, 87 (4).

Bisley, Nick (2013), 'An Ally For All The Years to Come: Why Australia is Not a Conflicted US Ally', *Australian Journal of International Affairs*, 67 (4).

Blackwill, Robert (2018), *Trump's Foreign Policies Are Better Than They Seem*, Council Special Report No. 84, www.cfr.org/sites/default/files/report_pdf/CSR%2084_Blackwill_Trump.pdf accessed 27 April 2020.

Campbell, Kurt M. and Ely Ratner (2018), 'The China Reckoning: How Beijing Defied American Expectations', *Foreign Affairs*, 97 (2).

Carney, Stephen A. (2011), *Allied Participation in Operation Iraqi Freedom*, Washington, DC: Center of Military History, United States Army.

Cave, Damien and Jamie Tarabay (2019). 'Suddenly, the Chinese Threat to Australia Seems Very Real', *New York Times*, 28 November, www.nytimes.com/2019/11/28/world/australia/china-spying-wang-liqiang-nick-zhao.html accessed 27 April 2020.

Chai, Tommy Sheng Hao (2020), 'How China Attempts to Drive a Wedge in the US–Australia Alliance', *Australia Journal of International Affairs*, in press.

Chellaney, Brahma (2002), *Feasibility of the Russia–China–India Strategic Triangle: Assessment of Theoretical and Empirical Issues*, Proliferation Papers, no. 5, Paris: Institut Francais des Relations Internationales.

Crawford, Timothy W. (2008), 'Wedge Strategy, Balancing, and the Deviant Case of Spain, 1940–41', *Security Studies*, 17 (1).

Crawford, Timothy W. (2011), 'Preventing Enemy Coalitions: How Wedge Strategies Shape Power Politics', *International Security*, 35 (4).

Department of Defence (2000), *Defence 2000: Our Future Defense Force*, www.defence.gov.au/publications/wpaper2000.pdf accessed 27 April 2020.

Department of Defence (2003), *The War in Iraq: ADF Operations in the Middle East in 2003*, www.defence.gov.au/Publications/Docs/Lessons.pdf accessed 27 April 2020.

Department of Defence (2016), *2016 Defence White Paper*, www.defence.gov.au/WhitePaper/Docs/2016-Defence-White-Paper.pdf accessed 27 April 2020.

Department of Defense (2018), *National Defense Strategy of the United States of America: Sharpening the American Military's Competitive Edge*, https://dod.defense.gov/Portals/1/Documents/pubs/2018-National-Defense-Strategy-Summary.pdf accessed 27 April 2020.

Department of Defense (2019), *Indo-Pacific Strategy Report*, Washington, DC: Department of Defense.

Department of Foreign Affairs and Trade (1996), 'Australia–United States Ministerial Consultations 1996 Sydney Statement, Joint Security Declaration', https://dfat.gov.au/geo/united-states-of-america/ausmin/Pages/australia-united-states-ministerial-consultations-1996-sydney-statement.aspx accessed 27 April 2020.

Department of Foreign Affairs and Trade (2019), 'Trade Statistical Pivot Tables, Australia Level', https://dfat.gov.au/about-us/publications/Pages/trade-statistical-pivot-tables.aspx accessed 27 April 2020.

Dibb, Paul (2007), 'Australia–United States', in Brendan Taylor (ed.), *Australia as an Asia-Pacific regional power: Friendships in Flux?*, London: Routledge.

Dittmer, Lowell (1981), 'The Strategic Triangle: An Elementary Game-Theoretical Analysis', *World Politics*, 33 (4).

Dittmer, Lowell (2005), 'The Sino-Japanese-Russian Triangle', *Journal of Chinese Political Science*, 10 (1).

Dittmer, Lowell (2012), 'Sino-Australian Relations: A Triangular Perspective', *Australian Journal of Political Science*, 47 (4).

Dittmer, Lowell and Baogang He (2014), 'Introduction: Australia's Strategic Dilemma', *Asian Survey*, 54 (2).

Dreyer, June Teufel (2012), 'The Shifting Triangle: Sino–Japanese–American Relations in Stressful Times', *Journal of Contemporary China*, 21 (75).

Edwards, Peter (2005), *Permanent Friends? Historical Reflections on the Australian-American Alliance*, Sydney: Lowy Institute.

Forgey, Quint and Caitlin Oprysko (2020). 'Trump Announces, The Reverses, Freeze On Funding for World Health Organization', *Politico*, 7 April, www.politico.eu/article/donald-trump-threatens-world-health-organization-funding/ accessed 27 April 2020.

General Office of the Chinese Communist Party (2013), 'Communiqué on the Current State of the Ideological Sphere' ('Document No 9'), English translation, www.chinafile.com/document-9-chinafile-translation accessed 27 April 2020.

Gill, Bates and Benjamin Schreer (2018). 'Countering China's "United Front"', *The Washington Quarterly*, 41 (2).

Glaser, Charles L. (2015), 'A US–China Grand Bargain? The Hard Choice between Military Competition and Accommodation', *International Security*, 39 (4).

Grattan. Michelle (2019), 'Kevin Rudd Urges Australia to Reduce its Economic Dependence on China', *The Conversation*, 26 November, https://theconversation.com/kevin-rudd-urges-australia-to-reduce-its-economic-dependence-on-china-127828 accessed 27 April 2020.

Haas, Richard (2017), 'America and the Great Abdication', *The Atlantic*, 28 December, www.theatlantic.com/international/archive/2017/12/america-abidcation-trump-foreign-policy/549296/ accessed 27 April 2020.

Heydarian, Richard Javad (2017), 'Evolving Philippines–US–China Strategic Triangle: International and Domestic Drivers', *Asian Politics & Policy*, 9 (4).

Hirschman, Albert O. (1945), *National Power and the Structure of Foreign Trade*. Berkeley, CA: University of California Press.

Holland, Jack and Matt McDonald (2010), 'Australian Identity, Interventionism and the "War on Terror"', in Asaf Siniver (ed.), *International Terrorism Post 9/11: Comparative Dynamics and Responses*, London: Routledge.

Hornung, Jeffery W. (2014), 'Japan's Growing Hard Hedge Against China', *Asian Security*, 10 (2).

Howard, John (2001), 'Transcript of the Prime Minister, the Hon John Howard MP, Joint Press Conference with the Deputy Prime Minister and the Minister for Foreign Affairs, Parliament House', 14 September, https://pmtranscripts.pmc.gov.au/release/transcript-12308 accessed 27 April 2020.

Howard, John (2003), 'Interview with Steve Liebmann, Today Show, Channel 9', 14 March, https://pmtranscripts.pmc.gov.au/release/transcript-20722 accessed 27 April 2020.

Howe, Katie (2019), 'A Quiet Kowari: US, Australia, and China Trilateral Military Exercise', *The Diplomat*, 30 September, https://thediplomat.com/2019/09/a-quiet-kowari-us-australia-and-china-trilateral-military-exercise/ accessed 27 April 2020.

Isakhan, Benjamin (2014), 'The Politics of Australia's Withdrawal From Iraq', *Australian Journal of Political Science*, 49 (4).

Izumikawa, Yasuhiro (2013), 'To Coerce or Reward? Theorizing Wedge Strategies in Alliance Politics', *Security Studies*, 22 (3).

Jiang Yong (2018). 'Theoretical Thinking on the Belt and Road Initiative', *Contemporary International Relations*, 28 (4) (July/August).

Kelton, Maryanne (2007), *More Than an Ally? Contemporary Australia–US Relations*, London: Routledge.

Kim, Woosang (1996) 'Power, Parity, Alliance, and War From 1648 To 1975', in Jacek Kugler and Douglas Lemke (eds), *Parity and War: Evaluations and Extensions of The War Ledger*, Ann Arbor, MI: The University of Michigan Press.

Kirshner, Johnathan (2009), 'Realist political economy: Traditional themes and contemporary challenges', in Mark Blyth (ed.), *Routledge Handbook of International Political Economy (IPE): IPE as a Global Conversation*. London: Routledge.

Kolstad, Ivar (2019), 'Too Big To Fault? Effects of the 2010 Nobel Peace Prize on Norwegian Exports to China and Foreign Policy', *International Political Science Review*, 41 (2).

Lai, Christina (2018), 'Acting One Way and Talking Another: China's Coercive Economic Diplomacy in East Asia and Beyond', *The Pacific Review*, 31 (2).

Lake, David A. (1997), 'Regional Security Complexes: A Systems Approach', in David A. Lake and Patrick M. Morgan (eds), *Regional Orders: Building Security in a New World*, University Park, PA: The Pennsylvania State University Press.

Leaver, Richard (2001), 'The Meanings, Origins and Implications of 'the Howard Doctrine', *The Pacific Review*, 14 (1).

Lemke, Douglas and William Reed (1996), 'Regime Types and Status Quo Evaluations: PTT and the Democratic Peace', *International Interactions*, 22 (2).

Liff, Adam P. (2018), 'China and the US Alliance System', *The China Quarterly*, 233.

Liu Weidong and Wang Bo (2013), 'The Roles of the United States in the China–US–Japan Trilateral Relations', *Journal of Global Policy and Governance*, 2 (2).

Lockyer, Adam (2012), 'The Logic of Interoperability: Australia's Acquisition of the F-35 Joint Strike Fighter', *International Journal: Canada's Journal of Global Policy Analysis*, 68 (1).

Lockyer, Adam (2017), *Australia's Defence Strategy: Evaluating Alternatives for a Contested Asia*, Melbourne: Melbourne University Press.

Luo Xi (2017), 'Formation, Tendency and Management of Sino-US Strategic Competition in Asian-Pacific Region', *Around Southeast Asia* [in Chinese], (5).

McDonald, Scott D. (2019). '战略竞争? – Strategic Competition?' in Scott D. McDonald and Michael C. Burgoyne (eds.), *China's Global Influence: Perspectives and Recommendations*, Honolulu, HI: Asia-Pacific Center for Security Studies.

Munro, Kelsey (2018), 'Australia's New Foreign-Influence Laws: Who is Targeted?' *The Interpreter*, 5 December, www.lowyinstitute.org/the-interpreter/australia-new-foreign-influence-laws-who-targeted accessed 27 April 2020.

Nebehay, Stephanie (2020), 'WHO Chief Says Widespread Travel Bans Not Needed to Beat China Virus', Reuters, 3 February, www.reuters.com/article/us-china-health-who/who-chief-says-widespread-travel-bans-not-needed-to-beat-china-virus-idUSKBN1ZX1H3 accessed 27 April 2020.

Norris, William J. (2016), *Chinese Economic Statecraft: Commercial Actors, Grand Strategy, and State Control*, Ithaca, NY: Cornell University Press.

Oneal, John R., Frances H. Oneal, Zeev Maoz, and Bruce Russett (1996), 'The Liberal Peace: Interdependence, Democracy, and International Conflict, 1950–85', *Journal of Peace Research*, 33 (1).

Pant, Harsh (2006), 'Feasibility of the Russia–China–India Strategic Triangle: Assessment of Theoretical and Empirical Issues', *International Studies*, 43 (1).

Pape, Robert A (1997), 'Why Economic Sanctions Do Not Work', *International Security* 22 (2).

Passy, Jacob (2014), 'Putin Plays Chicken with US Farmers – and Loses', www.cnbc.com/2014/09/25/vladimir-putins-import-sanctions-fail-to-hurt-us-chicken-farmers.html accessed 27 April 2020.

Pillsbury, Michael (2015), *The Hundred-Year Marathon: China's Secret Strategy to Replace America as the Global Superpower*, New York: Henry Holt and Co.

Pomfret, John (2020), 'The US–China Coronavirus Blame Game and Conspiracies are Getting Dangerous', *The Washington Post*, 18 March, www.washingtonpost.com/opinions/2020/03/17/us-china-coronavirus-blame-game-conspiracies-are-getting-dangerous accessed 27 April 2020.

Reilly, James (2012), 'China's Unilateral Sanctions', *The Washington Quarterly*, 35 (4).

Reilly, James (2013), 'China's Economic Statecraft: Turning Wealth Into Power', www.lowyinstitute.org/sites/default/files/reilly_chinas_economic_statecraft_web_0.pdf accessed 27 April 2020.

Ross, Robert S. (2019), 'On the Fungibility of Economic Power: China's Economic Rise and the East Asian Security Order', *European Journal of International Relations*, 25 (1).

Russett, Bruce (1998), 'A Neo-Kantian Perspective: Democracy, Interdependence, and International Organizations in Building Security Communities', in Emmanuel Adler and Michael Barnett (eds), *Security Communities*, Cambridge: Cambridge University Press.

Schweller, Randall L. (1993), 'Tripolarity and the Second World War', *International Studies Quarterly*, 37 (1).

Schweller, Randall L. (1998), *Deadly Imbalances: Tripolarity and Hitler's Strategy of World Conquest*, New York: Columbia University Press.

Smith, Paul J. (2013), 'The Tilting Triangle: Geopolitics of the China–India–Pakistan Relationship', *Comparative Strategy*, 32 (4).

Steff, Reuben and Francesca Dodd-Parr (2019), 'Examining The Immanent Dilemma Of Small States in the Asia-Pacific: The Strategic Triangle Between New Zealand, the US and China', *The Pacific Review*, 32 (1).

Tammen, Ronald L. *et al.* (2000), *Power Transitions: Strategies for the 21st Century*, New York: Chatham House.

Tow, William T. (2004), 'Deputy Sheriff or Independent Ally? Evolving Australian–American Ties in an Ambiguous World Order', *The Pacific Review*, 17 (2).

Walt, Stephen M. (1987), *The Origins of Alliances*, Ithaca, NY: Cornell University Press.

Waltz, Kenneth N. (1979), *Theory of International Politics*, New York: McGraw-Hill.

Waltz, Kenneth N. (2000), 'Structural Realism after the Cold War', *International Security*, 25 (1).

White House (2017). *National Security Strategy of the United States of America*, Washington, DC: White House.

Williams, Brock R. and Keigh E. Hammond (2019), 'US–China Tariff Actions by the Numbers', www.hsdl.org/?abstract&did=830458 accessed 27 April 2020.

Wong, Catherine (2018), 'US, Chinese Warships Within Metres of Collision in South China Sea, Leaked Pictures Show', *South China Morning Post*, 3 October, www.scmp.com/news/china/military/article/2166849/us-chinese-warships-within-metres-collision-south-china-sea accessed 27 April 2020.

Part III
The future

9 The US–Australian alliance and its implications for Australian defence strategy and procurement

Fred Smith, Yves-Heng Lim and Adam Lockyer

It has become a cliché to describe Australia's alliance with the United States as the cornerstone of its defence policy and strategy (Beeson 2003). This does not mean, however, that it is any less true. The United States remains central to Australian defence planning (Bell 1987; Bisley 2013; Cox and O'Connor 2012). Indeed, there are few stages within Australia's defence planning process where the US alliance is not a prominent – if not the primary – factor in the decision-making process. However, the US–Australia alliance is entering a new era and the expectations of each partner are shifting quickly (Lockyer 2017a; Lockyer 2017b; Lockyer 2015). The rise of Asia, in general, and People's Republic of China (PRC), in particular, is redefining the relationship (Ayson 2012). Australia's region is transforming from being a placid backwater during much of the later stages of the Cold War and post-Cold War era, to being increasingly contested.

The US–Australian alliance has a long and deep history. Australia has faithfully joined the United States in most of its combat operations since the end of the Second World War, including Korea, Vietnam, the Gulf War, Somalia, Afghanistan and Iraq. This history of working together on operations has led both sides – and particularly Australia – to emphasize technological, logistical and doctrinal interoperability when making procurement decisions. However, Australia's defence strategy is no longer simply looking at the United States for direction. The rise of other great powers within the region are increasingly casting their own shadow over the defence planning process. In particular, Australia is now equally concerned with how the United States and China will react to Canberra's decisions on procurement, doctrine and defence strategy.

The rapid changes in technology and the balance of capabilities in Asia mean that there is now only one certainty: the future will be different from the past (Baker 1991). This chapter sketches some likely possible futures for both the US–Australia alliance and procurement. Section One examines in more detail the historical antecedents of the relationship. Section Two outlines how changes in the military balance in Asia are affecting the US–Australia alliance. It continues by outlining three possible future options for the alliance:

- expanding US basing agreements;
- filling a gap – Australia developing 'niche' naval capabilities; and
- joint forward basing.

Each of these options will require a very differently tooled Australian Defence Force (ADF). This chapter will outline the procurement implications of the decisions.

A legacy: the alliance and patterns of acquisition for Australia

Although closely tied to the United States defence alliance since the Second World War and the signing of the Australia, New Zealand, United States Security Treaty (ANZUS) in 1951, the different services of the ADF have balanced defence system procurement in different ways. The Royal Australia Navy (RAN) and the Australian Army, for example, have balanced their procurement decisions between Europe, the United States and indigenously-produced weapon systems and platforms. The Royal Australian Air Force (RAAF), in contrast, has depended almost exclusively upon American built airframes.

As Table 9.1 shows, the RAN naval procurement has been a 'mixed bag' of platforms and systems from an array of national providers.

Despite this 'mixed bag' approach to ship platform procurement, the overarching requirement for RAN platforms and systems is that they be interoperable with their US counterparts. A good example of this is the US-supplied Aegis air-defence system (Radar tracking and weapon systems

Table 9.1 Royal Australian Navy – diversified procurement graph.

Built	Type	Class	Nation of Design
2009–2020	Air warfare destroyer	Hobart class	Spain
2009–2015	Landing helicopter dock (LHD)	Canberra class	Spain
2018–	Auxiliary oiler replenishment (AOR)	Supply class	Spain
1965	Destroyer	Perth class	US
1978–1992	Frigate	Adelaide class	US
1961	Destroyer escort	River class	UK
1957–1978	Conventional attack submarine	Oberon class	UK
2002–2007	Landing ship	Bay class	UK
1990–2003	Conventional attack submarine	Collins class	Sweden
-	Conventional attack submarine	Attack class	France
1993–2006	Frigate	ANZAC class	German

integration) employed on the Hobart-class destroyers (Air Defence Destroyers – AWD). The Aegis system allows for a shared secure datalink between RAN and US Navy ships and other C4ISR communications systems. This allows for the instantaneous sharing of data and ensures that the warships of the two nations have the same combat picture (Dominguez 2019). A second example of the RAN's tight interoperability procurement requirements is reflected in the current project-build of the Shortfin Barracuda attack submarine. The Shortfin Barracuda was selected by Australia through a competitive process in 2016. Despite being designed in France and built and fitted out in Australia, the United States will be responsible for supplying integrated combat systems for the new boats, as well as provide the submarine's weapons systems. These boats' bodies might be French, but they will think and speak in American English. These examples demonstrate that although the platforms themselves may be designed and built elsewhere, where warfighting systems are concerned, the RAN is fully interoperable with the United States.

In contrast, the RAAF is seamlessly integrated with United States' weapons platform and combat systems. Indeed, since 1945, Australia's warplanes have been almost exclusive supplied by the United States. The only time the RAAF has seriously looked beyond US suppliers has been when Australia's acquisition cycle has fallen outside the United States' cycle. For example, Australia was still operating the F-86 Sabre in the late-1950s. This was well after the United States had replaced their own Sabres with the F-100 Supersabre and F-105 Thunderchief. Australia was forced to purchase the French Mirage III largely because the US F-105 Thunderchief was coming to the end of its lifecycle, while the F-4 Phantom II was still in development. The RAAF learnt its lesson and has subsequently attempted to align its procurement cycle more directly with the United States. Indeed, it has shown a willingness to purchase warplanes 'off the plans'. The F-111C and the F-35 JSF were both acquired via this fashion.

The RAAF is currently procuring the United States' Lockheed Martin F-35 Lightening II fighter/attack aircraft and is already operating the following:

- Boeing F/A-18F Super Hornet;
- McDonnell Douglas F/A-18A/B Hornet fighter-attack aircraft;
- Boeing EA-18G Growler Electronic Warfare aircraft;
- Lockheed AP-3C Orion maritime patrol aircraft (MPA), (which is currently being replaced by Boeing P-8A Poseidon MPA);
- Boeing C-17 Globemaster;
- Lockheed C-130 Hercules transport aircraft;
- Boeing 737;
- E-7A AEW&C, Wedgetail Airborne Early Warning & Control aircraft; and
- Gulfstream MC-55A Peregrine Intelligence, Surveillance, Reconnaissance and Electronic Warfare (ISREW) aircraft.

The European Airbus KC-30A air refuelling tanker aircraft is the only significant exception to the otherwise exclusively American fleet. The future of the RAAF looks likely to resemble the past. In the new Unmanned Aircraft Systems (UAS) category, the RAAF plans to acquire Northrop Grumman's MQ-4C Triton maritime patrol UAS, a high altitude long endurance (HALE) aircraft and has shown interest in acquiring the US General Atomics Aeronautical MQ-9B Sky Guardian hunter-killer UAS.

So why does the RAAF mirror the US Airforce and US Navy fleet of aircraft so closely? There are three main reasons. First, the close alliance between the United States and Australia means that the supply chain and acquisition of sensitive and sophisticated combat systems is often streamlined compared with comparable possible procurement partners. Second, air combat requires seamless coordination and communication between allied aircraft. Operating the same aircraft facilitates the exchange of training and tactics, techniques and procedures (TTPs) between the RAAF and the US Air force (USAF) and US Navy (USN), Naval Aviation. Finally, on operations, it is likely that the RAAF will share airfields with the USAF and USN Naval Aviation. It improves operational efficiency and effectiveness being able to borrow parts and ordinance from the neighbouring hanger. Indeed, even further, there is substantial advantages to being able to help work on each other's aircraft while on operations.

To be truly integrated, however, Australia and US defence forces must 'train' as they would expect to 'fight' in a potential future conflict. This means that correctly manning, training, equipping and operating Australia's defence forces should go hand in hand with its US counterparts. All the sophisticated and interoperable C4ISR architectures, tied to combat weapons platforms and systems, will be of little use if the manning, training and equipping of these military forces does not keep pace. In the case of the US–Australia alliance, this means conducting combined and joint training exercises where the integration of these systems and capabilities is honed through the use of shared tactics, techniques and procedures (TTPs) and shared secure communications systems. Combined Joint Exercises such as biennial-held 'Talisman Sabre' and RAAF Combined biennial exercise 'Pitch Black' are examples of exercise training opportunities where problems and solutions to interoperability challenges presented can be identified and overall operational capabilities improved (McGhee 2019).

Operations where Australian and US defence forces work side-by-side also greatly improve interoperability. The RAN's Operation MANITOU, working within the US Navy's Fifth Fleet and under the Combined Maritime Force (CMF) Bahrain command and control architecture provides the RAN with superb operational experience and interoperable execution of day-to-day missions. Similarly, During Operation OKRA, the ADF contributed to the international efforts to fight to fight the ISIS in Iraq and Syria. The ADF deployed 780 personnel to the Middle East, including contributions to the Air Task Group (ATG), the Special Operations Task Group (SOTG) and Task

Group Taji (TG Taji). The RAN and RAAF forces are also deployed in support of US 'Maximum Pressure' operations in northeast Asia focused on enforcing UN Security Council Sanctions on North Korea, currently supported by HMAS Parramatta, RAAF MPA conducting surface surveillance missions, and with ADF intelligence support (McGuirk 2018; Lubold and Talley 2018). These current and recent real world, day-to-day operations enhance interoperability and tighten the relationship between the Australian Defence Force and its US defence force counterparts.

But what next? What is needed today to prepare for the future? What should be the next step be in strengthening capabilities while improving warfighting interoperability? And, in what strategic context is the Australia–US defence alliance framed now and into the near-to-midterm future?

The consequences of a changing Asia

Australia's strategic landscape is changing at a rapid pace. Put simply, Australia confronts a fast-changing region where the rise of China creates considerable uncertainties about the stability of the regional security environment over the near and far term. China's ascent has fundamentally shifted the balance of power in the region. There is an abundant literature on the causes and consequence of the extraordinary growth of China's military power (see, for instance, Heginbotham et al. 2015; Cliff 2016; Cole 2010; Pehrson 2006) and a detailed discussion is beyond the scope of this chapter, but the scale of the change can easily be grasped. In 1995, China's share of Asia's military expenditure was a mere 9.5 per cent; by 2018 it was 49.5 per cent (SIPRI 2020). In 1995, both the People's Liberation Army Navy and Air Force operated antiquated platforms whose design lagged two generations behind their Western counterpart. Twenty-five years later, the PLAAF operates more than nine hundred 4th-generation fighters (more than three times the number deployed by Japan) and is introducing a 5th generation fighter – the J-20 (IISS 2020). The PLAN operates today the largest fleet of modern diesel-electric submarines in the world, more than sixty modern major surface combatant – including the brand new 12,000-ton Type 055 large destroyer – and has a developing aircraft carrier program. Together with the rapid modernization of the Strategic Missile Force (Erickson 2019), these developments might not make China a peer competitor of the United States at the global level, but modern China possess a serious challenge to the United States across the political, economic and strategic domains within Asia (Heginbotham et al. 2015).

The geopolitical reverberations of the power shift to Asia, and the redistribution of military power within Asia, have resulted in an urgent need to revisit Australia's defence strategy (Thomas, Cooper and Rehman 2013). Rapid changes in the balance of power have resulted in increased pressure on one of Australia's primary areas of strategic concern, the Indo-Pacific Arc, defined broadly as the maritime gateway between the Indian and Pacific oceans which it captures Malaysia, Singapore, Indonesia and northern Australia (Lockyer 2017a, 2017b). The Indo-Pacific Arc is central to Australia's security. The region has traditionally been conceptualized as Australia's 'northern approaches' or the direction through, or from, any conventional attack on Australia would be most likely to come. In the Twenty-First Century, however, the Indo-Pacific Arc's value to the great powers is along its horizontal-axis rather than its vertical-axis (Lockyer 2017a: 247–250). As Robert Kaplan writes:

> The Strait of Malacca is the Fulda Gap of the twenty-first century multipolar world, the place where almost all of the shipping lanes between the Red Sea and the Sea of Japan converge at the most vital choke point of world commerce; where the spheres of naval influence of India and China meet; where the Indian Ocean joins the western Pacific.
>
> (Kaplan 2010: 261)

Despite this geopolitical change, the presence of a potentially hostile great power, or even strategic competition within, the Indo-Pacific Arc would be a major security concern for Australia.

As a middle power, Australia's ability to single-handedly counter China's expansive power and ambitions in the Indo-Pacific Arc is severely limited. Canberra has little choice but to rely on the involvement of its traditional ally. Fortunately, the United States has two major strategic interests in the Indo-Pacific Arc. First, the Indo-Pacific Arc is a vital fulcrum for swinging US military power between the Pacific and Indian oceans. The ability to quickly move and concentrate military power is fundamental to the United States' grand strategy (Posen 2003). Second, as a maritime trading power, the United States has a vital interest in ensuring that the world's main trading routes remain open, secure and free (Bradford 2011; Yoshihara 2013). It is hardly surprising, therefore, that the United States has repeatedly restated its commitment to the preservation of a favourable balance of power in the Indo-Pacific system (White House 2017). But, though the roots of US involvement in the Indo-Pacific run deep (Green 2017), Washington's involvement in the region remains, nonetheless, a strategic choice rather than a necessity. In other words, the US can – and might – ultimately decide that the costs of its commitment in the Indo-Pacific region exceed the benefit and opt for a strategy of 'retrenchment' or 'offshore balancing' (MacDonald and Parent 2011, 2018). Seen from an Australian perspective, the problem boils down to the classical risk of 'abandonment' (Snyder 1997: 181; Renouf 1979), a risk obviously compounded by Australia's relative weight in the region. In this sense, in spite of the convergence of strategic interests between Australia and the United States in regard to the future of the Indo-Pacific, Canberra has little choice but to try engineering a strategy that would lock in American presence and commitment to the region (O'Neil 2011).

For a small-middle power like Australia, a strategy designed to keep a great power like the US in can essentially be described as a strategy of influence (Schelling 2008 [1966]). Rarely will a small-middle power be able to force, or even compel, a great power to change their policy position. Instead, small-middle powers in their relations with great powers will need to groom, prompt, pressure, reassure, help and threaten the foreign capital's decision-making elite. A small-middle power's objective should be to manipulate the great power's will to fight. Confronted to a hostile great power, a middle power's influence strategy can be largely equated with a strategy of deterrence, that is a strategy that aims at manipulating the cost-benefit of the opponent to lessen its will to fight. An influence strategy can also be implemented to alter the will to fight of a friendly great power and a small-middle power will attempt to increase a friendly great power's will to fight over strategic interests vital to themselves through military exchanges, exercises and operational interoperability (Lockyer 2013). This can be achieved through either 'general' or 'immediate' influence activities.[1] General influence activities are used to shape the environment and how the great power views its relationship with the small-middle power. A small-middle power will use immediate influence activities when there might soon be needed to call upon the great power to defend its strategies interests. For instance, immediate influence activities might be attempted if a small-middle power identified an urgent threat to one of its strategic interests and had some doubts about the commitment of its more powerful ally.

General influence activities are a traditional objective of naval diplomacy. Port visits, personnel exchanges, conferences and joint exercises can be used to signal goodwill and benign intentions. Geoffrey Till points out, for instance, that ship 'visits can be a useful form of diplomatic exchange [to] help maintain or secure good relations and win popular favour' (Till 2004: 300). *Australian Maritime Operations* emphasizes that 'operational calls', 'goodwill visits' and exercises have an important role to play in fostering good relations between the visiting and the host nations (Royal Australian Navy 2017: 157). For small-middle power navies, these confidence-building measures can play an important role in consolidating the commitment of friendly great powers. To a certain extent these measures can play a role in shaping the great power preferences if only because reneging on commitments after having demonstrated friendship might entail significant reputational costs for the great power (Schelling 2008 [1966]).

Option 1: expanding US basing agreements

Beyond the manipulation of reputational costs, a small-middle power might be able to more directly manipulate the cost–benefit analysis of a friendly great power. The basing or permanent rotation of military assets (e.g. the US Navy's littoral combat vessels through Singapore) is arguably the most effective means of 'bonding' the great power to the interests of the small-middle power and convincing opponents of the commitment.[2] In addition to the resulting interdependence that basing decisions often create, they can also act as a 'trip wire' (Schelling 2008 [1966]: 111–116). That is, it will be difficult for an opposing great power to attack the hosting small-middle power's military forces without also damaging the friendly great power's military assets. This danger increases the risks of escalation and the aggressor finding itself in a war with a peer competitor.

Australia has already taken steps in this direction. The ongoing rotation of US Marines to Darwin is a potential template for how basing arrangements between Australia and the US could proceed. 'Rotations' avoid many of the traps and complication that always accompany foreign basing agreements. 'Rotations' would focus joint efforts on enhancing combat power, improving warfighting capabilities and facilitating the ability to operate jointly and seamlessly, rather than getting bogged-down on issues of payouts, money and legal liability, like the US bases in Japan often do (Newsham 2020).

James Holmes, a strategist at the US Navy War College, would agree with this concept and an even more aggressive US basing in Australia. Holmes contends that 'doubt will linger in allied minds unless they regard American commitments as irrevocable, but US deployments to Oz are skin in the game. Stationing military forces overseas inspires trust. In turn, an unbreakable bond between America and Australia could give China pause the next time it contemplates making mischief' (Holmes 2019; also see Holmes and Yoshi-hara 2008). Holmes continues by differentiating, yet connecting, military interoperability, capability and US stationing in Australia to deterrence:

> Capability and cohesion buttress deterrence. So, interoperability is good because it translates into capability, and because capability joined with common purpose transmits a message – disheartening potential foes, giving heart to allies, and helping win over doubters we would like to recruit as allies or coalition partners. Interoperability – a tactical function – has direct political import. But concentrating on tactics and politics obscures the strategic worth of stationing forces in Australia.
>
> (Holmes 2019)

US Navy presence in the immediate vicinity of the Indo-Pacific Arc and its ability to react quickly, flexibly and decisively to contingencies arising in the region is also key to a credible deterrence. Greater US military presence in Australia could, in this sense, directly contribute to the stability of the Indo-Pacific Arc and help lock the US in. An often-cited 2012 report by the CSIS suggests that:

> Australia's geography, political stability, and existing defense capabilities and infrastructure offer strategic depth and other significant military advantages to the United States in light of the growing range of Chinese weapons systems, US efforts to achieve a more distributed force posture,

and the increasing strategic importance of Southeast Asia and the Indian Ocean An enhanced US defense presence in Australia would expand potential opportunities for cooperation with Indonesia, other Southeast Asian countries, and India, and it would complement parallel initiatives such as rotationally deploying Littoral Combat Ships in Singapore and increased US military access to the Philippines.

(Berteau et al. 2012)

The Center for Strategic and Budgetary Assessments (CBSA), writing in its study *Tightening the Chain: Implementing a Strategy of Maritime Pressure in the Western Pacific*, emphasizes that in any potential conflict with China, 'the US ability to operate from Australia would be invaluable', going on to discuss the value of north Australia both to marshal any NATO allies that might support the US and Australia with military forces in a contingency, as well as to use northern airbases for US tactical fighter/attack and long-range bomber aircraft, air tanker refuelling, maritime patrol aircraft and UAS operations in a South China Sea scenario (Mahnken, Sharp, Fabian and Kouretsos 2019).

Discussion in US military academic and 'think tank' circles has focused increasingly on the need for the US to increase its presence and military support to friendly nations along the second island chain in the western Pacific, even referring it not as a 'chain' but as a 'cloud', and although not officially connected to northern Australia, certainly both Manus Island off northern Papua New Guinea (PNG) and Darwin on the northern coast of Australia are close enough to be considered geographically synonymous, deserving the same consideration (Rhodes 2019a). In fact, Rhodes suggests that the US strategy should abandon the narrower focus of the 2nd island 'chain' constraint altogether and instead emphasize the larger 'cloud' concept, highlighting a broader US regional role buttressed by increased investment and an enduring presence (Rhodes 2019b).

Beyond the joint US–Australia–PNG Manus Island naval base redevelopment and improvement initiative announced by US Vice President Pence in 2018 during the APEC Summit in PNG (Whiting 2018), Darwin in particular stands out as a logical focus of US–Australia defence improvement and forward basing efforts, particularly when considering that the distance from Manus Island to Haikou, Hainan, China is 4,692 kilometres (km) or 2,529 nautical miles (nm), while the distance from Darwin to Haikou is 4,239 km or 2,228 nm, even closer – although the strategic value of an additional axis of approach Manus Island provides is also important.

Using what's known as 'Mahan's Yardstick', an approximate 'standard distance' of 3,500 nm (roughly the distance from Hawaii to Guam) for naval planning, recognizing that not all naval capability can be measured in terms of readiness, budgets, numbers of ships, even warfighting capabilities but also on the distance from home ports to potential areas of operations or conflict, distance matters greatly in measuring effectiveness (Rhodes 2019b). Today, based on modern warfighting capabilities, that 'critical distance' for both strategic and operational planning is considerably shorter, potentially down to 1,000 nm, placing greater emphasis on 'range, reach, and distance in force planning', making the forward basing challenge even more pressing.

Future Australian procurement under Option 1

If the 'Expanding US Basing Agreements' option was to be pursued, then Australia's future procurement would likely change in three ways:

- an expanded amphibious capability based in Darwin;
- if US Navy nuclear-powered submarines were based in Australia, then this would increase the likelihood that the RAN would acquire nuclear powered attack submarines; and
- if US long ranged bombers were to be based at RAAF Tindal, then the RAAF would likely either acquire similar bombers or the ability for their fighters to escort the USAF bombers.

This would mean Australia would likely focus its naval and army procurement on amphibious capabilities. The ADF would likely consider establishing a combined amphibious force in Darwin, supported by amphibious ships from both nations home-ported in Darwin, moving some US Marine forces outside potential weapon engagement zones and facilitating engagement out to potential southeast Asian partner nations for training and exercises (Roberts 2019).

If the US decided to permanently station nuclear powered submarines in Australia (possibility at HMAS Stirling in Western Australia), then this would significantly increase the chances that Australia would decide to acquire nuclear powered attack submarines. Currently, the main arguments against Australia acquiring nuclear powered submarines are (a) a lack of mechanical and technical knowledge in regards to the maintenance and up keep, (b) nuclear reactor facilities suitable to maintain a nuclear power fleet and (c) the Australian peoples' reluctance to have nuclear power near population centres. The permanent stationing of US Navy boats would overcome many of these problems as the facilities would need to be built, Australian sailors could learn how to maintain the boats by working alongside their American colleagues and – presumably – the Australian public would have become accustomed to having nuclear powered warships port at HMAS Stirling, which open the door to Australia's acquisition. Australia has already committed to buying 12 French Shortfin Barracuda attack submarines, but unlike the French boats Australia's will be conventionally powered. It would be a relatively simple switch to have later boats to be built as nuclear-powered boats.

Similarly, there have been discussions of basing USAF long-range bombers from RAAF Tindal in the Northern Territory. Australia would likely seek to leverage this opportunity by either procuring their own long-range bombers to operate alongside the USAF fleet or focus their F-35 JSF for long-range escort duties, possibly with additional in-flight refuelling capabilities and airborne early-warning and command (AWAC) aircraft. This would provide Australia with a new deterrence by punishment capability, which has been missing since the retirement of the F-111C in 2010 (Babbage 1980, 1990, 2008).

Option 2: filling a gap – Australia developing 'niche' naval capabilities

Crafty small-middle powers have, at times, developed niche capabilities that a great power has become reliant upon. In Australia's quest to tie the United States to the region, it may procure capabilities that provide it with considerable intra-alliance leveraged at critical times. For instance, the US Navy momentarily found itself in a delicate position during the Tanker War (1984–1988) when the initial reluctance of its European allies to engage in minesweeping operations exposed the shortcomings of the US Navy in this domain (Cordesman 1990). Decades of viewing minesweeping as a peripheral activity that could be farmed-out to the smaller Europeans allies almost crippled the entire United States' operation. By deliberately developing niche capabilities, small-middle powers can increase the great power's dependency on them which, in turn, can be leveraged by the small-middle power to manipulate the great power's will to fight at critical times. A shrewd small-middle power can make abandonment a two-way street.

In the Australian context, the development of 'niche' capabilities could essentially mean developing the navy around 'pockets of excellence' in domains where the United States is at a relative weakness. In theory, such a niche navy would contribute to bolstering US–Australia's deterrence against encroachments on the Indo-Pacific Arc, but also enhance Australia's influence on its ally as Australia's non-participation would, at least, entail significant additional costs for the United States. In a way, Canberra seems to have already taken steps in that direction with its future submarine program. Milan Vego emphasizes (2010) that United States nuclear attack submarine were not the optimal platform to operate in littorals and that the United States might need to add diesel-electric submarines to its fleet. With major investments in the *Barracuda-Shortfin*, Australia is set to acquire precisely the type of capabilities that maximize synergies between national and coalition needs.

Conventional submarine options

Conventional diesel-electric submarines (designated SSK) have the advantage of being able to operate quietly while running on battery-power in the shallow-water of the littorals of East Asia and in strait choke-points of maritime Southeast Asia. They can then recharge their batteries at night or during lower vulnerability periods. Their advantage is in their stealth and ability to operate in relatively swallow water. Their vulnerability, however, is their slower speed and more limited range. Indeed, if discovered, an SSK would need to switch from stealthily battery propulsion to its relatively loud and noisy diesel engine(s). Even then, under diesel power the submarine will not be able to travel more 20 knots (kn).

The arguments for and against nuclear versus conventional submarines are legendary, but suffice it to say there are advantages and disadvantages to each and Australia has chosen the conventional option, while the United States has chosen to develop a purely nuclear submarine force (Ohff 2017; Walker and Krusz 2018). These two forces are complimentary and, indeed, the RAN and USN submarine forces will be able to perform different functions better than the other. Overtime, these close working partners could become increasingly dependent upon each other. It may well develop into a 'long sword', 'short sword', interoperable strategy within a single operational planning architecture.

Logistics and sustainment options

One niche naval capability focus area where Australia could assist the US, and it seems the USN could use and would appreciate the help, is in the area of sustainment through improved naval logistics support. Logistics and sustainment requirements in a combat contingency in the South China Sea or East Asia would be extensive, as discussed in the CSBA study, *Tightening the Chain,* which calls for support to distributed military operations in a contested environment along the First Island Chain relying on 'greater use of prepositioned stocks of munitions and sustainment materiel, manned and unmanned air and sea assets for mobility and resupply, and emerging technologies' (Mahnken, Sharp, Fabian and Kouretsos 2019: 55).

In particular, the US Navy's 14 Maritime Prepositioning Ships (MPS), US Naval Ship (USNS) contingent, part of the Military Sealift Command's (MSC) Prepositioning Program, are in need of significant recapitalization and potential replacement. These ships preposition US Marine Corps vehicles, equipment and ammunition throughout the world, with prepositioned logistics ships forward deployed in the Indian Ocean at Diego Garcia and in the Western Pacific at Guam and Saipan. Based on a September 2019 readiness exercise or 'stress test' of the sealift fleet, with 33 of 61 sealift ships activated simultaneously, less than half were fully prepared to get underway for a major sealift operation in a crisis, demonstrating that the fleet is in urgent need of recapitalization if it is to be relied upon (Larter 2019).

Admiral Davidson, Commander US INDOPACOM, recently testified to Congress stating that his operational plans are critically reliant on logistics support, the logistics support provided by sealift: 'Clearly recapitalization of our sealift system is going to be critically important, as its aging out and really has propulsion plants that [are] expiring in capability and our ability to maintain them', Davidson said. 'It's [a] risk to our troops and all of our people that are forward in the region if there is any delay in our ability to deliver the logistics in accordance with the [operation] plans' (Larter 2019). Despite this pressing requirement, sealift recapitalization is under threat due to projected costs of the Common Hull Auxiliary Multi-Mission Platform (CHAMP), a key initiative in the sealift recapitalization effort, made even more pressing as the sealift fleet is either becoming obsolete or is nearing the end of its service life (Larter 2019).

Australia has several ways in which it could contribute to support the alliance's logistics, sustainment 'tail'. The Australian shipbuilder, Austral, has recently announced that it is has been approved by the US to have its shipyards in Australia bid for and provide services to USN and MSC ships. Leveraging off this approval and close shipbuilding and maintenance relationship with the USN, Austral can support logistics and MPS ships based or operating in the Indo-Pacific region. Potentially, Australia could offer to upgrade the port of Darwin to facilitate basing and maintenance there for existing USNS MPS ships or their follow-on MSC successors. Working with US planners, Australia could also invest in building more robust logistics storage and maintenance facilities in Darwin, equipping them with the right mix of stores and munitions for a potential Indo-Asia-Pacific contingency. Although more costly, the RAN could consider investing more heavily in logistics ships and sustainment that would support both the RAN and USN in a conflict.

ISR and autonomous vehicles – air, surface, subsurface

On January 26, 2020, the US Navy forwardly deployed MQ-4C Tritons Unmanned Aerial Vehicles (UAV) to Guam. This signals that the US Navy is preparing for a far more aggressive role for autonomous platforms and unmanned vehicles – in the air, on the surface and beneath the waves – in the future (Vercellone 2020). In CBSA's *'Tightening the Chain'* study, unmanned platforms (air, surface and subsurface) – are described as conducting operations from ISR and communications, to strike and logistics support in sea denial and air denial campaigns (Mahnken, Sharp, Fabian and Kouretsos 2019: 32–34).

Australia could contribute in this area. Commander Paul Hornsby, the RAN lead on 'maritime remotes' (autonomous vehicles that will complement and interact with manned platforms in the maritime domain), points to the *2018 Australian Robotics Roadmap* as an indicator of the Australian approach to cross-leveraging robotic systems and AI, as the report stated: 'Robotics can be the force multiplier needed to augment Australia's highly valued human workforce and to enable persistent, wide-area operations in air, land, sea, subsurface, space and cyber domains' (Laird 2020). Already Australia is working with core 5-Eyes partner allies to consolidate R&D efforts and collaborate to better develop and manage autonomous vehicles in a shared C2 system integrated with allied combat systems (Laird 2020).

Option 3: dividing the Darwin–Manus–Guam line

The ports of Darwin, Manus Island (in Papua New Guinea) and Guam represent the south eastern extent of the Second Island Chain. These three ports could possibly become an interconnected defensive network designed to track any air, surface or subsurface platform transiting from East Asia into the South Pacific. An allied A2/AD strategy that can counter China's expansionist tendencies (Biddle and Oelrich 2016; Lockyer and Symons 2019; Lockyer in press; Lockyer and Cohen 2017). Under this framework, Australia would take responsibility for the Darwin to Manus area of operations, while the US Navy assumes primary responsibility for the Guam to Manus area of operations. This 'possible future' for the alliance envisages each of the allies to take responsibility for a different section of the line of containment (Gaddis 2005). The result for Australia would be far more air and naval forces deployed to the port of Darwin and RAAF Tindal, which would constantly be transiting to and from Manus Island on surveillance tasks.

The US Navy Submarine Squadron 15 could be used for a template. Here, the US Navy forward bases submarines to Guam on a rotational basis. The RAN could follow suit, with two to three SSK submarines permanently on rotation through Darwin and Manus Island. The remaining fleet could be undergoing training and maintenance back at HMAS Stirling. Under this plan, Australia SSK submarines would be nearer the potential region of conflict and transit to and arrive on station in chokepoints or critical sea lines of communication (SLOC) operating areas in less time, helping overcome the tyranny of distance and slow platform speed.

As discussed previously, conventional submarines may operate well in the shallow waters while patrolling on battery-power at slower speeds (3–5 kn), but they are notoriously slow when transiting, with a nominal sustained forward speed of advance of approximately 10–15 kn. The sea between Darwin and Manus Island is primarily shallow and characterized by islands and straits, which is perfect terrain for an SSK to operate. In contrast, the ocean between Guam and Manus Island is deep open ocean, which is more the preferred hunting ground of the SSNs of the US Navy. So, this division of labour also plays to comparative advantages of each alliance partner.

Surface combatants, such as the Hobart-class AWD, with a top SOA of 28+ kn are better capable of moving quickly from their home base in Sydney to Darwin. However, in the bigger scheme of things, they are still relatively slow and would benefit from being forward based in Darwin on a rotational basis along with the SSKs.

In addition to increased RAN focus on the Darwin-Manus line, the RAAF would also need to move additional resources to RAAF Tindal. RAAF Tindal has already been cited for upgrades to its runways and facilities to support new F-35 Joint Strike Fighters and possibly US Air Force longer-range bomber aircraft and air tanker. (Packham 2020). With the addition of seven new RAAF MQ-4C Triton UAS, the RAAF should consider forward basing one to two patrol ready airframes forward, either at RAAF Tindal or RAAF Base Darwin, operating out of Darwin International Airport, as the US Navy has done in Guam.

Future Australian procurement under Option 3

Arguably the greatest advantage of Option 3 is that both Australia and the United States current and planned procurement strategies closely match those that would be required for patrolling the Darwin–Manus–Guam line. As discussed above, Australia's conventional submarine and surface forces are well suited for operations through and around the Papua New Guinean straights and islands; while the US Navy prefers the open ocean like that between Guam and Manus Island.

The main changes to Australia's procurement strategy within Option 3 would mainly relate to basing. Darwin port would require major upgrades to be able to handle the rotation of a significant amount of the RAN's fleet. Similarly, Manus Island would need to be upgraded to be able to port both Australian and American submarines and major surface combatants. The facilities would also need to be upgraded to support command, control and communication between the RAN and US Navy. In addition, the island would also likely require anti-aircraft, anti-ship and anti-ballistic missile capabilities.

Conclusion

As Peter Jennings (2020) recently wrote: 'A much sharper strategic competition for influence is building in Asia between the US and China. Australia can't opt out from this reality. Washington and its key allies, Japan and Australia, need to give the wider region some confidence that collectively we can push back against Beijing's bullying'. He explains why geography matters – that Southeast Asia was the strategic fulcrum during the Second World War and it is today, as the PRC clearly shows its intent to supplant US security leadership in the region.

In this chapter we have sketched some of the possible futures for the US–Australian alliance and what the implications of these different roads will mean for Australia's future military procurement. We argue that there are broadly three main avenues: Expanding US Basing Agreements; Filling a Gap; or Joint Forward Basing. Of these three different futures, arguably joint basing along the Darwin–Manus–Guam line would require the less change in each alliance partners' current fleet of warships, submarines and aircraft. It would also make a valuable strategic contribution to blocking China's political and strategic encroachment towards the South Pacific.

Notes

1 'General' and 'immediate' influence activities is adopted from Patrick Morgan's distinction between general and immediate deterrence (see Morgan 1977; Morgan 2009).
2 Bonding behaviour is a classic means of 'bandwagoning'. For a discussion, see Walt (2005: 191–194) and Walt (1997).

References

Ayson, Robert (2012), 'Choosing Ahead of Time? Australia, New Zealand and the US–China Contest in Asia', *Contemporary Southeast Asia*, 34 (3).
Babbage, Ross (1980), *Rethinking Australia's Defence*, St Lucia: University of Queensland Press.
Babbage, Ross (1990), *A Coast Too Long: Defending Australia Beyond the 1990s*, North Sydney: Allen and Unwin.
Babbage, Ross (2008), 'Learning to Walk Amongst Giants', *Security Challenges*, 4 (1).
BakerIII, James A. (1991), 'America in Asia: Emerging Architecture for a Pacific Community', *Foreign Affairs*, 70 (5).
Beeson, Mark (2003), 'Australia's Relationship with the United States: The Case for Greater Independence', *Australian Journal of Political Science*, 38 (3).
Bell, Coral (1987), *Dependent Ally: A Study in Australian Foreign Policy*, Melbourne: Oxford University Press.
Berteau, David J., Michael J. Green, Gregory T. Kiley, Nicholas F. Szechenyi, Ernest Z. Bower, Victor Cha, Karl F. Inderfurth, Christopher K. Johnson, Gary A. Powell, and Stephanie Sanok (2012), *US Force Posture Strategy in the Asia Pacific Region: An Independent Assessment*, Washington, DC: CSIS.
Biddle, Stephen and Ivan Oelrich (2016), 'Future Warfare in the Western Pacific: Chinese Antiaccess/Area Denial, US AirSea Battle, and Command of the Commons in East Asia', *International Security*, 41 (1).
Bisley, Nick, (2013), '"An Ally for All the Years to Come": Why Australia is Not a Conflicted US Ally', *Australian Journal of International Affairs*, 67 (4).
Bradford, John F. (2011), 'The Maritime Strategy of the United States: Implications for Indo-Pacific Sea Lanes', *Contemporary Southeast Asia*, 33 (2).
Cliff, Roger (2016), *China's Military Power: Assessing Current and Future Capabilities*, Cambridge: Cambridge University Press.
Cole, Bernard D. (2010), *The Great Wall at Sea*, Annapolis, ML: Naval Institute Press.
Cordesman, Anthony H. (1990), *The Lessons of Modern War, Volume II*, Washington, DC: Center for Strategic and International Studies.
Cox, Lloyd and Brendan O'Connor, (2012), 'Australia, the US, and the Vietnam and Iraq Wars: "Hound Dog, Not Lap Dog"', *Australian Journal of Political Science*, 47 (2).
Dominguez, Gabriel (2019), 'Final Hobart-class Destroyer to be Delivered to RAN in February 2020', *Jane's Defence Weekly*, 11 November.
Erickson, Andrew S. (2019), 'China's Massive Military Parade Shows Beijing is a Missile Superpower', *The National Interest*, 1 October.
Gaddis, John Lewis (2005), *Strategies of Containment: A Critical Appraisal of American National Security Policy During the Cold War*, Oxford: Oxford University Press.

Green, Michael (2017), *By More Than Providence: Grand Strategy and American Power in the Asia Pacific Since 1783*, New York: Columbia University Press.

Heginbotham, Eric*et al.* (2015), *The US–China Military Scorecard: Forces, Geography, And The Evolving Balance Of Power, 1996–2017*, Santa Monica, CA: RAND.

Holmes, James R. and Toshi Yoshihara (2008), *Chinese Naval Strategy in the 21st Century: A Turn to Mahan*, London: Routledge.

Holmes, James (2019), 'America Needs A Navy Base in Australia – For More Than Just Countering China', *The National Interest*, 9 December.

IISS (2020), *The Military Balance*, London: Routledge/IISS.

Jennings, Peter (2020), 'Letting the Beijing Bully Know This is Our Neighbourhood', *The Australian*, 21 February.

Kaplan, Robert (2010), *Monsoon: The Indian Ocean and the Battle for Supremacy in the 21st Century*, Collingwood, VIC: Black Inc.

Laird, Robbin (2020), 'Shaping an Australian Navy Approach to Maritime Remotes, Artificial Intelligence and Combat Grids', *Second Line of Defence*, 2 March.

Larter, David B. (2019), 'The US Military Ran The Largest Stress Test of its Sealift Fleet in Years. It's in Big Trouble', *Defense News*, 31 December.

Lockyer, Adam (2017a), *Australia's Defence Strategy: Evaluating Alternatives for a Contested Asia*, Melbourne: Melbourne University Press.

Lockyer, Adam (2017b), 'The Future of Australian Defence Strategy', *United Services*, 64 (4).

Lockyer, Adam (2013), 'The Logic of Interoperability: Australia's Acquisition of the F-35 Joint Strike Fighter', *International Journal*, 68 (1).

Lockyer, Adam (2015), 'An Australian Defence Policy for a Multipolar Asia', *Defence Studies*, 15 (3).

Lockyer, Adam (in press), 'The Future of Deterrence and the Arms Trade', in Andrew T. H. Tan, (ed.) *Research Handbook on the Arms Trade*, Cheltenham: Edward Elgar.

Lockyer, Adam, and Michael D.Cohen (2017), 'Denial Strategy in Australian Strategic Thought', *Australian Journal of International Affairs*, 71 (4).

Lockyer, Adam and Jonathan Symons (2019), 'The National Security Implications of Geoengineering: An Australian Perspective', *Australian Journal of International Affairs*, 73 (5).

Lubold, Gordon and Ian Talley (2018), 'Seven Countries Join to Hunt Ships Smuggling Fuel to North Korea', *The Wall Street Journal*, 14 September.

Mahnken, Thomas G., Travis Sharp, Billy Fabian and Peter Kouretsos (2019), *Tightening the Chain: Implementing a Strategy of Maritime Pressure in the Western Pacific*, Center for Strategic and Budgetary Assessments (CSBA), 23 May, https://csbaonline.org/research/publications/implementing-a-strategy-of-maritime-pressure-in-the-western-pacific/publication/1 accessed 16 July 2020.

MacDonald, Paul K. and Joseph M. Parent, (2011), 'Graceful Decline? The Surprising Success of Great Power Retrenchment', *International Security*, 35 (4), 7–44.

MacDonald, Paul K. and Joseph M. Parent, (2018), *Twilight of the Titans: Great Power Decline and Retrenchment*, Ithaca, NY: Cornell University Press.

McGhee, Rachel (2019), 'Talisman Sabre War Gaming Sees Largest Australian-led Beach Invasion Exercise', *ABC News*, 17 July.

McGuirk, Rod (2018), 'Australia Assigns Warship to Enforce North Korean Sanctions', *Associated Press*, 12 October.

Morgan, Patrick M. (1977), *Deterrence: A Conceptual Analysis*, Beverly Hills, CA: Sage Publications.

Morgan, Patrick M. (2009), *Deterrence Now*, New York: Cambridge University Press.

Newsham, Grant (2020), 'Can US–Japan Avoid Train Wreck on Defense Costs? Washington Wants Tokyo to Quadruple The Amount it Pays For Military Protection Under the Special Measures Agreement', *Asia Times*, 6 March.

O'Neil, Andrew (2011), 'Conceptualising Future Security Threats to Australia's Security', *Australian Journal of Political Science*, 46 (1).

Ohff, Hans J. (2017), 'Nuclear Versus Diesel-Electric: The Case for Conventional Submarines for the RAN', *The Strategist*, (ASPI blog), 11 July.

Packham, Ben (2020), 'Strategist Paul Dibb Calls For Long-Range Top End Missiles', *The Australian*, 21 February.

Pehrson, Christopher J. (2006), *String of Pearls: Meeting the Challenge of China's Rising Power Across the Asian Littoral*, Carlisle: Strategic Studies Institute, US Army War College.

Posen, Barry (2003), 'Command of the Commons: The Military Foundation of US Hegemony', *International Security*, 28 (1).

Renouf, Alan, (1979), *The Frightened Country*, Melbourne: Macmillan.

Rhodes, Andrew (2019a), 'The Second Island Cloud: A Deeper and Broader Concept for American Presence in the Pacific Islands', *Joint Force Quarterly*, 95 (4).

Rhodes, Andrew (2019b), 'Go Get Mahan's Yardstick', *Proceedings*, 145 (7).

Roberts, Seth (2019), 'Former Marine Colonel Pitches Australian–American Amphibious Force in Western Pacific', *Stars and Stripes*, 31 December.

Royal Australian Navy (2017), *Australian Maritime Operations*, Canberra: Sea Power Centre.

Schelling, Thomas C. (2008 [1966]), *Arms and Influence*, New Haven, CT: Yale University Press.

SIPRI (2020), 'SIPRI Military Expenditure Database', www.sipri.org/databases/milex accessed 22 April 2020.

Snyder, Glenn H. (1997), *Alliance Politics*, Ithaca, NY: Cornell University Press.

Thomas, Jim, Zack Cooper and Iskander Rehman (2013), *Gateway to the Indo-Pacific: Australian Defence Strategy and the Future of the Australia–US Alliance*, Washington, DC: Center for Strategic and Budgetary Assessments.

Till, Geoffrey (2004), *Seapower: A Guide for the Twenty-First Century*, London: Routledge.

Vego, Milan (2010), 'The Right Submarine for Lurking in the Littorals', *Proceedings*, June.

Vercellone, Chiara (2020), 'US Navy's First Triton Drones Arrive in Guam', *Defense News, 28* January.

Walker, Michael and Austin Krusz (2018), 'There's a Case for Diesels', *Proceedings*, June, 144 (6).

Walt, Stephen M. (2005), *Taming American Power: The Global Response to US Primacy*, New York: W. W. Norton.

Walt, Stephen (1997), 'Why Alliances Endure or Collapse', *Survival*, 39 (1).

White House (2017), 'National Security Strategy of the United States of America', www.whitehouse.gov/wp-content/uploads/2017/12/NSS-Final-12-18-2017-0905.pdf accessed 16 July 2020.

Whiting, Natalie (2018), 'Joint US–Australian Naval Base on Manus Island a "Significant Pushback" Against China's Pacific Ambitions', *ABC News*, 18 November.

Yoshihara, Toshi (2013), 'The US Navy's Indo-Pacific Challenge', *Journal of the Indian Ocean Region*, 9 (1).

10 The future of Australia–US strategic and defence cooperation

An Australian perspective

Andrew O'Neil

Introduction

America's global alliance network stands at a crossroads. Under the Trump administration, US engagement with allies in Europe and the Indo-Pacific has been turbulent and characterized by a resurgent transactionalism on the part of Washington. The 'America First' mantra of the administration, coupled with Trump's own fixation on the 'cost' of alliances, has produced an environment where Washington's political relations with most allies remain fractious and edgy. President Trump's directive to the Pentagon in June 2020 to reduce US force numbers in Germany by 10,000 personnel was a unilateral move with no consultation with Berlin or other NATO capitals (Pancevski 2020). Similarly, the earlier cancellation in 2018 by the White House of joint US–South Korean military exercises followed Trump's repeated questioning in private of the rationale for keeping US forces deployed on the Korean peninsula (Kim and Snyder 2020: 86). Despite the best efforts of the US foreign policy and defence establishments to reassure allies that institutions are more powerful than agents, NATO members and bilateral US allies in the Indo-Pacific have been knocked off balance by President Trump's approach to alliance management.

However, this is not the first time US allies have been under pressure from Washington, with burden sharing tensions in NATO remaining a recurring sore point for the US going back to the 1950s. The notion of Europeans free-riding on a generous US benefactor retains serious purchase in policy making circles in Washington, and all US administrations have grappled with how to turn around low defence spending among NATO allies. In the Indo-Pacific, uncertainties about long-term US commitment to allies runs deep. The last crisis of confidence in US regional staying power followed the 1969 Guam Doctrine, but concerns about Washington's commitment to Asia emerged after the Cold War and were not allayed until the 1995 Nye Review. Despite repeated reassurances about a continued US presence since that time, concerns persist about whether the US might be tempted to retreat to an offshore balancing posture if Washington judges the costs of maintaining primacy as excessive.

Moreover, the Trump administration is not the first US administration to treat US allies with disrespect in public. In the 1970s, the Nixon and Carter administrations withdrew significant US military components from South Korea with little if any consultation of the government in Seoul. Only after elements of his own administration pushed back did Carter retreat from his intention to pull out all US forces (including nuclear weapons) in the face of opposition from South Korea. In the NATO context, the Nixon administration periodically floated ideas about the US pulling back its military commitment to NATO unless European allies increased spending on their conventional forces. In quintessential Trumpian rhetoric, in March 1974 President Nixon informed an audience of European leaders that they 'cannot have it both ways. They cannot have the US participation and cooperation on the security front and then proceed to have confrontation and even hostility on the economic and political front' (quoted in Sayle 2019: 187).

One of the curious features of the Trump period is that, in spite of the tough rhetoric from the White House, in a number of significant respects the US has effectively deepened its military commitments worldwide between 2017 and 2020. This has aligned with the 2018 National Defense Strategy, which underscored the importance of reinforcing the role of alliances in the Indo-Pacific and Europe (US Department of Defense 2018). Within NATO, the Trump administration has continued to harden the US forward presence in eastern Europe and the Baltic states through the increased rotation of US forces (including nuclear-capable assets), and joint exercises (Emmott and Chalmers 2020). In the Indo-Pacific, although it ended the basing of nuclear-capable aircraft in Guam in 2020 (Trevithick 2020), the Trump administration has focused on reassuring allies by strengthening the extended deterrence dialogues with Tokyo and Seoul, regularly reaffirming the nuclear umbrella, and eschewing nuclear no-first-use while endorsing lower-yield warhead capabilities in the 2018 NPR (Office of the Secretary of Defense 2018). With Australia, the US has expanded the Force Posture Initiative finalized under the Obama administration, which has included expanding basing options for US strategic bombers.

US political commitments to alliances may have weakened under the Trump administration, but on the ground America's alliances have in fact been strengthened since 2017. How is this likely to evolve in coming years? And where does the Australia–US alliance fit? In this chapter, I discuss the key drivers of the alliance from Australia's perspective and sketch three potential options for Australian strategic policy over the next decade. These options are by no means exhaustive, but they do illustrate the constraints confronting Canberra as governments look to navigate a security climate in the Indo-Pacific that will be rougher and possibly more dangerous over the next decade. Australia's strategic anxieties are likely to stem mainly (as they do today) from concerns over the behaviour of the People's Republic of China; concerns that exist independently from the alliance relationship with the US. More aggressive Chinese espionage and cyber-attacks targeted at Australia's national assets have exacerbated existing anxiety about Beijing's assertive conduct in the region where it has sought, inter alia, to limit freedom of navigation through declaring territorial control of islands in the South China Sea and through the declaration of an air defence identification zone in the East China Sea. Yet, China's conduct is not the only factor exercising the minds of Australian strategists. Growing awareness of the Trump administration's treatment of other US allies has underscored the potentially tenuous nature of long-term US commitments. But, like all junior US allies, Australia is equally conscious of the risks of alliance entrapment, which have risen appreciably as the Obama and Trump administrations have embraced more muscular approaches to China in the Indo-Pacific and elsewhere.

Drivers of the Australia–US alliance

Since the formal end of the trilateral ANZUS alliance in 1986, the bilateral security alliance between Australia and the US has evolved within a framework that prioritizes close defence and intelligence cooperation. As the late Desmond Ball (2001) noted, the intelligence relationship between the two countries remains the 'strategic essence' of the alliance, providing as it did the foundation of cooperation during the Pacific War that led to the ANZUS treaty in 1951. The Five-Eyes intelligence agreement, which frames much of the intelligence cooperation between Canberra and Washington, predated the ANZUS treaty by four years and provided the foundation for much of the Cold War cooperation on intelligence collection, exchange, and analysis. Defence cooperation within the alliance reflects the intimate military-to-military ties between the countries' armed services. These are supplemented and reinforced by the Australian Defence organization's close ties to US Indo Pacific Command (INDOPACOM) and the embedding of ADF personnel in various US combatant commands. There is a high degree of interoperability between the US and Australian militaries, which has deepened further as a result of the Afghanistan and Iraq commitments, while Australia's force structure and procurement decision mirror a presumption for acquiring US equipment and platforms.

All of this is underpinned by a strong normative framework of shared democratic values and a political narrative that emphasizes '100 years of mateship' and an 'unbreakable alliance' between the two countries. At times verging on the sentimental, this narrative features heavily in elite rhetoric on both sides that cites shared wartime experiences and 'genuine cultural affinity and a spirit of collaboration'.[1] This is further reinforced by the strongly favourable popular perceptions of both countries among their respective populations. In the most recent Lowy Institute poll, for instance, more than three-quarters of respondents said they regarded the US alliance as 'very important' or 'fairly important' for Australia's security. This level of support has remained relatively consistent since the poll began in 2005, despite falls under the Bush and Trump administrations (Lowy Institute 2020a). While the emphasis on shared values is not unusual in US alliances (NATO's survival in the decade after the Cold War was due in no small part to shared norms among member states), the degree to which Australian elites – who are not generally renowned for their sentimentality – seize on emotive rhetoric about the alliance is noteworthy.

Yet, as with all security alliances, the core purpose of the Australia–US alliance is to formalize reciprocal commitments to use force. Indeed, the prospect of using military force in unison with other states to achieve common goals is the *raison d'être* of alliances. As Paul Schroeder (1976: 227) has observed, 'whether offensive or defensive, limited or unlimited, equal or unequal, bilateral or multilateral, alliances must involve some measure of commitment to use force to achieve a common goal'. Like all junior allies of the United States, Australia has tried to fashion alliance arrangements that yield benefits disproportionate to the input costs of maintaining the alliance. A major plank in the approach of successive Australian governments has been to provide modest support to the US militarily outside theatres of immediate security concern to Australia with a view to building up a stock of credit in Washington that can be leveraged if and when Australia's core security interests are ever threatened. The ANZUS treaty provides few, if any, reassurance touchpoints for Australia that US support in such an event would necessarily be forthcoming. The treaty itself is vague on obligations, and the US has a track record of specifying limitations to its commitments under the treaty. In a functional sense, moreover, and in contrast with other US alliances worldwide, the Australia–US alliance has little institutional depth and is characterized by a high degree of informal bargaining based on personal relationships.

Thus, despite the potent nature of the political narrative underpinning the alliance, along with the clear defence and intelligence benefits that flow from being allied with the world's strongest power, Australian policymakers have grounds to be uncertain about a future US commitment to use force to protect Australia's core interests. Disappointment about the absence of forthcoming US support in West Papua, *Konfrontasi*, and even the initial reluctance of the US to support Australia in East Timor in 1999 has been a recurring theme in Australian defence policy (Cohen and O'Neil 2015). This has led to Australian officials being somewhat wary of seeking clarifications that 'could result in a more limited US commitment than would serve Australia's interests' (Defence Committee 2009 [1976]: 604). Equally, Australian officials have been reticent to engage the US in direct dialogue on deterrence issues, which is almost certainly due to awareness of potential entrapment risks and concern that the US may not provide Australia with the sorts of reassurances it asks for.[2]

While Australia cannot be sure the US would necessarily come to its defence *in extremis*, would-be adversaries cannot be sure the US would not. As with all junior allies outside NATO, it is this ambiguity that provides a degree of reassurance for Australia rather than any iron clad security guarantee. Chinese strategists have indicated they believe Washington would be just as focused on restraining allies with a view to de-escalation as it would be on intervening in a conflict between a US ally and China because of concerns about escalation to a nuclear conflict (Cunningham and Fravel 2019: 75). When one reviews the cautious US reaction to the North Korean strikes on South Korean territory in 2010, and Washington's view that Japan should resist pushing back against Beijing in East China Sea, these Chinese strategists may have a point (see Ramstad 2010; Hughes 2016: 139). On the other hand, given the high levels of bipartisanship in Washington about the scale of the long-term great power challenge from Beijing, there is likely to be a groundswell of support for US intervention if China is seen as the aggressor in any conflict. Indeed, at the time of writing, it is difficult to think of a scenario where an Indo-Pacific ally of the United States would be engaged in a conflict with China without the US already being involved militarily due to its presence in the region.

Although ambiguity of US commitment may provide some reassurance, the threshold for US intervention remains unclear. The depth of defence and intelligence cooperation with the US has accelerated dramatically since the 1970s, and the normative currency of the alliance has increased among elites on both sides, but Australian policy makers have every reason to abide by the assessment contained in the 1976 Defence White Paper that 'it is possible to envisage a range of situations in which the threshold of direct US combat involvement [in support of Australia] could be quite high' (Killen 1976: 10). Since the end of the Cold War, Australian strategic guidance has made no public reference to US intervention on Australia's behalf, with the sole exception of protecting Australia against nuclear threats.[3] Unlike other US allies, Australia invokes the nuclear umbrella for the sole purpose of deterring nuclear threats, but does not reference any role for US conventional or nuclear forces deterring large-scale conventional military threats to Australia. Significantly, Australia is the only major US ally that claims the applicability of the nuclear umbrella with no corresponding confirmation from Washington and does not have a formal nuclear policy consultation process with the US (Fruhling and O'Neil 2020: 142–143).

Future options?

As Australia's security environment continues to evolve in ways that are hard to predict, policy makers may be tempted to recalibrate the country's strategic posture, and with it the nature of the alliance with the United States. What sort of options will Australia have in the medium to longer term? Below, I sketch three possible options, each with varying degrees of plausibility. As a middle power, Australia is not necessarily master of its strategic destiny, but it does have some options in the years ahead. The road Australia takes will depend largely on the evolving security environment in the Indo-Pacific, in particular how China interacts with countries in the region, but it will also be

186 of Andrew O'Neil

contingent on US alliance management and domestic factors in Australia itself, including whether centre-right or centre-left governments are in power at critical junctures of strategic decision making.

Armed neutrality

Despite the long-standing alliance with the US, the concept of armed neutrality has a well-established presence in the history of Australian strategic discourse. While the roots of armed neutrality can be traced back to Australia's role in the British Empire, in a contemporary context, 'the idea has drawn strength from its having provided an alternative to the dominance of the US alliance in Australian strategic thinking' (Dean 2019: 190). The idea that Australia should eschew its alliance with the United States and base its strategic policy on neutrality reached a peak in the late 1960s when serious doubts emerged about the willingness and ability of the US to support its Asian allies in the face of looming defeat in Vietnam. This perspective never acquired mainstream appeal, but the Gorton government – in particular Prime Minister Gorton himself, who had inherent distrust of great powers – was sympathetic to the concept. The serious thought given in the late 1960s to what it would take for Australia to achieve a threshold nuclear weapons capability should be seen in this light (Lyon 2008: 435–446).

Advocates of armed neutrality in Australia's current strategic debates are relatively hard to find, in part because it is rare for analysts to argue that Australia should strive for greater independence from the United States *and* substantially increase its defence expenditure to safeguard long-term security. In recent times, Hugh White (2019) is one of the few mainstream defence experts to mount a serious case for Australia investing in the military capabilities (including long-range strike forces) it would require to become 'a strategically independent middle power over coming decades'; notably, White's book on the subject includes a chapter devoted to an independent nuclear capability. Others have detected the re-emergence of Gorton era doubts about US extended deterrence in the 2020 Defence Strategic Update's call for Australia to 'take greater responsibility for our own security' and the prescription that 'the ADF [Australian Defence Force] grow its self-reliant ability to deliver deterrent effects' (Lyon 2020). Doubts about the Trump administration's commitment to allies in general, coupled with (re)emerging doubts about US staying power in the Indo-Pacific in the wake of coronavirus disease 2019 (COVID-19), hardly render discussion about armed neutrality mainstream, but they do make it less of a fringe activity than it has been in recent years.

However, conceptual discussions and hints in Defence documents at greater self-reliance do not mean that armed neutrality will be at the heart of Australia's strategic policy anytime soon. Firstly, Australia remains acutely dependent on US military platforms to equip the ADF. This has been a deliberate approach by successive Australian governments, going back to the

Menzies period, to promote interoperability with US forces in joint operations. Indeed, the long-range anti-ship missile (AGM 158C) touted by the 2020 Defence Strategic Update as a new capability acquisition to enhance the ADF's 'deterrent effects' is purpose built for the US Air Force and US Navy (Navy Recognition 2020) and has the effect of further locking Australia into the US military procurement network. In any crisis requiring the use of Australian forces (with or without the US being involved), Canberra would remain acutely reliant on uninterrupted supplies from the US, potentially in a high level combat environment where integrated logistics would inevitably become an issue. In short, without a defence industry base that can safeguard self-reliance during crises, credible armed neutrality for Australia is little more than wishful thinking.

Second, while the US alliance may have frayed around the edges under the Trump administration, it has not frayed to the extent that core assumptions about US reliability have changed in Australia's strategy. Rightly or wrongly, Australian policy makers still operate on the assumption that the US alliance will probably 'deliver' in a crisis; as noted, the key uncertainty is at what threshold this would occur if the US was not directly involved. While it is not beyond the bounds of possibility for this assumption to be revised, it would require a significant loss of confidence in the US security alliance, potentially triggered by Washington failing to back another ally under threat. The third reason why armed neutrality will struggle to gain traction in the Australian context is an aversion among policy makers and the public to spend what it takes to acquire the military capabilities to achieve genuine self-reliance. The 2009 Defence White Paper laid out an ambitious plan for acquiring a host of maritime and air capabilities that came closer than any White Paper since the 1970s to embracing self-reliance (Department of Defence 2009), but enthusiasm waned among policy makers as the extent of the proposed costs became clear. Modest levels of defence spending despite a worsening strategic climate in the Indo-Pacific demonstrate that, at least for the foreseeable future, successive Australian governments remain content to free ride on the US alliance for as long as possible.[4]

Bandwagoning with China

Bandwagoning has traditionally been defined among realists as weaker states submitting to rising great powers and is typically juxtaposed with balancing, where states either unilaterally or with other likeminded states seek to constrain the rise of the new great power (Waltz 1979). But as Randall Schweller (1994: 74) has argued, this dichotomy overlooks that different states have different reasons to either balance or bandwagon: 'The aim of balancing is self-preservation and the protection of values already possessed, while the goal of bandwagoning is usually self-extension: to obtain values coveted'. As the bilateral relationship between Canberra and Beijing continues to deteriorate, it seems fanciful to ponder the option of Australia bandwagoning with

China; indeed, Australia's current behaviour appears to align with the text-book definition of balancing. Moreover, there seems to be a negligible pro-spect of this changing in the face of increasingly shrill rhetoric from Beijing directed towards those states that directly, or even implicitly, challenge China's behaviour. Growing public opinion in Australia seems to back the Morrison government's willingness to challenge Beijing on issues as diverse as human rights in Hong Kong, freedom of navigation in the South China Sea, and the origins of COVID-19. While most Australians still regard China more as an economic partner than as a security threat, this gap has been rapidly narrowing since 2018 (Lowy Institute 2020b).

However, Australia's ongoing, and acute, economic dependence on China persists. Around one-third of all Australian exports are bound for Chinese markets and over one-quarter of Australia's two-way trade is with China (DFAT 2020a: 5). There are no serious rivals to China in terms of trade and although foreign direct investment from the US (which accounts for roughly one-quarter of inbound FDI; DFAT 2020b) can be seen as being just as important as trade with China, trade delivers more immediate employment and income benefits than FDI, and the tangible benefits are therefore more 'visible' for communities. And despite calls from some analysts for Australia to wean itself off its economic dependence on China (Xu 2020), there are very few if any plausible proposals for how this might be done without punching a major hole in the Australian economy. Beijing has demonstrated an awareness of the sensitivity of this dependence by issuing threats that it may advise Chinese consumers to avoid Australian goods and not travel to or study in Australia (tourism and education have been two of the biggest Chinese dominated markets in Australia). Although Chinese authorities deny drawing any link, these threats typically accompany periods of political tension in the Sino-Australian relationship.

The prospect of Australia bandwagoning with China is a scenario that has in the past exercised some US observers. Writing in the final years of the Bush administration, Joshua Kurlantzick (2007: 214) warned that China had the potential 'to drive a wedge' between the US and Australia while Robert Kagan (2008: 38) claimed that Australia was 'tilting towards China and away from the United States and other democratic powers in the region'. Echoes of this anxiety are still evident and potentially remain a point of underlying sensitivity in the Australia–US relationship. In widely publicized remarks during a visit to Sydney in 2019, Secretary of State Mike Pompeo responded to a question referring to the benefits Australia gains from its economic rela-tionship with China by noting: 'Yeah, look, you can sell your soul for a pile of soybeans, or you can protect your people' (Department of State 2019). From Washington's perspective, the zero-sum logic of great power competition with Beijing means that there is little tolerance for US allies hoping to compart-mentalize economic and political relations with China. This is not good news for Australia, which has been pursuing a strategy that seeks to bracket com-mercial from political relations with Beijing. Although Canberra's willingness to accommodate China has declined as evidence grows of Beijing's inter-ference in Australian domestic affairs, there is no evidence of a genuine appetite to emulate the US approach of linking security and commercial relations. Even the Morrison government has been careful to avoid endorsing closer strategic collaboration with the US in areas that would provoke China, such as joint freedom of navigation operations (FONOPS) and endorsing the future deployment of US intermediate range missiles to northern Australia (Packham and Aikman 2019).

How likely is a future Australian decision to bandwagon with China? As far-fetched as it seems at the time of writing, this scenario is something that cannot be ruled out. There can be no doubt that Canberra's willingness to challenge China publicly is based on genuine values and a desire not to be pushed around by an authoritarian great power, but there must be a question about whether future governments will continue with such an approach in the event the US withdraws to an offshore balancing posture and/or if the cred-ibility of US security assurances dissipate over time. Australian policymakers undoubtedly see the US alliance as something of a safety net in their dealings with China; without confidence in the alliance, Australia's willingness to stand up to China may decline over time. Assuming the established aversion to outlaying significantly higher defence expenditure to achieve a greater degree of genuine self-reliance remains, it is unlikely future governments will feel sufficiently confident in pushing back against China if the US dials down its presence in the Indo-Pacific. Combined with a lack of any realistic options to offset trade dependence on China, this may result in a gradual shift on the part of Australian policy makers to a position that is more sympathetic to Beijing's worldview when it comes to the regional order in the Indo-Pacific, which may ultimately result in bandwagoning.

Deeper commitment to the alliance

Of the three options presented here, Australia deepening its strategic rela-tionship with the United States within the alliance is the most plausible in the years ahead. It is one of the striking paradoxes of the Australia–US alliance that the key initiatives to embed Australia in the US global military network took place just as doubts about the alliance were reaching their peak in the late 1960s and early 1970s. Yet, more than any other initiative, the advent of US satellite ground stations at Nurrungar and Pine Gap (known colloquially as 'the bases' and formally as 'the joint facilities') bound Australia to the United States in a tangible strategic sense. Unlike many other US allies, Australia never stationed US forces or nuclear weapons on its soil, but for all intents and purposes the joint facilities were just as effective in assuring Aus-tralian policy makers that the US would defend continental Australia by dint of the presence of these bases. Since the 1970s when Soviet officials made thinly veiled references to nuclear strikes on the joint facilities, successive Australian governments have been aware that these would almost certainly be targets in the event of a war, including in any conflict between the US and China (Fruhling and O'Neil 2020: 142).

However, in contrast to US alliances elsewhere, the Australia–US alliance is characterized by a degree of detachment in relation to joint planning, strategic policy coordination, and the physical stationing of US military assets on the junior ally's territory. As one analyst has noted, '[a] heavy reliance on personal relationships at the political and working levels; the effectiveness of ad hoc cooperation; an aversion on the part of each country to ask much of the other regarding future commitments; the low-cost, decentralized, informal cooperation between them; and a heavy emphasis on past conflicts and common values to shore up political support have traditionally been considered strengths of the US–Australian relationship' (Fruhling 2018: 199–200). This has obscured the relative dearth of institutional ballast underpinning the alliance when compared to the NATO, South Korean, and Japanese examples. Although many critics and supporters of the alliance in Australia claim that the security relationship is as intimate as any other alliance, this does not stand up to close scrutiny; in reality, there is significant scope for deeper alliance cooperation between Australia and the US.

NATO-like military cooperation, including nuclear-sharing and joint operational planning may be out of the question for a variety of reasons, but closer operational cooperation in the form of a more ambitious rotation of US strategic bomber assets through northern Australia, the home porting of a US aircraft carrier task force, and the stationing of US missiles on Australian territory are all potential options. Also, increased joint air and naval patrols in the Indo-Pacific with the US and other allies such as Japan is an area that remains underdeveloped (Townshend, Thomas-Noone and Steward 2019). In 2012, the Gillard government agreed to the US–Australia Force Posture Initiative that included a 'rotational' deployment of US marines to Darwin, additional pre-positioning of equipment, space surveillance sensors, and increased US air operations from Australia. Full implementation, however, has been hampered by protracted negotiations on cost-sharing (Crane 2019) as well as Australian reluctance to confirm closer involvement in US long-range offensive operations in the Indo-Pacific. Yet, the Morrison government announced in February 2020 that it would be investing $1.1 billion at RAAF base Tindal to help enable operation of tanker aircraft in addition to the operation of US strategic bombers (Doran 2020).

There are three key reasons why deeper alliance cooperation remains the most likely option for Australian policy makers, notwithstanding the perennial concern on the part of junior allies about potential entrapment in US military operations. The first and most obvious reason is path dependence. Despite its under-institutionalized nature, the Australia–US alliance has evolved in such a way that has resulted in deepening security cooperation over time. This is because the values and inherent properties of all alliances are geared towards closer defence cooperation the longer they remain in existence. In the case of the Australia–US alliance, deeper cooperation is a logical step in accordance with its established trajectory, and for this reason can be seen as the path of least resistance domestically for Australian policy makers; it starts looking attractive when juxtaposed with significant tax hikes to underwrite the military spending required to achieve armed neutrality or the backlash to perceived 'kowtowing' to China likely to result from bandwagoning with Beijing. The second reason is that Beijing is likely to become more assertive in its demands that Australia comply with China's policy preferences. A major theme permeating the 2020 Defence Strategic Update was the need for Australia to reinforce its deterrence capabilities; some of this can be achieved through the acquisition of specific military capabilities, but given the widening differential with Chinese capabilities, looking to how extended deterrence can contribute to filling the capability gap in relation to China makes sense. Third, and related to the point about path dependence, deeper cooperation with the US is relatively straightforward for governments to 'sell' to the Australian public and to various stakeholders within the national bureaucracy. The bigger challenge would come with convincing some regional neighbours that home porting a carrier strike group or stationing intermediate range missiles on Australian soil necessarily aligns with their security interests. That said, the subdued response in the region (including from Jakarta) to the new long-range strike capabilities outlined in the 2020 Defence Strategic Update may point to an era when concerns in Southeast Asia over China outweigh those about specific military acquisitions by Australia (Massola 2020).

Conclusion

Despite a lack of institutional depth in the Australia–US alliance and doubts over the threshold at which the US would intervene to defend Australia, successive governments in Canberra regard the alliance as central to strategic policy. Australia's defence and intelligence capabilities are deeply enmeshed in US and US-led networks, which has promoted a degree of dependence that would make it difficult for any Australian government to withdraw from the alliance, even if it wanted to. The transaction costs alone of shifting defence procurement flows would be huge and the potential loss of access to the Five Eyes intelligence network would have deleterious implications for Australia's long-term security. Seen in this light, the Australia–US alliance appears here to stay. However, whether it continues to evolve as it has over the past few decades is more of an open question. Periodic soul-searching within the US over the cost of global leadership is likely to intensify as the scale of the costs of COVID-19 become clearer, and alliances will undoubtedly be in this mix. At the very least, burden sharing expectations will grow as the US public demands a greater emphasis on putting America first in resource allocation terms (as distinct from the Trump administration's principal use of 'America First' as a slogan). Even if Donald Trump proves to be a one-term president, some of his overtly transactional approach to alliance management will remain. Put simply, the US will become an even more demanding ally in coming years, irrespective of who is in the White House.

Does Australia possess the material capabilities and strategic creativity to adapt to this environment? Although the 2020 Defence Strategic Update paints a Hobbesian picture of Australia's evolving strategic environment, as Hugh White (2020) points out, the Morrison government has in fact devoted little additional spending to underwrite a defence force that is capable of deterring would-be adversaries or imposing serious costs if conflict occurs. This suggests that, despite the growing emphasis on the need to deter China militarily, Australia is still to come to terms with the strong probability the US will increasingly look to shift the burden of underwriting allies' security on to allies themselves. Even in the likely event that future Australian governments decide against pursuing armed neutrality or bandwagoning with Beijing, the cost of maintaining the alliance with the United States will become a lot higher in the years ahead.

Notes

1 The website of the Australian mission in Washington has a web page solely devoted to the topic of 'Mateship'. See https://usa.embassy.gov.au/mateship
2 A senior US official has confirmed that Australian officials have been largely unresponsive to US overtures for a bilateral strategic dialogue covering issues relating to extended deterrence. Author's discussion with US official, Washington DC, September 2019.
3 The 2020 Defence Strategic Update notes that: 'Only the nuclear and conventional capabilities of the United States can offer effective deterrence against the possibility of nuclear threats against Australia' (Department of Defence 2020).
4 As a percentage of overall government spending, Australia's defence expenditure was 5.1% in 2019 compared to 5.2% in 2015 (SIPRI 2020).

References

Ball, Desmond (2001), 'The Strategic Essence', *Australian Journal of International Affairs*, 55 (2).

Cohen, Michael and Andrew O'Neil (2015), 'Doubts Down Under: American Extended Deterrence, Australia, and the 1999 Timor Crisis', *International Relations of the Asia Pacific*, 15 (1).

Cunningham, Fiona and Taylor Fravel (2019), 'Dangerous Confidence? Chinese Views on Nuclear Escalation', *International Security*, 44 (2).

Crane, Michael (2019), 'Boosting the US Presence in Northern Australia – Slowly But Surely', *The Strategist*, 21 March, www.aspistrategist.org.au/boosting-the-us-presence-in-northern-australia-slowly-but-surely accessed 10 July 2020.

Dean, Peter (2019), 'Armed Neutrality? Dependence, Independence and Australian Strategy', in Peter Dean, Stephan Fruhling and Brendan Taylor (eds), *After American Primacy: Imagining the Future of Australia's Defence*, Melbourne: Melbourne University Press.

Defence Committee (2009[1976]), 'Australian Strategic Analysis and Defence Planning Objectives, 2 September', in Stephan Fruhling (ed.), *A History of Australian Strategic Policy Since 1945*, Canberra: Commonwealth of Australia.

Department of Defence (2020), *Defence Strategic Update 2020*, www.defence.gov.au/Stra tegicUpdate-2020/docs/2020_Defence_Strategic_Update.pdf accessed 10 July 2020.

Department of Defence (2009), *Defending Australia in the Asia Pacific Century: Force 2030*, https://defence.gov.au/whitepaper/2009/docs/defence_white_paper_2009.pdf acces-sed 10 July 2020.

Department of State (2019), 'Speech by Secretary of State Michael Pompeo, Sydney, 4 August: The US and Australia – The Unbreakable Alliance', www.state.gov/ the-u-s-and-australia-the-unbreakable-alliance/ accessed 10 July 2020.

DFAT (2020a), *Australia's Composition of Trade 2018–2019*, Canberra: Commonwealth of Australia.

DFAT (2020b), 'Foreign Investment Statistics', www.dfat.gov.au/trade/resources/investm ent-statistics/Pages/statistics-on-who-invests-in-australia accessed 10 July 2020.

Doran, Mathew (2020), 'Federal Government Spends $1.1 Billion on Northern Terri-tory Airbase, Expanding Reach into the Indo-Pacific', *ABC News Online*, 21 Feb-ruary, www.abc.net.au/news/2020-02-21/federal-government-spends-1.1-billion-on-top -end-air-base/11986904 accessed 10 July 2020.

Emmott, Robin and John Chalmers (2020), 'Trump Troop Pullout Would Still Leave Hefty US Footprint in Europe', *Reuters*, 9 June, www.reuters.com/article/us-usa -germany-military-analysis/trump-troop-pullout-would-still-leave-hefty-us-footprint- in-europe-idUSKBN23F29P accessed 10 July 2020.

Fruhling, Stephan (2018), 'Is ANZUS Really an Alliance? Aligning the US and Australia', *Survival*, 60 (5).

Fruhling, Stephan and Andrew O'Neil (2020), 'Institutions, Informality and Influence: Explaining Nuclear Cooperation in the Australia–US Alliance', *Australian Journal of Political Science*, 55 (2).

Hughes, Christopher (2016), 'Japan's "Resentful Realism" and Balancing China's Rise', *Chinese Journal of International Politics*, 9 (2).

Kagan, Robert (2008), 'The September 12 Paradigm: America, the World and George W. Bush', *Foreign Affairs*, 87 (5).

Killen, The Hon.D. J. (1976), *Australian Defence*, Canberra: Australian Government Publishing Service.

Kim, Sung-ham and Scott Snyder (2020), 'Denuclearizing North Korea: Time for Plan B', *Washington Quarterly*, 42 (4).

Kurlantzick, Joshua (2007), *Charm Offensive: How China's Soft Power is Transforming the World*, New Haven, CT: Yale University Press.

Lowy Institute (2020a), 'Lowy Institute Poll 2020 – Importance of US Alliance', http s://poll.lowyinstitute.org/charts/importance-of-the-us-alliance accessed 10 July 2020.

Lowy Institute (2020b), 'Lowy Institute Poll 2020 – China: Economic Partner or Security Threat?', https://poll.lowyinstitute.org/report/#h2-relations-with-superp owers-china-and-united-states accessed 10 July 2020.

Lyon, Rod (2020), 'Defence Update Signals Australia's Waning Faith in US Extended Deterrence', *The Strategist*, 6 July, www.aspistrategist.org.au/defence-update-signa ls-australias-waning-faith-in-us-extended-deterrence/ accessed 10 July 2020.

Lyon, Rod (2008), 'Australia: Back to the Future?', in Muthiah Alagappa (ed.), *The Long Shadow: Nuclear Weapons and Security in 21st Century Asia*, Stanford, CA: Stanford University Press.

Massola, James (2020), 'Long-range Missiles Likely to Earn a Quiet "Thank You" from Neighbours', *Sydney Morning Herald*, 2 July, www.smh.com.au/world/asia/long-range-missiles-likely-to-earn-a-quiet-thank-you-from-neighbours-20200702-p558g8.html accessed 10 July 2020.

Navy Recognition (2020), 'US Approves a Sale to Australia of 200 AGM-158C Long Range Anti-Ship Missiles', *Navy Recognition'*, 8 February, www.navyrecognition.com/index.php/news/defence-news/2020/february/8029-us-approves-a-sale-to-australia-for-200-agm-158c-long-range-anti-ship-missiles-lrasm.html accessed 10 July 2020.

Office of the Secretary of Defense (2018), *Nuclear Posture Review 2018*, https://media.defense.gov/2018/Feb/02/2001872886/-1/-1/1/2018-NUCLEAR-POSTURE-REVIEW-FINAL-REPORT.PDF accessed 10 July 2020.

Packham, Ben and Amos, Aikman (2019), 'Hosting US Missiles Not on the Agenda: PM', *The Australian*, 6 August, www.theaustralian.com.au/nation/defence/hosting-us-missiles-not-on-the-agenda-pm/news-story/c6d852434bc11abb8ddc6ac64f69c0c3 accessed 10 July 2020.

Pancevski, Bojan (2020), 'Trump's Planned Troop Withdrawal from Germany Leaves Berlin Cold', *Wall Street Journal*, 26 June, www.wsj.com/articles/trumps-planned-troop-withdrawal-from-germany-leaves-berlin-cold-11593184247 accessed 10 July 2020.

Ramstad, Evan (2010), 'Firing Drill Increases Tension in Korea', *Wall Street Journal*, 20 December, www.wsj.com/articles/SB10001424052748704138604576029240348016046 accessed 10 July 2020.

Sayle, Timothy Andrews (2019), *Enduring Alliance: A History of NATO and the Postwar Global Order*, Ithaca, NY: Cornell University Press.

Schroeder, Paul (1976), 'Alliances, 1815–1945: Weapons of Power and Tools of Management', in Klaus Knorr (ed.), *Historical Dimensions of National Security Problems*, Lawrence, KS: University of Kansas Press.

Schweller, Randall (1994), 'Bandwagoning for Profit: Bringing the Revisionist State Back In', *International Security*, 19 (1).

SIPRI (2020), 'SIPRI Military Expenditure Database', www.sipri.org/databases/milex accessed 10 July 2020.

Townshend, Ashley, Brendan Thomas-Noone, and Matilda Steward (2019), *Averting Crisis: American Strategy, Military Spending and Collective Defence in the Indo-Pacific*, Sydney: US Studies Centre, University of Sydney, August, www.ussc.edu.au/analysis/averting-crisis-american-strategy-military-spending-and-collective-defence-in-the-indo-pacific#america%E2%80%99s-superpower-mindset-and-the-problem-of-strategic-prioritisation accessed 10 July 2020.

Trevithick, Joseph (2020), 'The Air Force Abruptly Ends its Continuous Bomber Presence on Guam After 16 Years', *The Drive*, 17 April, www.thedrive.com/the-war-zone/33057/the-continuous-strategic-bomber-presence-mission-to-guam-has-abruptly-ended-after-16-years accessed 10 July 2020.

US Department of Defense (2018), *Summary of the 2018 National Defense Strategy*, https://dod.defense.gov/Portals/1/Documents/pubs/2018-National-Defense-Strategy-Summary.pdf accessed 10 July 2020.

Waltz, Kenneth (1979), *Theory of International Politics*, Long Grove, IL: Waveland Press.

White, Hugh (2019), *How to Defend Australia*, Carlton: La Trobe University Press.

White, Hugh (2020), 'Why Australia's Strategic Situation is Far Worse Than We Think', *Australian Financial Review*, 6 July, www.afr.com/policy/foreign-affairs/why-australia

-s-strategic-situation-is-far-worse-than-we-think-20200705-p5594m accessed 10 July 2020.

Xu, Vicky Xiuzhong (2020), 'Why Australia Must Not Bow to China But Seek Wider Trade Options', *Sydney Morning Herald*, 21 May, www.smh.com.au/national/why-australia-must-not-bow-to-china-but-seek-wider-trade-options-20200521-p54v2o.html accessed 10 July 2020.

11 The future of Australia–US strategic and defence cooperation

A US perspective

Scott D. McDonald

Introduction

Three decades after the end of the Cold War, it is well past time to reorient and reinvigorate the Australia–US Alliance. This does not require a renegotiation of the ANZUS Treaty, but a candid conversation regarding shared goals and methods of cooperation. In other words, what are the strategic *ends* we hope to achieve together, and what are the broad *ways* we can agree on in pursuit of those ends. With the threats that drove formation of the alliance gone, the parties should use this period of relative peace to establish a forward-looking alliance, which aims to create the world we chose to live in. In short, Australia and the US should design a framework for mutually building and maintaining the regional order that benefits them.

This chapter will argue for a renewed alliance built on four foundational principles. In the twenty-first century, military alignment is insufficient for protecting state security and shaping the environment it needs to prosper. Therefore, the alliance must move beyond a military partnership and become bilaterally integrated at the level of *grand strategy*. Second, it must be framed specifically as *pursuing a vision* for regional order, rather than combatting one. As US Ambassador Culvahouse observed, '[w]e believe that everyone deserves a fair go, and that by working hard and playing by the rules, everyone should have a fair shot at prosperity. These are the values that make the US–Australia alliance unbreakable and will carry it into our next century of partnership' (Nicholson 2019). Having determined an allied vision of the future, the alliance must then seek an unprecedented level of *integration*. This will involve accepting allied input in policy generation, as well as upgrading the extent to which execution of policy is integrated across the region and across departments. Finally, Australia and the US should work together to break the paradigm that common interest is built on 'fear of other states' (Waltz 1979: 166). Instead, this chapter argues the alliance should serve as a catalyst to weave a web of multilateral *partnerships* with the goal of building a multilateral security architecture.

After describing an alliance built on the principles of grand strategy, vision, integration and partnerships, the chapter will examine some of the factors presenting risks of Australia–US divergence. In doing so, the chapter will call attention to the fact that the best preventative care for these threats lays within the increased communication and coordination required to reinvigorate the alliance and nurture the regional order that meets their shared interests.

An alliance of grand strategy

When in 1951 the Australia–US alliance was codified in the ANZUS Treaty, the parties were less interested in developing a region than they were with securing themselves from a resurgent Japanese Empire or other expansionist powers (Australia and New Zealand), thwarting the worldwide spread of communism (the US) and securing input to allied decision-making (McLean 1990; Young 1999: 6; Brown and Rayner 2001; Robb and Gill 2015: 156–157). In short, the alliance was narrowly focused on collective defence to preserve the status quo (ANZUS Treaty 1952: Preamble).

The world that confronts Australia and the US today is not one of imminent military threat. While security issues remain, they tend to be of a less existential nature and require tools and solutions other than the military. Even the re-emergence of great power competition noted in the *US National Security Strategy* (White House 2017) is playing itself out across the elements of national power.[1] Consequently, an alliance solely oriented on military security is not well suited to the regional strategic environment. As Edel (2019) notes, 'a rules-based order means that it is not simple raw power that determines outcomes'.

The Australia–US alliance must, therefore, be elevated from one focused on defence, to a grand strategic partnership, which will require a better alignment of national policies and priorities across the elements of national power. This is not to belittle the extensive bilateral coordination that already occurs between the two governments beyond the security realm; rather the purpose is to emphasize that the states must cooperate at the level of grand strategy and effectively synchronize their efforts in shaping the Indo-Pacific across diplomatic, informational, military and economic lines of effort.

Alliance for a vision

Neither Australia nor the US face an imminent existential threat. However, this is not a reason to scrap the relationship; rather it represents an opportunity to take the initiative and craft the future. The bilateral relationship was rooted in shared values well before the exigencies of the Second World War forced the nations together in self-defence. Shared heritage and frontier spirt create a natural kinship. More importantly, these values underwrite a shared view of the future.

Australia and the US desire an Indo-Pacific that is free from coercive force and open to trade. Both states depend on trade for their prosperity and are integrated with the global supply chains that pass through the Indo-Pacific. This shared vision requires no threat for motivation, but carries within it the seeds of a cooperative partnership for mutual benefit. These ideals and the absence of an existential military threat provide the allies strategic space to step back and design an alliance that is pro-value, rather than anti-adversary.

Too often in recent years have headlines heralded the need to counter a revisionist People's Republic of China (PRC). Regardless of Beijing's intentions, this second-handed orientation is detrimental to sound strategy and policy. In that regard, arguments over whether or not Australia or the US would militarily aid the other in a future hypothetical crisis are moot. Such a decision would be taken under the terms of the ANZUS Treaty 'in accordance with [the state's] constitutional processes' (ANZUS Treaty 1952: Article IV). More importantly, developing a strategic approach based on a threat rather than a vision leads one to cede initiative and cognitive control to one's adversary (McDonald 2017). This is ultimately a strategic dead-end that leads at best to drift and at worst to unnecessary conflict.

The Free and Open Indo-Pacific (FOIP) provides an existing, positive regional vision that Australia, the US and many regional partners already accept and can support. This concept first entered the international lexicon in a speech by Japanese Prime Minister Shinzo Abe to the Sixth Tokyo International Conference on African Development (Soeya 2017: 16). According to Soeya, this concept is a 're-branding of the long-held Japanese regional policies that had evolved during the three decades since the end of the Cold War. These regional policies have emphasized the principle of multilateralism with a view to creating a rule-based and non-exclusive regional order through promoting relations of functional cooperation with primarily, if not exclusively, ASEAN [Association of Southeast Asian Nations] and its member states' (Soeya 2017: 17).

FOIP became a mainstay of regional discourse when US President Donald Trump promoted it at the 2017 Asia-Pacific Economic Cooperation CEO Summit in Da Nang, Vietnam. Unfortunately, the lack of details led to some confusion about what it entailed. It was not until a May 2018 Senate hearing that Deputy Assistant Secretary of State Alex Wong and Assistant Secretary of Defense Randall Schriver jointly described FOIP. Specifically, they defined four principles the US seeks to protect as the foundation for regional security: international rules-based order, ASEAN centrality, promotion of the common values of 'free' and 'open', and cooperative pursuit of prosperity, security and liberty that excludes no nation (US Senate 2018). In short, they offered strategic *ends* that combine state security and economic prosperity to enable a cooperative region.[2] This was supplemented with strategic *ways* in June when Secretary of Defense James Mattis outlined four themes for implementing FOIP: expanding attention on the maritime space; increasing interoperability with partner militaries; strengthening the rule of law, civil society and transparent governance; and promoting private sector-led development. Taken together, these statements establish FOIP as a grand-strategic approach to regional security. It is not imposed, but seeks cooperation and participation of the region, for mutual benefit. It is a pro-values approach to building a regional architecture.

This concept also complements ideas already resident in the region. In addition to being based on a Japanese concept, FOIP mirrors efforts ongoing within ASEAN. For example, 'dynamic equilibrium' proposed by Indonesia's Minister for Foreign Affairs, Marty Natalegawa, sees no country as preponderant, preferring inclusivity: 'the more, the merrier; and for countries to be engaged in multisectoral issues, not only security but also political and also environment, economic, social-cultural, et cetera' (Natalegawa 2010). He envisions a region defined not by 'bloc politics and often self-fulfilling geopolitical fault lines; rather, a new kind of international relations with its emphasis on common security, common prosperity and common stability' (Natalegawa 2011). ASEAN has integrated these concepts in the 'ASEAN Outlook on the Indo-Pacific', which envisions four key elements of the region: A perspective of viewing the Asia-Pacific and Indian Ocean regions as a closely integrated and interconnected region, with ASEAN playing a central and strategic role; an Indo-Pacific region of dialogue and cooperation instead of rivalry; an Indo-Pacific region of development and prosperity for all; and the importance of the maritime domain and perspective in the evolving regional architecture (ASEAN 2019). In short, ASEAN views the region developing along similar lines as FOIP. In fact, the US government hosted two workshops in Honolulu to solicit input from regional leaders and found broad consensus regarding FOIPs underlying principles (Yamin 2018).

Given the volume of publicity surrounding Xi Jinping's 'One Belt, One Road' (OBOR) initiative, it is understandable that some view FOIP in opposition to it. However, this orientation must be rejected. As Palit and Sano note, transforming FOIP into such a counterpoint runs the risk of making it overly focused on security and placing the US in a security dilemma (Palit and Sano 2018: 3). In contrast, the promotion of trade and development corridors across the region is fully endorsed by FOIP. In fact, it is the relatively free and open architecture built and supported by the US and its allies over the past 75 years that makes the positive aspects OBOR possible. It is the attempt leverage corrupt practices to coerce states into hewing to a Beijing line is fundamentally opposed to the values of FOIP. Reinforcing an open and free architecture will aid in reducing those practices, to the benefit of the people of the PRC and every other regional state. Therefore, the Australia–US alliance should neither be against the PRC nor its initiatives, rather it should organize and act to promote the positive vision embodied in FOIP.

From aligned to combined

After agreeing to shared strategic ends, Australia and the US must better coordinate not only the development of the strategic ways they intend to pursue those ends, but their actual implementation as well. In order to accomplish this and create combined[3] efforts, they must be integrated from the policy perspective, as well as in the operationalization of their strategy.

Integrated regional policy

Closer policy coordination was one of the chief objectives sought by Australia in negotiating the ANZUS treaty (Robb and Gill 2015: 152–157). In fact, it was viewed as the most important element of the treaty (National Archives of Australia 1952). However, the US resisted being tied too tightly to their allies and Secretary of State Dulles ensured 'the treaty was limited in nature and scope, disappointing Australian and New Zealand officials who had sought to establish joint staff talks and integrated military planning' (Robb and Gill 2015: 137). Despite continued pressure at the first meeting of the ANZUS council, the US resisted allied requests for representatives to the Joint Chiefs of Staff (JCS) as 'unprecedented and undesirable' (Mabon 1984). While this has in some sense been corrected by the many Australian officers embedded at the working level of the joint staff, policy is still made at the senior levels of government. As Frühling notes, there remains a lack of mechanisms to address political-military questions and 'coordinate their efforts for collective defence for the preservation of peace and security' (Frühling 2018: 200).

To ensure shared grand-strategic ends are achieved, Australia and the US must increase combined policy planning. This does not mean they cannot have independent foreign policies or even disagree. In fact, it is likely they will not agree on everything, but as Edel and Lee note, if frank discussions are not held about important issues among those who make policy 'alliance management can easily devolve into papering over differences and a seeking of the lowest common denominator' (Edel and Lee 2019: 2).

In fact, to achieve grand-strategic ends, integration with the JCS envisioned in the early days of ANZUS is insufficient; rather coordination bodies must be established within the US National Security Council (NSC) and the Australian Department of Prime Minister and Cabinet (PM&C). Under Article VII of the ANZUS Treaty, the parties established a council of Foreign Ministers for similar, if less ambitious, purposes. According to Brown and Rayner, the Australia–US ministerial meeting (AUSMIN) held annually between the foreign and defence minister for each state, now takes the place of that body (Brown and Rayner 2001). They observe that the regular bilateral access it provides 'has been judged by successive Australian governments to be a valuable opportunity for wide ranging discussions on a number of issues, and to gain insight to US thinking, especially to changes in its defence policy'. However, because of its episodic nature, AUSMIN coordinates, but does not integrate policy development. As Edel and Lee argue, '[b]ringing Australia into the conversation earlier will give Canberra the confidence that US policymakers are taking into account their interests as well' (Edel and Lee 2019: 12). To facilitate this, the allies must integrate liaisons into their senior security policy staffs. Moreover, the perennial issue of over-classification must be finally resolved. The inability of the two governments to talk to each other about matters of mutual concern continues to be an irritant to leaders on both sides, and prevents them from planning and operating together as well as they could.

Functional integration

While Australian and US forces already operate together, by synchronizing their actions at the grand strategic level and integrating policy planning, combined operations will become better focused and further operational integration possible. This will increase their efficiency and allow them to tailor engagement packages to maximize the value of interactions across the region.

Previously, Australia and the US tried to share the work and focus on different sub-regions. This concept was codified for wartime naval forces in the Radford-Collins Agreement of 1951 (text available in Forbes and Lovi 2007: 45–67). This was not a treaty, but a working-level agreement to facilitate fighting a common enemy (Brown n.d.). Fortunately, this territorial division never had to be exercised in conflict, however, both the contemporary integrated security environment and complementary nature of the allies suggest dividing to region into areas of responsibility is a suboptimal strategy. In fact, the two states benefit from having varied outlooks, capabilities and relationships across the region. This allows them to complement, reinforce and cover gaps the other might miss or not be best prepared to address. Traditional problems of duplication or unnecessary overlap are certainly undesirable, but they are resolvable through better planning and closer coordination.

In fact, having a close ally examining the same situations, participating in strategic-level planning and providing alternative viewpoints promotes critical thinking and improves prioritization. Furthermore, tasks can be distributed to individual governments and departments where deemed most effective, as well as designated for combined execution where more appropriate for the task or environment. In other words, strategic-level and functional-level integration are mutually complementary. However, in order to be impactful on a grand-strategic level, this integration must take place across the elements of national power.

Diplomatic

As the Australian *2016 Defence White Paper* notes, growing prosperity of the Indo-Pacific is built on active engagement by the US and regional states in building a rules-based global order (14). As the *2017 Foreign Policy White Paper* argues,

> [o]ur ability to protect and advance our interests rests on the quality of our engagement with the world. This includes the ideas we bring to the table, our ability to persuade others to our point of view and the strength

of the relationships we build with other governments and, increasingly, with influential non-government actors.

(Government of Australia 2017: 17)

This sentiment is recognized in the *US National Security Strategy*, which calls for 'expanding and deepening relationships with new partners that share respect for sovereignty, fair and reciprocal trade and the rule of law' (White House 2017: 46–47). The *Foreign Policy White Paper* also calls attention to the importance of tying regional cooperation to existing institutions to build norms and peaceful resolution of disputes (Government of Australia 2017: 38). In fact, one of those institutions – Asia-Pacific Economic Cooperation (APEC) – was the result of an Australian initiative (Kelton 2007: 258).

Integrated diplomacy also helps the alliance function better. Frühling argues that greater policy dialogue between the Australian Department of Foreign Affairs and Trade and the US Department of State, 'would go some way towards addressing current points of friction, and create arrangements that have proved useful in other alliances, including standing working groups and enduring agenda items at strategy, policy and political levels' (Frühling 2018: 210). In other words, getting better aligned diplomatically will improve the functioning of the alliance itself, as well as its ability to shape the region.

Informational

If diplomacy is the foundation, information is its key enabler. In a digitally interconnected world, the speed of information has increased the importance of understanding and operating in the information environment. Success can rapidly become failure if the battle of the narrative is lost. As the 2017 *Foreign Policy White Paper* recognizes,

> the greater ability in a globalised world of individuals and non-state actors to shape outcomes on issues of importance to Australia. Digital communication also allows nongovernment actors and nation states alike to influence public attitudes at a pace and scale not witnessed before, for good and ill.

(Government of Australia 2017: 110)

Consequently, both governments, individually and together, need to be on the forefront of communication and disseminate their message to the world before it is done by actors that wish them ill.

Most importantly, the alliance must communicate a vision for the future of the Indo-Pacific. While this process has begun, it must be comprehensive and routine. The fact that the Foreign Minister of Singapore could respond in May 2018 – six months after FOIP's introduction – that he did not know exactly what it was, is an indictment of US information management (Yong 2018). Since then, news of FOIP and what it means has trickled out. If it is to be the organizing principle for the alliance's approach to the region, it must be discussed regularly, not in vacuous platitudes, but in terms of real actions that are being planned and visibly implemented.

The communication effect of actions or non-action has played out starkly in Southeast Asia, where US attendance at regional fora is closely watched and reported on as an expression of US interest and intent. The absence of the US at meetings of regional leaders during the Bush administration was a constant news item. More recently, President Trump's decision to skip the East Asia Summit and US-ASEAN Summit in November 2019, garnered press and speculation among some in the region that 'the US does not see ASEAN as important' (Raksaseri and Sabpaitoon 2019). While it may seem unfair to argue that a power with global interests should attend every regional meeting, when the US claims to be placing a priority on the region, people from that region expect a certain level of representation. Whether the US agrees with this evaluation or not, it is the lens through which leaders in the region view their participation. In fact, Tow argues 'ASEAN's brittleness in the absence of a regionally engaged United States ranks as perhaps Australia's most fundamental concern about Southeast Asia' (Tow 2017: 51).

Military

With almost 600 Australians on secondment within the US military and over a century of cooperation, they are as close as any two militaries in the world. However, from the perspective of increasing the ability of the alliance to positively influence the Indo-Pacific, the many existing bilateral activities need to be explicitly tied to FOIP and the scope of partnerships broadened and overlapped wherever possible.

At the operational level, military services are already experimenting with this model. One example is the 2012 establishment of an additional Deputy Commanding General billet at US Army Pacific, filled by an Australian Army Major General. The first occupant, Major General Richard Burr, oversaw the command's logistics functions, but also focused on engagement with Oceania and South Asian countries (Guardian 2012). This role allowed an experienced Australian officer to directly advise the US Army on how it engaged the region. The success of this integration has led to an expanded role for the Australian general, who now leads many multi-lateral exercises and engagements on behalf of US Army Pacific. In addition to sharing experiences, this role brings an inherently international face to regional engagements.

While further efforts at integration are underway across the military services, the establishment and operation of the Marine Rotational Force-Darwin (MRF-D) provides an excellent example of the benefits, challenges and solutions provided by increased integration. MRF-D reached its full strength of 2,500 Marines in 2019 after 8 years of gradual growth in personnel and equipment (Robson 2019). One benefit of the deployment is its role in integrating Australian Army and US Marine Corps operations with each other and their Navies. This has been enhanced by the parallel development of Australia's amphibious capability and integration of the *Canberra* class LHD (landing helicopter dock). In 2018 Marines assisted during the first full scale Sea Series exercise, certifying 8/9 Royal Australian Regiment as Australia's first Amphibious Readiness Unit (Wetzel 2018). This success was built upon when Australia, Japan and the US conducted combined amphibious operations during Exercise Talisman Sabre 2019 (Harkins 2019).

By developing this capability, MRF-D is nurturing a combined force that can ensure stability during steady state, or Phase Zero, operations. US amphibious forces routinely transit the Indo-Pacific and conduct training and security cooperation with partner countries. Naturally, these cruises are also designed to improve the training and readiness of US forces. However, simply by demonstrating will and capability, it reminds malign actors that the US has the ability to respond wherever its interests are threatened. These operations also provide reassurance to partners while assisting them in improving their own militaries. By conducting this engagement with *combined* forces, every security cooperation event has an inherently international face. To leverage the benefits of this experiment, every time an Australian amphibious ship conducts security cooperation in the Indo-Pacific, there should be US Marines embarked. Likewise, every US ship should have a contingent of Australian soldiers. Unless a host nation's attitudes towards one or the other prohibit it, Australian and US amphibious forces should step into every exercise shoulder to shoulder, demonstrating not only the relationship between the two, but the commitment to approach the region multilaterally.

Another benefit of this amphibious cross-pollination is the mitigation of a chronic shortage of US amphibious ships. For the last decade, US Navy inventory of amphibious ships has hovered in the low 30s, while estimated annual need has exceeded 50, based on combatant commander requests for ships to support operational requirements (Leed 2014: 4–5). By integrating allied amphibious ships into the regional engagement plan, the alliance can expand the number of combined units routinely cruising the region and conducting engagements.

Regardless of how third parties are brought onboard, Australian and US forces need to increase their integration as combined forces. However, some fear that embedding Australian forces in US formations 'effectively abrogates any visible Australian political influence' (Frühling 2018: 209). One solution is to increase the number of combined formations commanded by Australian officers, even where they do not represent the preponderance of forces. Assigning a US deputy will help assuage national-command issues as long as the proper strategic and policy coordination advocated above occurs. Making this sort of command relationship routine is necessary to build truly combined forces and approach the region in an integrated fashion. Although the example used here is amphibious, this solution can be applied across military services and engagement types. Through expanded cooperation and ability to bring others on board, Australia–US combined forces can demonstrate that shared interests and cooperative security are a value, thus increasing regional stability.

Another concern regarding increased integration is that national caveats or policy proscriptions that prevent specific types of activities will prevent a truly combined amphibious task force. However, Australia and the US have shown flexibility in working through these issues in the past. The key is to plan early and set clear rules each country's leadership can accept. This is facilitated by better strategic-level integration. If both parties understand each other, agree to the general plan, have the opportunity to object and plan alternatives in advance, many of the actual implementation problems can be overcome. The bias should be towards solutions that enable combined amphibious patrols, rather than looking for problems that prevent it. Fortunately, this orientation towards overcoming problems reflects a culture Aussie Diggers and US Marines (and the two countries' militaries in general) already share.

Economic

The economic instrument is viewed as the most difficult for liberal states to wield, due to their principled abhorrence of governmental interference in the free economic decision-making of individuals. However, when properly understood, this dedication to economic liberty is a much more potent tool than the destructive remit of state interference. As Secretary Pompeo noted 'the US Government doesn't tell American companies what to do. But we help build environments that foster good, productive capitalism' (Pompeo 2018b). This environment of free exchange and open commerce enables the creation of wealth and lifts millions out of poverty.

Of course, that principle must be concretized through actions that demonstrate a commitment to a system of free exchange. As Tow notes, the US withdrawal from the Trans-Pacific Partnership (TPP) was a blow to Australia, because it 'undercut Australia's commitment to regional order-building by pursuing multilateral free trade arrangements and promoting an "inclusive" approach to shaping future rules for security conduct in Asia' (Tow 2017: 51). To Australia and others, US withdrawal communicated political and economic detachment, when the region wanted engagement.

However, as beneficial as trade liberalization is, deals such as TPP are still managed trade. Despite the marginal gains in economic liberty, they still entail governments picking what sectors of their economies will be winners and losers and determining the terms by which individuals exchange value. As Palit and Sano note, the PRC's experience with OBOR suggests 'top-down investment commitments are not enough to get FOIP the desired sanctity' (Palit and Sano 2018: 4). Rather, liberal states should uphold the principle that, 'the right of free trade applies not only within our borders, but also in our trade with foreign nations' (Binswanger 2018: 156). That is to say that economic liberty does not exist solely within states nor is it exercised vis-à-vis other states; rather individuals have the right to trade wherever they see fit, on terms they mutually negotiate. In other words, *'there is no such thing as "unfair" trade.* The so-called 'unfairness' here is not to the buyer or to the seller but to a third party who objects ... A third party has no right to intervene in a transaction between a willing buyer and a willing seller' (Binswanger 2018: 159). Therefore, if the goal is an Indo-Pacific that is free and open, then the allies should promote the destruction of the barriers to individual liberty that hobble trade, instead of making adjustments to those barriers. They should commit themselves to unilateral elimination of trade barriers, monetary or otherwise, with only limited caveats for security-related technology.

Similarly, Australia and the US should not try to match the PRC's infra-structure hand-outs. By engaging in it, they undermine the very principles that define the FOIP's private sector led development and free societies more broadly. Instead, the Australia–US alliance should promote a positive economic vision for the region. This is done by showing that trade and investment is valued by removing barriers that prevent it. Australian and US companies have long invested in the region and will continue to do so if the governments get out of the way and focus on maintaining a stable environment for them to do so. As a result, these companies and private individuals will serve as better ambassadors for free and open trading regimes than governments ever could.

Partnerships for a purpose

The case for functional integration does not explain what allied engagements should actually do – a gap in FOIP as well. Functional integration is a strategic *way*. From an alliance management perspective, it does not speak to the *means*, or the tools that will be used to put the strategy into place. In military strategy, *means* look like ships and tanks or specific initiatives – things that can be employed through the designed *ways* in order to achieve strategic *ends*.

FOIP has clear *ends* – as enumerated in its four key principles – it seeks to achieve through its declared *ways* – the themes laid out by Secretary Mattis. However, beyond several small pots of money pledged on 30 July 2018 (Pompeo 2018b), there have been few *means* announced. Unfortunately, this financial 'me too-ism' plays into the hands of those who see FOIP as a counter to OBOR. In late 2018, McDonald argued the US, in conjunction with any willing partner, needed to begin actively operating in support of FOIP principles through 'Communities of Common Interest'. This concept advocates establishing small groups of like-minded partners to cooperate on multiple issue-specific partnerships. This idea is embodied in the Department of Defense's 'Parnerships for a Purpose'. According to the 2019 *Indo-Pacific Strategy Report*, these will weave together 'a networked security architecture – with shared values, habits of cooperation and compatible and complementary capabilities – will form a strong free and open fabric that knits the region together, preserving sovereignty and regional peace and stability for years to come' (Department of Defense 2019: 44–45).

Combined alliance strategy should seek to explicitly approach the region as a catalyst for establishing these partnerships, working together where possible and separately – but in coordination – where desirable. This conforms with Edel's call to 'think globally – in a strategic and collaborative manner. This means seeking out more coalitions of the willing, drawn from the Atlantic, Indian and Pacific Ocean regions, who see a need, have the will and possess the capabilities that can sustain an open and free order' (Edel 2019). This sentiment is also echoed in the 2017 *Foreign Policy White Paper*: 'Australia will also work within smaller groupings of these countries, reflecting our shared interests in a region based on the principles described' (Government of Australia 2017: 40).

This is not '*ad hoc*' multilateralism, but done purposefully, around issues of specific benefit to the alliance and regional security, with a long-range vision for achieving the principles of FOIP. Partnerships must be sought that cover issues across the components of national power and that ultimately include every country in the region in one or more partnerships, thus creating an overlapping lattice work of partnerships that build relationships and promote common interests, thereby reducing stark cleavages between states and building stability (McDonald 2018). Thus, the Partnership for a Purpose construct can be used to demonstrate that the alliance's vision of the future is non-exclusionary, rather it seeks a regional architecture in which all parties work towards common values.

Multilateral, issue-specific partnerships allow Australia and the US to undertake actions that build collective security, but that may be less appetizing if pursued by the alliance in isolation. For example, Australian Prime Minister Turnbull demurred from combined South China Sea patrols with Indonesia out of the fear that it could increase tensions (Reuters 2017). However, by building a Partnership for a Purpose around regional sea lane security more broadly, the alliance could create a framework that may eventually move into the South China Sea in a manner that is inherently less provocative, while achieving the aim of building broader groupings of regional partners.

To reinforce the FOIP principle of ASEAN centrality, each partnership must be tied to at least one ASEAN state and linked to an ASEAN-centred forum. This will ensure the fulcrum of the Indo-Pacific has a stake in each partnership. In fact, these linkages are more important than Australia or the US being a member of every partnership. They will encourage and support the partnerships, but the key is to use their combined influence to buttress ASEAN as the centre of a regional security architecture.

While the number of new partnerships is limited only by imagination, the initiatives need not be new or expensive. For example, Australia is already planning on updating patrol boats in 12 South Pacific countries through the Pacific Maritime Security Program (Government of Australia 2016: 74). As it does so, it should coordinate with regional partners to ensure it builds partnerships for common threats facing the region, such as trafficking in persons (TIP), that these boats can be used to support. It can then tie these operations to its own rotation of Offshore Patrol Vessels through the Lombrum Naval Base it is refurbishing on Manus Island, Papua New Guinea (Fish 2018). This is an example of an existing bilateral initiative to improve security that can be turned into a means to link other states in the region with similar interests together. The network can then be tied to ASEAN through the Jakarta Centre for Law Enforcement Cooperation – whose founding was also assisted by Australia – thus bringing counter-TIP cooperation in Oceania into broader cooperation across the Indo-Pacific.

One way to bring partnerships together at low cost is expansion of ship-rider programs. Indonesia and Australian have done this under Operation Gannet, targeting illicit activity on both sides of their shared maritime border (Australian Border Force 2019). The US also has ship rider agreements that allow 11 Pacific Island nations to exercise sovereignty in their exclusive economic zone by leveraging US Coast Guard and Navy ship deployments (Department of Defense 2019: 41). Overall, Australian law enforcement and the US Coast Guard are increasingly involved in regional security cooperation, especially in partner countries that have no military. The next step is to explicitly tie their actions to regional strategy and highlight the principles they support and the partnerships they build.

The idea of partnerships is not new. The innovation of Partnerships for a Purpose is to consciously pursue partnerships with the goal of weaving a networked architecture together out of nations that have no interest in broader formal alliances, but do share many common interests. However, this concept cannot be confined to the military; Partnerships for a Purpose must stretch across elements of national power. In the words of the 2017 *Foreign Policy White Paper*, 'our security and prosperity will be enhanced in a region characterized by respect for international law and other norms, and by open markets' (Government of Australia 2017: 37).

Managing risk to the relationship

The foundation of the Australia–US relationship in shared values has proven resilient through many leaders and challenges. However, the whims of individuals have often surprised the theorists and even the strongest relationships break. Therefore, in looking to the future, it is important to also consider potential risks so they can be mitigated. Some of the current risks that emerge from within the alliance include: a lack of straight talk, forcing a choice and poor communication.

Lack of straight talk

Many in both Australia and the US rightly regard shared frankness and willingness to speak openly as one of the alliance's strengths. As Foreign Minister Bishop noted in 2018, Australia and the US do not always agree, but are able to work through differences in a constructive and positive way

(Pompeo 2018a). One of the values of a close partner is the ability to tell them the truth they do not want to hear. As Curran notes, the relatively contentious relationship between the US and the Whitlam government during the 1970s, was ultimately beneficial to the US, providing 'an important part of its adjustment to new realities in both Australia and the Asia-Pacific. For the first time in nearly a decade it realized that it could not take the interests of its junior ally for granted' (Curran 2014: 407). Only by having disagreements directly addressed, could the partners better understand each other and what was necessary for alliance maintenance.

The size of the US foreign policy establishment means it sometimes spends all its time coordinating with itself and loses touch with the world outside. A friend who can tell the US it does not understand the region keeps the US policy establishment from succumbing to groupthink. It also reminds policy-makers in Washington that Australia is not a sycophant that will go along with any bad idea. Should Australia stop giving unwelcome news, its importance will be forgotten and its insights ignored. It will slowly slip further away and begin to distrust the US as much as the US will begin to ignore it.

A related problem would occur if dialogue continues but one party begins censoring its words or actions to please the other. For example, McMullin (2018) fears Australia has gotten involved in wars that were not otherwise in its interests because it was more concerned with 'currying favour with America' than developing good policy. Such behaviour is not only dangerous for Australia – in terms of wasting lives and treasure on something that it does not value – but for the US, which gains a false sense of support that proves ephemeral. Both parties must be on guard for this type of behaviour and maintain the tradition of speaking frankly with one another.

The recommendation for further integration within the NSC and PM&C will help to mitigate this risk. In fact, it serves to emphasize the importance of a US embed in PM&C, as well as an Australian in the NSC. Cross-pollination builds shared understanding and institutionalizes assumption challenging. Ensuring this happens in both capitals not only broadens alliance experience and ensures both capitals have a sounding board, but provides each with a reality check on what their own embed shares.

Forcing a choice?

Some see risk to the alliance in a presumed US desire to force Australia to choose between it and the PRC. This seems rather short sighted and often premised on a mercantilist view of economics. Australia has no need to choose, as long as the US maintains a liberal trade orientation. Moreover, though the PRC may believe Australia should have to choose, the US has no need to worry about such an eventuality, as long as Australia maintains a liberal trade orientation. The only economic choices that matter regard finding the best value for the dollar, are made by individuals and are unique for each transaction. In free states, countries do not trade, individuals do. If both

Australia and the US maintain liberal economies, they have no reason to worry about who trades with whom, and every reason to maintain a security relationship based on a free and open order.

The real threat in this regard is what Gyngell and Wesley argue is a consequence of Australia's dependence on alliances: the classic dilemma between 'entrapment' and 'abandonment' (Gyngell and Wesley 2007: 211). It is not that they will have to choose between friends, but that the friend they have tied themselves to draws them in to a war they do not want. This threat can be avoided, because the treaty states only that an attack in the Pacific Area is a danger to each state's peace and that each party will 'meet the common danger in accordance with its constitutional processes' (ANZUS Treaty 1952: Article IV). The actual risk here is again the lack of straight talk. Allies must be willing to disagree, do so forcefully and as early in the policy planning process as possible.

Australia can also combat this by demonstrating continued value to the US, independent of any specific security threat. This speaks to the importance of being 'for' values, rather than 'anti-' any particular adversary. Meanwhile, as the larger partner, the US must redouble its efforts to ensure it hears its partner's objections. The strategic-level integration measures discussed above are designed, in part, to encourage that level of discourse.

Understand what you communicate

The US could risk alienating Australia, or vice versa, and encouraging it to seek security elsewhere simply by not understanding how its actions are perceived in Canberra. Issues that seem peripheral in the US can have an outsized effect and communicate unintended messages about the value of the relationship. For example, cutting the US government's plan to spend USD76 million on bulk fuel storage in Darwin was identified as a cost saving to fund President Trump's border wall (Coyne 2019). While Coyne presents this as a reason that Australia must do a better job demonstrating the value of MRF-D, it is also incumbent on the US to understand action such as this send a message, unintended though it may be, that MRF-D is not a priority. In short, both parties can put the alliance at risk by not understanding the message their actions send about how they value the alliance.

Writing in the middle of the longest period without a US ambassador since diplomatic relations were established, Corben (2018) notes the deleterious effect of not having an ambassador. Though relations continued, such absences send a message that the US takes the relationship for granted. During another gap of 18 months from 2005 to 2006, Australian interlocutors routinely noted the slight during official meetings (Personal experience of author). While often done in a joking tone, the prevailing sense from many departments was that the US took them for granted.

To avoid these slights, both states must have a clear understanding of what the alliance means to each other and the world. As Gill and Switzer note, 'for

Washington, the US–Australian partnership has become a special relationship with few equivalents in the world. But few outside a small circle of policy elites seem to have noticed' (Gill and Switzer 2015). Australia has tried to address the importance of the alliance through the '100 years of Mateship' campaign, which highlights the interconnectedness of Australia and the US dating back to operations in World War One, as well as cultural and economic links. Cooper worries this could backfire, making Americans think the relationship is so strong that it does not need careful tending (Cooper 2018).

Ultimately, both parties run the risk of undermining the relationship if they do not pay attention to the manner in which their actions have unintended communication effects. Once again, this type of mistake is best combated by talking constantly and having the partner's officials embedded in their senior policy planning staff. This level of placement allows them to provide feedback on policy while still in development so the meaning and impact of specific policy options are understood before they are enacted and the damage is done.

Constant tending

In summing up the risks to the alliance, this section almost appears too rosy, noting that for every risk, there is a simple and easy solution based on the nature of the alliance. In proposing a more integrated, grand-strategic alliance, there is a risk of dreaming so big that it inadvertently takes the alliance for granted and falls into the traps outlined here. This, of course, is not what is being advocated. Good relationships do not simply exist, rather they are constantly nurtured and sustained through good communication, frank discussion and constant interaction. Although Australia and the US share much, it can all be squandered for lack of effort in alliance maintenance. It is by constantly and continuously 'muddling through' together than the relationship will remain strong and focused on shared values.

Conclusion

The Australia–US alliance is strong, but requires more effort and attention because the challenges of the Indo-Pacific require a combined effort. Frühling (2018: 215) worries 'strengthening the alliance will require devoting more time and effort to an ally that Washington has customarily valued precisely because it did not require the same level of attention as US alliances in Europe and Northeast Asia'. This chapter has argued that more attention serves US interests, both in terms of maintaining the alliance and in providing the routine contact across the region that is required to show regional states that the US is involved, a valuable partner and a force for good. In short, it should want to give Australia this level of attention, because its own and combined interests are served by it. In fact, the future vision of the alliance proposed by this chapter cannot come into being without bilateral engagement that is more regular, more integrated and more constructive to regional architecture. Moreover, the risks that exist in the alliance stem from inadvertent effects of not giving enough attention to actions that affect this important partner. That is why going forward, the Australia–US alliance must become a grand-strategic partnership that works together for values, integrates its actions and brings the countries the Indo-Pacific region together in partnerships that pursue shared prosperity.

Notes

1   The element of national power is a US military term for the idea that all the tools of statecraft are necessary to address complex security issues. Coordinating these tools generally requires coordination across the whole-of-government and is essential at the grand-strategic level of inter-state relations. The elements of national power are traditionally represented with the acronym DIME (Diplomatic, Informational, Military, and Economic).
2   In US military doctrine strategy can be defined as 'the art and science of determining a future state/condition (ends), conveying this to an audience, determining the operational approach (ways), and identifying the authorities and resources (time, forces, equipment, money, etc.) (means) necessary to reach the intended end state, all while managing the associated risk' (Department of Defense 2017).
3   In US military doctrine, 'combined' identifies 'two or more forces or agencies of two or more allies operating together', as opposed to joint, which designates forces from two or more military departments of a single country operating together (Department of Defense 2016: 40).

References

ANZUS Treaty (1952), 'ANZUS Treaty', effective 29 April, https://australianpolitics.com/1951/09/01/anzus-treaty-text.html accessed 10 January 2020.

ASEAN (2019), 'ASEAN Outlook on the Indo-Pacific', ASEAN Communique, 23 June, https://asean.org/asean-outlook-indo-pacific/ accessed 6 January.

Australian Border Force (2019), 'Joint Australia-Indonesia Maritime Patrols in Timor Sea', Joint media release of Australian Border Force and Fisheries Management Authority, 30 September, www.afma.gov.au/news-media/media-releases/joint-australia-indonesia-maritime-patrols-timor-sea accessed 10 January 2020.

Baldino, Daniel (2014), 'Interview: Whither the Australia–US Alliance?' *Policy* 30 (1).

BBC.com (2003), 'Bush Hails "Sheriff" Australia', 16 October, http://news.bbc.co.uk/2/hi/asia-pacific/3196524.stm accessed 13 January 2020.

Beeson, Mark (2003), 'Australia's Relationship with the United States: the Case for Greater Independence', *Australian Journal of Political Science* 38 (3).

Beeson, Mark and Alan Bloomfield (2019), 'The Trump Effect Downunder: US Allies, Australian Strategic Culture, and the Politics of Path Dependence', *Contemporary Security Policy* 40 (3).

Binswanger, Harry (2018), '"Buy American" Is Un-American', in Jonathan Hoenig (ed.), *A New Textbook of Americanism: The Politics of Ayn Rand* (pp. 151–167), Chicago, IL: Capitalistpig Publications.

Brooks, Stephen G. and William C. Wohlforth (2008), *World Out of Balance: International Relations and the Challenge of American Primacy*, Princeton, NJ: Princeton University Press.

Brown, Andrew (n.d.), 'The History of the Radford-Collins Agreement', www.navy.gov.
au/history/feature-histories/history-radford-collins-agreement accessed 5 June 2020.

Brown, Gary and Laura Rayner (2001), 'Upside, Downside: ANZUS: After Fifty
Years', *Current Issues Brief*, no. 3, 28 August, www.aph.gov.au/About_Parliament/
Parliamentary_Departments/Parliamentary_Library/Publications_Archive/CIB/cib0
102/02CIB03 accessed 10 January 2020.

Carr, Andrew (2019), 'Sharing the Burden in Alliances: It Isn't Just About Money,
Mate', *The Strategist*, 6 June, www.aspistrategist.org.au/sharing-the-burden-in-allia
nces-it-isnt-just-about-money-mate/ accessed 9 January 2020.

Channel News Asia (2019), 'Trump Invites ASEAN Leaders to "Special Summit" in
US After Skipping Bangkok Meet', *Channel News Asia*, 4 November, www.cha
nnelnewsasia.com/news/asia/trump-invites-asean-leaders-special-summit-us-after-ski
p-bangkok-12061480 accessed 13 January 2020.

Cooper, Zack (2018), 'Hard Truths About the US–Australia Alliance', *The Strategist*,
9 July, www.aspistrategist.org.au/hard-truths-about-the-us-australia-alliance/ accessed 4 January 2020.

Corben, Tom (2018), 'US Ambassadors to Australia: A Brief History', United States
Studies Centre, 28 June, www.ussc.edu.au/analysis/us-ambassadors-to-australia
accessed 13 January 2020.

Cossa, Ralph A., Brad Glosserman, Michael A. McDevitt, Nirav Patel, James
Przystrup, and Brad Roberts (2009), *The United States and the Asia-Pacific Region:
Security Strategy for the Obama Administration*, Washington, DC: Center for a
New American Security.

Coyne, John (2019), 'It's Time To Make Good On Defence Commitments To Northern Australia', *The Strategist*, 24 May, www.aspistrategist.org.au/its-time-to-ma
ke-good-on-defence-commitments-to-northern-australia/ accessed 9 January 2020.

Curran, James (2014), 'The Dilemmas of Divergence: The Crisis in American-
Australian Relations, 1972–1975', *Diplomatic History* 38 (2).

Department of Defense (2019), *Indo-Pacific Strategy Report*, Washington, DC:
Department of Defense.

Department of Defense (2016), *Joint Publication 1-02: Department of Defense Dictionary
of Military and Associated Terms*, Washington, DC: Department of Defense.

Department of Defense (2017), *Joint Publication 5-0: Joint Planning*, Washington,
DC: Department of Defense.

Dibb, Paul (2019), 'Revisiting the North in the Defence of Australia', *The Strategist*,
27 June, www.aspistrategist.org.au/revisiting-the-north-in-the-defence-of-australia/
accessed, 9 January 2020.

Edel, Charles (2019), 'The Future of the US–Australia Alliance', *The Strategist*, 3
July, www.aspistrategist.org.au/the-future-of-the-us-australia-alliance/ accessed 15
May 2019.

Edel, Charles and John Lee (2019), *The Future of the US–Australia Alliance In An Era
Of Great Power Competition*, Sydney: United States Studies Centre.

Fish, Tim (2018), 'Australia, US Set to Expand Papua New Guinea Naval Base',
USNI News, 23 November, https://news.usni.org/2018/11/23/australia-u-s-set-expa
nd-papa-new-guinea-naval-base accessed 6 January 2020.

Forbes, Andrew and Michelle Lovi (eds) (2007), *Australian Maritime Issues 2006:
SPC-A Annual* (pp. 45–67) Canberra: Sea Power Centre.

Frühling, Stephan (2018), 'Is ANZUS Really an Alliance? Aligning the US and
Australia', *Survival* 60 (5).

Gill, Bates and Tom Switzer (2015), 'The New Special Relationship: The US–Australia Alliance Deepens', *Foreign Affairs Online*, 19 February.www.foreignaffairs.com/arti cles/australia/2015-02-19/new-special-relationship accessed 10 January 2020.

Government of Australia (2016) *Defence White Paper*, Canberra: Government of Australia.

Government of Australia (2017) *Foreign Policy White Paper*, Canberra: Government of Australia.

Guardian (2012), 'Australian General to Help Lead US Military Push Into Pacific', *The Guardian*, 20 August, www.theguardian.com/world/2012/aug/21/australia n-general-us-army-pacific accessed 10 January 2020.

Gyngell, Allan and Michael Wesley (2007), *Making Australian Foreign Policy*, 2nd ed, Melbourne, VIC: Cambridge University Press.

Harkins, Gina (2019), 'Japan's Brand-New Amphibious Force Just Practiced Hitting the Beach With US, Australian Troops', 26 July, www.military.com/daily-news/2019/07/26/japans-new-island-defending-marines-stormed-beach-us-aussie-tro ops.html accessed 10 January 2020.

Kelton, Maryanne (2007), 'Global Trade', in Richard Devetak, Anthony Burke, and Jim George (eds), *An Introduction to International Relations: Australian Perspectives* (pp. 248–259) Melbourne, VIC: Cambridge University Press.

Leed, Maren (2014), *Amphibious Shipping Shortfalls: Risks and Opportunities to Bridge the Gap*, Washington, DC: CSIS.

Mattis, James N. (2018), 'Remarks by Secretary Mattis at Shangri-La Dialogue', 2 June, www.defense.gov/Newsroom/Transcripts/Transcript/Article/1538599/remarks-by-secreta ry-mattis-at-plenary-session-of-the-2018-shangri-la-dialogue/ accessed 2 June 2018.

Mabon, David W. (ed.) (1984), *Foreign Relations of the United States, 1952–1954, Volume XII, Part 1: East Asia and the Pacific*, Conference files, lot 59 D95, CF116, Document 58, Washington, DC: United States Government Printing Office, https:// history.state.gov/historicaldocuments/frus1952-54v12p1/d58 accessed 10 January 2020.

McDonald, Scott D. (2017), *'Forthcoming Asia Strategy Should Avoid Second-handed Pitfalls'*, *The National Interest*, 26 December, https://nationalinterest.org/feature/the-trump-administration-isnt-putting-america-first-23813 accessed 9 January 2020.

McDonald, Scott D. (2018), 'Wanted: A Strategy for the Indo-Pacific Region', *The National Interest*, 7 August, https://nationalinterest.org/feature/wanted-strategy-in do-pacific-region-28182 accessed 9 January 2020.

McLean, David (1990), 'ANZUS Origins: A Reassessment', *Australian Historical Studies* 24 (94).

McMullin, Ross (2018), 'The Truth Behind Australia's "100 Years Of Mateship" With the US', *Sydney Morning Herald*, 1 April, www.smh.com.au/national/the-truth-behind-a ustralia-s-100-years-of-mateship-with-the-us-20180314-p4z4bz.html accessed 18 December 2019.

Medcalf, Rory (2018), 'Australia's Foreign Policy White Paper: Navigating Uncertainty in the Indo-Pacific', *Security Challenges* 14 (1).

Miller, Charles (2015), 'Public Support For ANZUS: Evidence of a Generational Shift?' *Australian Journal of Political Science* 50 (3).

Muramatsu, Yohei (2019), 'Trump Skips ASEAN Summit Again, Ceding Influence to China', *Nikkei Asian Review*, 1 November, https://asia.nikkei.com/Politics/ International-relations/Trump-skips-ASEAN-Summit-again-ceding-influence-to-Chi na accessed 13 January 2020.

Natalegawa, Marty (2010), 'A Conversation with Marty Natalegawa', 20 September, www.cfr.org/event/conversation-marty-natalegawa-0 accessed 21 December 2019.

Natalegawa, Marty (2011), 'Statement by H.E. Dr. R. M. Marty M. Natalegawa, Minister for Foreign Affairs, Republic of Indonesia at the General Debate of the 66th Session of the United Nations General Assembly', 26 September, https://ga debate.un.org/sites/default/files/gastatements/66/ID_en.pdf accessed 21 December 2019.

National Archives of Australia (1952), Cablegram, Casey to Spender, 18 March, CRS A1838, item 532/13/2.

Nicholson, Brendan (2019), '"Unbreakable" Alliance: Ambassador Says US Is Here To Stay', *The Strategist*, 16 August, www.aspistrategist.org.au/unbreakable-allia nce-ambassador-says-us-is-here-to-stay/ accessed 9 January 2020.

O'Neil, Andrew (2011), 'Conceptualising Future Threats to Australia's Security', *Australian Journal of Political Science* 46 (1).

Palit, Amitendu and Shutaro Sano (2018), 'The United States' Free and Open Indo-Pacific Strategy: Challenges for India and Japan', *ISAS Insights*, 524.

Phillips, Andrew and Eric Hiariej (2016), 'Beyond the "Bandung Divide?" Assessing the Scope and Limits of Australia-Indonesia Security Cooperation', *Australian Journal of International Affairs* 70 (4).

Pompeo, Michael (2018a), 'Press Availability with Secretary of Defense James Mattis, Australian Foreign Minister Julie Bishop, and Australian Defense Minister Marise Payne', 24 July, www.state.gov/secretary/remarks/2018/07/284471.htm accessed 13 March 2019.

Pompeo, Michael (2018b), 'Remarks on 'America's Indo-Pacific Economic Vision', 30 July, www.state.gov/remarks-on-americas-indo-pacific-economic-vision/ accessed 5 January 2020.

Raksaseri, Kornchanok and Patpon Sabpaitoon (2019), 'Trump Skips ASEAN Summit Once Again', *Bangkok Post*, 31 October, www.bangkokpost.com/thailand/general/1783449/trump-skips-asean-summit-once-again accessed 13 January 2020.

Reuters (2017), 'Australia Says No Plan for Joint South China Sea Patrols with Indo-nesia', 6 March, www.reuters.com/article/us-southchinasea-indonesia-australia-idU SKBN16E0D0 accessed 10 January 2020.

Robb, Thomas K. and David James Gill (2015), 'The ANZUS Treaty during the Cold War: A Reinterpretation of US Diplomacy in the Southwest Pacific', *Journal of Cold War Studies* 17 (4).

Robson, Seth (2019), 'US Military Presence in Northern Australia Will Grow, Former Defense Official Says', *Stars and Stripes*, 21 October, www.stripes.com/news/pacific/us-military-presence-in-northern-australia-will-grow-former-defense-official-says-1.6 03959 accessed 10 January 2020.

Soeya, Yoshihide (2017), 'Indo-Pacific: From Strategy to Vision', in Ron Huisken (ed.), *Regional Security Outlook 2020*, Canberra: Council for Security Cooperation in the Asia Pacific.

Tomkins, Damien (2012), 'Two-Star Australian General Appointed Deputy Com-mander of US Army Pacific', *Asia Matters for America*, 24 August, https://asiama ttersforamerica.org/articles/two-star-australian-general-appointed-deputy-command er-of-us-army-pacific accessed 10 January 2020.

Tow, William T. (2017), 'President Trump and the Implications for the Australia–US Alliance and Australia's Role in Southeast Asia', *Contemporary Southeast Asia: A Journal of International & Strategic Affairs* 39 (1).

Tow, William T. and Leisa Hay (2001), 'Australia, the United States and a "China Growing Strong": Managing Conflict Avoidance', *Australian Journal of International Affairs* 55 (1).

Trump, Donald J. (2017), 'Remarks by President Trump at APEC CEO Summit | Da Nang, Vietnam', 10 November, www.whitehouse.gov/briefings-statements/remarks-p resident-trump-apec-ceo-summit-da-nang-vietnam/ accessed 10 January 2020.

US Senate (2018), 'American Leadership in the Asia Pacific, Part 5: The Asia Reassurance Initiative Act: Testimony before the Subcommittee on East Asia, The Pacific, and International Cybersecurity Policy', Senate, 115th Cong. Accessed 20 May 2018, www.foreign.senate.gov/hearings/american-leadership-in-the-asia-pacific-part-5-the-as ia-reassurance-initiative-act-051518.

Waltz, Kenneth N. (1979), *Theory of International Politics*, New York: McGraw Hill.

Wetzel, Daniel (2018), 'Aussies, Marines Take on Amphibious Warfare', 2 July, www. marines.mil/News/News-Display/Article/1565220/aussies-marines-take-on-amphibio us-warfare accessed 10 January 2020.

White House (2017), *National Security Strategy of the United States*, Washington, DC: White House.

Yamin, Saira (2018), 'DKI APCSS hosts second Indo-Pacific Strategy Workshop', 1 November, https://apcss.org/dki-apcss-hosts-second-indo-pacific-strategy-workshop/ accessed 10 June 2020.

Yong, Charissa (2018), 'Singapore Not Joining US, Japan-led Free And Open Indo-Pacific For Now: Vivian Balakrishnan', *Straits Times*, 14 May, www.straitstimes. com/singapore/singapore-not-joining-us-japan-led-free-and-open-indo-pacific-for-no w-vivian-balakrishnan accessed 16 May 2018.

Young, Peter Lewis (1999), 'The ANZUS Treaty: Is It Still Needed in A Post-Cold War World?' *Asian Defence Journal*, 1–2.

Index